A BRAND-NEW YEAR—
A PROMISING NEW START

With expert readings and forecasts, you can chart a course to romance, adventure, good health, or career opportunities while gaining valuable insight into yourself and others. Offering a daily outlook for 18 full months, this fascinating guide shows you:

- The important dates in your life
- What to expect from an astrological reading
- How the stars can help you stay healthy and fit
  And more!

Let this sound advice guide you through a year of heavenly possibilities—for today and for every day of 2007!

SYDNEY OMARR'S® DAY-BY-DAY
ASTROLOGICAL GUIDE FOR

ARIES—March 21–April 19
TAURUS—April 20–May 20
GEMINI—May 21–June 20
CANCER—June 21–July 22
LEO—July 23–August 22
VIRGO—August 23–September 22
LIBRA—September 23–October 22
SCORPIO—October 23–November 21
SAGITTARIUS—November 22–December 21
CAPRICORN—December 22–January 19
AQUARIUS—January 20–February 18
PISCES—February 19–March 20

IN 2007

SYDNEY OMARR'S®

DAY-BY-DAY ASTROLOGICAL GUIDE FOR

GEMINI

MAY 21–JUNE 20

2007

By Trish MacGregor
with Carol Tonsing

ⓢ

A SIGNET BOOK

SIGNET
Published by New American Library, a division of
Penguin Group (USA) Inc., 375 Hudson Street,
New York, New York 10014, USA
Penguin Group (Canada), 90 Eglinton Avenue East, Suite 700, Toronto,
Ontario M4P 2Y3, Canada (a division of Pearson Penguin Canada Inc.)
Penguin Books Ltd., 80 Strand, London WC2R 0RL, England
Penguin Ireland, 25 St. Stephen's Green, Dublin 2,
Ireland (a division of Penguin Books Ltd.)
Penguin Group (Australia), 250 Camberwell Road, Camberwell, Victoria 3124,
Australia (a division of Pearson Australia Group Pty. Ltd.)
Penguin Books India Pvt. Ltd., 11 Community Centre, Panchsheel Park,
New Delhi - 110 017, India
Penguin Group (NZ), cnr Airborne and Rosedale Roads, Albany,
Auckland 1310, New Zealand (a division of Pearson New Zealand Ltd.)
Penguin Books (South Africa) (Pty.) Ltd., 24 Sturdee Avenue,
Rosebank, Johannesburg 2196, South Africa

Penguin Books Ltd., Registered Offices:
80 Strand, London WC2R 0RL, England

First published by Signet, an imprint of New American Library,
a division of Penguin Group (USA) Inc.

First Printing, June 2006
10 9 8 7 6 5 4 3 2 1

PUBLISHER'S NOTE
While the author has made every effort to provide accurate telephone numbers
and Internet addresses at the time of publication, neither the publisher nor the
author assumes any responsibility for errors, or for changes that occur after publication. Further, publisher does not have any control over and does not assume
any responsibility for author or third-party Web sites or their content.

CONTENTS

INTRODUCTION

Astrology to Use Every Day

Are you living your life to the fullest? Whether you want a more rewarding career, financial freedom, better relationships, or a romantic love life, astrology can help you make it happen. No matter what your goal, astrology's age-old techniques work just as well today as they did thousands of years ago. You can apply them to so many areas of your life to make the best decisions concerning your career, love, money, health, and even clothing and vacations.

In relationships, astrology can help you understand every sun-sign combination, which is very handy when you meet someone special. You'll be amazed at how knowing only the person's sun sign can help resolve a conflict or improve communication. What's more, astrology gives you a way to troubleshoot potential problems in advance and, if they crop up, find a way to turn them around.

On a deeper level, astrology can be a tool for personal growth and insight into your own special place in the cosmos. Like your genetic imprint, your astrology chart is unique. It is a map of your moment in time, which has its own code, based on the sun, moon, and planets at the time and place you were born. What is especially intriguing is that this system can offer specific, practical guidance, even when using only one of the elements of the code, your sun sign.

For those who would like to know more about astrology, this book provides user-friendly information to start you on your astrological journey. Then you can put your whole astrological portrait together by looking up the other planets in your horoscope. If you want to delve deeper, we'll show you the best astrology Web sites, where you can find sophisticated software and free education. If you're interested in connecting with other astrologers, we provide an extensive resource list of contacts and organizations, as well as computer program recommendations for fun or serious study.

As the saying goes, "Timing is everything." We'll deal in many ways with the question of timing: the difficult times (which also present positive challenges), times with potential for delays and misunderstandings, and the best times to take risks and to kick back and relax. You will learn when to use the downtime when Mercury is retrograde to reconnect with old friends, troubleshoot, and reevaluate where you're going and with whom.

This guide provides the tools you need to plan the best year ever, to enhance every aspect of your life, plus astonishingly accurate day-by-day forecasts to follow along in your own activities. Let it empower you to make 2007 a year of growth and prosperity!

CHAPTER 1

The Big Trends of 2007

Prepare for Changes Ahead

Astrologers judge the trends of a year by following the slow-moving planets, from Jupiter through Pluto. A change in sign indicates a new cycle, with new emphasis. The farthest planets (Uranus, Neptune, and Pluto), which stay in a sign for at least seven years, cause a very significant change in the atmosphere when they change signs. Shifts in Jupiter, which changes every year, and Saturn, every two years, are more obvious in current events and daily lives. Jupiter generally brings a fortunate, expansive emphasis to its new sign, while Saturn's two-year cycle is a reality check, bringing tests of maturity, discipline, and responsibility.

Sagittarius Is the Sign to Watch

In the final year of Pluto's transit of Sagittarius, it will be accompanied and intensified by Jupiter, the planet of expansion. This duo is superpowerful because Sagittarius is the sign Jupiter rules, making 2007 the grand finale for many of the key trends that began in 1995, when Pluto first entered Sagittarius.

Until January 2008, slow-moving Pluto will be emphasizing everything associated with Sagittarius to prepare us philosophically and spiritually for things to come. Perhaps the most pervasive sign of Pluto in Sagittarius over the past few years has been globalization in all its forms. We are re-forming boundaries, creating new forms of travel, inter-acting with exotic cultures and religions as never before.

In truth-telling Sagittarius, Pluto has shifted our emphasis away from acquiring wealth to a quest for the meaning of it all, as upward strivers discover that money and power are not enough and religious extremists assert themselves. We search the cosmos for something to believe in when many lies and scandals are brought to public view, exposing leaders in the corporate, political and religious domains. When ideals and idols are shattered, we reevaluate our goals and ask ourselves what is really important.

Sagittarius is the sign of linking everything together; therefore, the trend has been to find ways to connect on spiritual, philosophical, and intellectual levels. The spiritual emphasis of Pluto in Sagittarius has filtered down to our home lives, as religion and religious controversy have entered local communities. Vast church complexes that combine religious activities with sports centers, health clubs, malls, and theme parks are being built. Religious education and book publishing have expanded as well.

Sagittarius is known for love of animals, especially horses. It's no surprise that horse racing has become popular again and that America has never been more pet happy. Look for extremes related to animal welfare, such as vegetarianism as a lifestyle. As habitats are destroyed, the care, feeding, and control of wild animals will become a larger issue, especially when deer, bears, and coyotes invade our backyards.

The Sagittarius love of the outdoors combined with Pluto's power has already promoted extreme sports, especially those that require strong legs, like rock climbing, trekking, or snowboarding. Expect the trend toward more adventurous travel to continue, as well as fitness- or sports-oriented vacations. Exotic hiking trips to unexplored territories, mountain-climbing expeditions, spa vacations, and sports-associated resorts are part of this trend.

Publishing, which is associated with Sagittarius, has been transformed by global conglomerates and the Internet. Look for more inspirational books aimed at those who are interested in spirituality outside of traditional religions.

What's Next? Capricorn Brings Us Down to Earth

Next year, Pluto will join Jupiter in Capricorn, which marks a major shift in emphasis to Capricorn-related themes. Capricorn is a practical, building, healing earth sign. It is an active, cardinal sign that symbolizes rising from the waters of the emotions to the top of the mountain, surmounting obstacles all the way, demanding maturity and down-to-earth common sense. Capricorn relates to structures, institutions, order, mountains and mountain countries, mineral rights, issues involving the elderly and growing older—all of which will be emphasized in the coming years.

This shift begins in December 2007, which starts activating all the cardinal signs (Aries, Cancer, Libra, Capricorn). At the end of 2007, you should feel the rumblings of change in the Capricorn area of your horoscope and in the world at large. The last time Pluto was in Capricorn was the period of the Revolutionary War. Therefore this may be an important time in U.S. politics, as well as a reflection of the aging and maturing of American society in general.

Saturn Moves from Leo to Virgo: The Maturing of the Baby Boomers, Reforms in Care and Maintenance

Saturn, the planet of limitation, testing, and restriction, has been transiting Leo since mid-July 2005, forcing us to grow up and get serious in the Leo areas of our lives. Many of the fun things in life fall under the banner of Leo: entertainment, show business, children, play, recreation, love affairs, hobbies, performing, talent, the creative arts, and recognition by others. Since Saturn tends to put a damper on Leo's fun, expect some restrictions on the entertainment business, shows with more serious themes and actors. Leo is associated with children, and with Saturn come the burdens and responsibilities of bringing them up.

The subject of aging in general belongs to Saturn, and

the Leo archetype in this area is the aging film star determined to hold on to youth. Love affairs and flirtations, part of Leo's sunny side, may this year involve older people. Maturing baby boomers will demand more awareness from the media. Therefore we will see more older people on television and in films, more entertainment tailored to an aging population, a harbinger of the even stronger Saturnian trends coming up in 2008. Since Leo is also associated with speculation and gambling, in fact all games, expect more stringent regulation and controversy around big-time casinos and sports.

Saturn in Leo demands hard work in creative ventures, responsibility when interacting with others. Leo types can't get away with casual love affairs, or with being high-handed, arrogant, or divalike in any way. Leo divas will have to earn their applause. This could tone down the blatant celebrity-worshipping culture that has arisen over the past few years. No longer will it be enough to be famous for being famous. The emphasis will be on true values rather than the trappings of success. Flashy lifestyles, bling bling jewelry, and showing off will be out.

Saturn moves into Virgo on September 2, 2007, which is followed soon after by a solar eclipse in Virgo on September 11. This is a time when Virgo issues—health care and maintenance and moral standards and controls—will come to the fore. We will adjust the structures of our lives, making changes so that we can function at an efficient level. We'll be challenged with a reality check in areas where we have been too optimistic or expansive.

Jupiter in Sagittarius

During the year that Jupiter remains in a sign, the fields associated with that sign—comedy, fun, travel, laughter—will be the ones that arouse excitement and enthusiasm, usually providing excellent opportunities for expansion, fame, and fortune. Jupiter remains in fun-loving Sagittarius, the sign it rules, until December 18.

One place we will notice the Jupiter influence is in fashion, which should have a cheerful, colorful look. Sagittarius

6

has great fashion flair, which should show up in ethnic influences and exciting new sportswear.

Those born under Sagittarius should have many opportunities during the year. However, keep your feet on the ground. The flip side of Jupiter is that there are no limits. You can expand off the planet under a Jupiter transit, which is why the planet is often called the Gateway to Heaven. If something is going to burst (such as an artery) or overextend or go over the top in some way, it could happen under a supposedly lucky Jupiter transit. So be aware.

Those born under Gemini may find their best opportunities working with partners this year, as Jupiter will be transiting their seventh house of relationships.

Continuing Trends

Uranus and Neptune continue to do a kind of astrological dance called a mutual reception. This is a supportive relationship where Uranus is in Pisces, the sign ruled by Neptune, while Neptune is in Aquarius, the sign ruled by Uranus. When this dance is over in 2011, it is likely that we will be living under very different political and social circumstances.

Uranus in Pisces

Uranus, known as the Great Awakener, tends to cause both upheaval and innovation in the sign it transits. During previous episodes of Uranus in Pisces, great religions and spiritual movements have come into being, most recently Mormonism and Christian Fundamentalism. In its most positive mode, Pisces promotes imagination and creativity, the art of illusion in theater and film, the inspiration of great artists. A water sign, Pisces is naturally associated with all things liquid—oceans, oil, alcohol—and with those creatures that live in the water—fish, the fishing industry, fish habitats, and fish farming. Currently there is a great debate going on about overfishing, contamination of fish, and fish farming. The underdog, the enslaved, and the disenfranchised should also benefit from Uranus in Pisces.

Since Uranus is a disruptive influence that aims to challenge the status quo, the forces of nature that manifest will most likely be in the Pisces area: oceans, seas, and rivers. We have seen unprecedented rainy seasons, floods, mud slides, and disastrous hurricanes. Note that 2005's devastating Hurricane Katrina hit an area known for both the oil and fishing industries.

Pisces is associated with the prenatal phase of life, which is related to regenerative medicine. The controversy over embryonic stem cell research should continue to be debated. Petroleum issues, both in the oil-producing countries and offshore oil drilling, will come to a head. Uranus in Pisces suggests that development of new hydroelectric sources may provide the power we need to continue our current power-thirsty lifestyle.

As in previous eras, there should continue to be a flourishing of the arts. We are seeing many new artistic forms developing now, such as computer-created actors and special effects. The sky's the limit on this influence.

Those who have problems with Uranus are those who resist change, so the key is to embrace the future.

Neptune in Aquarius

Neptune is a planet of imagination and creativity, but also of deception and illusion. Neptune is associated with hospitals, which have been the subject of much controversy. On the positive side, hospitals are acquiring cutting-edge technology. The atmosphere of many hospitals is already changing from the intimidating and sterile environment of the past to that of a health-promoting spa. Alternative therapies, such as massage, diet counseling, and aromatherapy, are becoming commonplace, which expresses this Neptune trend. New procedures in plastic surgery, also a Neptune glamour field, and anti-aging therapies are restoring the illusion of youth.

However, issues involving the expense and quality of

health care and the evolving relationship between doctors, drug companies, and HMOs reflect a darker side of this trend.

What About the New Planets?

Our solar system is becoming more complex; astronomers continue to discover new objects circling the sun. In addition to the familiar planets, there are comets, cometoids, asteroids, and strange icy bodies in the Kuiper Belt beyond Neptune. The newest object at this writing is a planetlike orb that has a tiny moon. It is tentatively nicknamed Xena, after the TV heroine. Once Xena's orbit is established, astrologers will observe what effect this planet has on our horoscopes. Astrologers have long hypothesized about distant planets on the outer reaches of the solar system, but most astrologers stop with Pluto, which itself is quite controversial. Some scientists insist that tiny Pluto, only one-fifth the size of Earth, is not a full-fledged planet. However, anyone experiencing a zap to the horoscope from this little object knows that it is a force to be reckoned with! Time will tell about Xena and her yet to be discovered siblings!

CHAPTER 2

Your Best Times This Year

Have you ever felt that success is a matter of timing, that you could set your schedule on a successful course if you coordinated your activities with times when the planets give you the green light? On the other hand, it's useful to know when not to act, when it would be better to kick back and review where you're going.

For instance, when mischievous Mercury creates havoc with communications and you can't seem to make progress with projects, you'll use the time to best advantage by backing up your vital computer files, clearing out your files and closets and reading between the lines of contracts. That's the time to be extra patient with coworkers and double-check all messages. Mark your social calendar when Venus passes through your sign—that's when you're the flavor of the month. You've got extra sex appeal, so it's time to get a knockout new outfit or hairstyle. Then ask someone you'd like to know better to dinner. Venus timing can also help you charm clients with a stunning sales pitch or make an offer they won't refuse.

In this chapter, you will learn how to find your best times as well as which times to avoid. You will also learn how to read the moods of the moon and make them work for you. Use the information and tables in this chapter and the planet tables in this book, and also use the moon sign listings in your daily forecasts.

Here are the happenings to note on your agenda:

- Dates of your sun sign (high-energy period)
- The month previous to your sun sign (low-energy period)
- Dates of planets in your sign this year

- Full and new moons (pay special attention when these fall in your sun sign!)
- Eclipses
- Moon in your sun sign every month, as well as moon in the opposite sign (listed in daily forecast)
- Mercury retrogrades
- Other retrograde periods

Your High-Power Time

Every birthday starts off a new cycle of solar energy for you. You should feel a new surge of vitality as the powerful sun enters your sign. This is the time when predominant energies are most favorable to you. So go for it! Start new projects, make your big moves (especially when the new moon is in your sign, doubling your charisma) You'll get the recognition you deserve now, when everyone is attuned to your sun sign. Look in the tables in this book to see if other planets will also be passing through your sun sign at this time. Venus (love, beauty), Mars (energy, drive), and Mercury (communication, mental sharpness) reinforce the sun and give an extra boost to your life in the areas they affect. Venus will rev up your social and love life, making you seem especially attractive. Mars amplifies your energy and drive. Mercury fuels your brainpower and helps you communicate. Jupiter signals an especially lucky period of expansion.

There are two downtimes related to the sun. During the month before your birthday period, when you are winding up your annual cycle, you could be feeling especially vulnerable and depleted. So at that time get extra rest, watch your diet, and take it easy. Don't overstress yourself. Use this time to gear up for a big "push" when the sun enters your sign.

Another downtime is when the sun is in a sign opposite your sun sign (six months from your birthday). That's when the prevailing energies are very different from yours. You may feel at odds with the world. You'll have to work harder for recognition because people are not on your wavelength.

However, this could be a good time to work on a team, in cooperation with others, or behind the scenes.

Plan Your Day with the Moon

The moon is a powerful tool to divine the mood of the moment. You can work with the moon in two ways. Plan by the *sign* the moon is in; plan by the *phase* of the moon. The sign will tell you the kind of activities that suit the moon's mood. The phase will tell you the best time to start or finish a certain activity.

Working with the phases of the moon is as easy as looking up at the night sky. During the new moon, when both the sun and moon are in the same sign, begin new ventures—especially activities that are favored by that sign. Then you'll utilize the powerful energies pulling you in the same direction. You'll be focused outward, toward action, and in a doing mode. Postpone breaking off, terminating, deliberating, or reflecting—activities that require introspection and passive work. These are better suited to a later moon phase.

Get your project under way during the first quarter. Then go public at the full moon, a time of high intensity, when feelings come out into the open. This is your time to shine—to express yourself. Be aware, however, that because pressures are being released, other people will also be letting off steam. Since confrontations are possible, take advantage of this time either to air grievances or to avoid arguments. Traditionally, astrologers often advise against surgery at this time, which could produce heavier bleeding.

About three days after the full moon comes the disseminating phase, a time when the energy of the cycle begins to wind down. From the last quarter of the moon to the next new moon, it's a time to cut off unproductive relationships, do serious thinking, and focus on inward-directed activities.

You'll feel some new and full moons more strongly than others, especially those new moons that fall in your sun sign and full moons in your opposite sign. Because that full moon happens at your low-energy time of year, it is likely to be an especially stressful time in a relationship, when any hidden problems or unexpressed emotions could surface.

Full and New Moons in 2007

All dates are calculated for eastern standard time and eastern daylight time.

Full Moon—January 3 in Cancer
New Moon—January 18 in Capricorn

Full Moon—February 2 in Leo
New Moon—February 17 in Aquarius

Full Moon—March 3 in Virgo (lunar eclipse)
New Moon—March 18 in Pisces (total solar eclipse)

Full Moon—April 2 in Libra
New Moon—April 17 in Aries

Full Moon—May 2 in Scorpio
New Moon—May 16 in Taurus

Full Moon—May 31 in Sagittarius
New Moon—June 14 in Gemini

Full Moon—June 30 in Capricorn
New Moon—July 14 in Cancer

Full Moon—July 29 in Aquarius
New Moon—August 12 in Leo

Full Moon—August 28 in Pisces (lunar eclipse)
New Moon—September 11 in Virgo (solar eclipse)

Full Moon—September 26 in Aries
New Moon—October 11 in Libra

Full Moon—October 26 in Taurus
New Moon—November 9 in Scorpio

Full Moon—November 24 in Gemini
New Moon—December 9 in Sagittarius
Full Moon—December 23 in Cancer

How to Time by the Moon Sign

To forecast the daily emotional "weather," to determine your monthly high and low days, or to synchronize your activities with the cycles of the moon, take note of the moon sign under your daily forecast at the end of the book. Here are some of the activities favored and the moods you are likely to encounter under each moon sign.

Moon in Aries: Get Moving!

The new moon in Aries is an ideal time to start new projects. Everyone is pushy, raring to go, rather impatient, and short-tempered. Leave details and follow-up for later. Competitive sports or martial arts are great ways to let off steam. Quiet types could use some assertiveness, but it's a great day for dynamos. Be careful not to step on too many toes.

Moon in Taurus: Lay the Foundations for Success

Do solid, methodical tasks like follow-through or backup work. Make investments, buy real estate, do appraisals, do some hard bargaining. Attend to your property. Get out in the country or spend some time in your garden. Enjoy creature comforts, music, a good dinner, sensual lovemaking. Forget starting a diet—this is a day when you'll feel self-indulgent.

Moon in Gemini: Communicate

Talk means action today. Telephone, write letters, fax! Make new contacts, stay in touch with steady customers.

14

You can juggle lots of tasks today. It's a great time for mental activity of any kind. Don't try to pin people down—they, too, are feeling restless. Keep it light. Flirtations and socializing are good. Watch gossip—and don't give away secrets.

Moon in Cancer: Pay Attention to Loved Ones

This is a moody, sensitive, emotional time. People respond to personal attention, to mothering. Stay at home, have a family dinner, call your mother. Nostalgia, memories, and psychic powers are heightened. You'll want to hang on to people and things (don't clean out your closets now). You could have shrewd insights into what others really need and want. Pay attention to dreams, intuition, and gut reactions.

Moon in Leo: Be Confident

Everybody is in a much more confident, warm, generous mood. It's a good day to ask for a raise, show what you can do, dress like a star. People will respond to flattery, enjoy a bit of drama and theater. You may be extravagant, treat yourself royally, and show off a bit—but don't break the bank! Be careful you don't promise more than you can deliver.

Moon in Virgo: Be Practical

Do practical down-to-earth chores. Review your budget, make repairs, be an efficiency expert. Not a day to ask for a raise. Tend to personal care and maintenance. Have a health checkup, go on a diet, buy vitamins or health food. Make your home spotless. Take care of details and piled-up chores. Reorganize your work and life so they run more smoothly and efficiently. Save money. Be prepared for others to be in a critical, faultfinding mood.

15

Moon in Libra: Be Diplomatic

Attend to legal matters. Negotiate contracts. Arbitrate. Do things with your favorite partner. Socialize. Be romantic. Buy a special gift, a beautiful object. Decorate yourself or your surroundings. Buy new clothes. Throw a party. Have an elegant, romantic evening. Smooth over any ruffled feathers. Avoid confrontations. Stick to civilized discussions.

Moon in Scorpio: Solve Problems

This is a day to do things with passion. You'll have excellent concentration and focus. Try not to get too intense emotionally. Avoid sharp exchanges with loved ones. Others may tend to go to extremes, get jealous, overreact. Great for troubleshooting, problem solving, research, scientific work—and making love. Pay attention to those psychic vibes.

Moon in Sagittarius: Sell and Motivate

A great time for travel, philosophical discussions, setting long-range career goals. Work out, do sports, buy athletic equipment. Others will be feeling upbeat, exuberant, and adventurous. Risk taking is favored. You may feel like taking a gamble, betting on the horses, visiting a local casino, buying a lottery ticket. Teaching, writing, and spiritual activities also get the green light. Relax outdoors. Take care of animals.

Moon in Capricorn: Get Organized

You can accomplish a lot now, so get on the ball! Attend to business. Issues concerning your basic responsibilities, duties, family, and elderly parents could crop up. You'll be expected to deliver on promises. Weed out the deadwood from your life. Get a dental checkup. Not a good day for gambling or taking risks.

Moon in Aquarius: Join the Group

A great day for doing things with groups—clubs, meetings, outings, politics, parties. Campaign for your candidate. Work for a worthy cause. Deal with larger issues that affect humanity—the environment and metaphysical questions. Buy a computer or electronic gadget. Watch TV. Wear something outrageous. Try something you've never done before. Present an original idea. Don't stick to a rigid schedule—go with the flow. Take a class in meditation, mind control. yoga.

Moon in Pisces: Be Creative

This can be a very creative day, so let your imagination work overtime. Film, theater, music, ballet could inspire you. Spend some time alone, resting and reflecting, reading or writing poetry. Daydreams can also be profitable. Help those less fortunate. Lend a listening ear to someone who may be feeling blue. Don't overindulge in self-pity or escapism, however. People are especially vulnerable to substance abuse now. Turn your thoughts to romance and someone special.

Retrogrades: When the Planets Seem to Backstep

All the planets, except for the sun and moon, have times when they appear to move backward—or retrograde—as it seems from our point of view on earth. At these times, planets do not work as they normally do. So it's best to "take a break" from that planet's energies in our life and to do some work on an inner level.

Mercury Retrograde: The Key Is in "Re"

Mercury goes retrograde most often, and its effects can be especially irritating. When it reaches a short distance ahead of the sun several times a year, it seems to move backward from our point of view. Astrologers often compare retrograde motion to the optical illusion that occurs when we ride on a train that passes another train traveling at a different speed—the second train appears to be moving in reverse.

What this means to you is that the Mercury-ruled areas of your life—analytical thought processes, communications, scheduling—are subject to all kinds of confusion. Be prepared. Communications equipment can break down. Schedules may be changed on short notice. People are late for appointments or don't show up at all. Traffic is terrible. Major purchases malfunction, don't work out, or get delivered in the wrong color. Letters don't arrive or are delivered to the wrong address. Employees will make errors that have to be corrected later. Contracts don't work out or must be renegotiated.

Since most of us can't put our lives on "hold" during Mercury retrogrades, we should learn to tame the trickster and make it work for us. The key is in the prefix *re-*. This is the time to go back over things in your life, *re*flect on what you've done during the previous months. Now you can get deeper insights, spot errors you've missed. So take time to *re*view and *re*evaluate what has happened. *Re*st and *re*ward yourself—it's a good time to take a vacation, especially if you *re*visit a favorite place. *Re*organize your work and finish up projects that are backed up. Clean out your desk and closets. Throw away what you can't *re*cycle. If you must sign contracts or agreements, do so with a contingency clause that lets you *re*evaluate the terms later.

Postpone major purchases or commitments for the time being. Don't get married (unless you're *re*marrying the same person). Try not to *re*ly on other people keeping appointments, contracts, or agreements to the letter; have several alternatives. Double-check and *re*ad between the lines. Don't buy anything connected with communications or transportation (if you must, be sure to cover yourself).

Mercury retrograding through your sun sign will intensify its effect on your life.

If Mercury was retrograde when you were born, you may be one of the lucky people who don't suffer the frustrations of this period. If so, your mind probably works in a very intuitive, insightful way.

The sign in which Mercury is retrograding can give you an idea of what's in store—as well as the sun signs that will be especially challenged.

Mercury Retrogrades in 2007

Mercury has three retrograde periods this year.
   February 14 to March 8 from Pisces back to Aquarius
   June 15 to July 9 in Cancer
   October 11 to November 1 from Scorpio back to Libra

Venus Retrograde: Relationships Move Backward

Retrograding Venus can cause your relationships to take a backward step, or it can make you extravagant and impractical. Shopping till you drop and buying what you cannot afford are problems at this time. It's *not* a good time to redecorate—you'll hate the color of the walls later. Postpone getting a new hairstyle. Try not to fall in love either. But if you wish to make amends in an already troubled relationship, make peaceful overtures at this time.

Venus Retrogrades in 2007

Venus turns retrograde in Virgo from July 27 until September 8, when it turns direct in Leo.

Use the Go Power of Mars

Mars shows how and when to get where you want to go. Timing your moves with Mars on your side can give you a big push. On the other hand, pushing Mars the wrong way can guarantee that you'll run into frustrations in every corner. Your best times to forge ahead are during the weeks when Mars is traveling through your sun sign or your Mars sign (look these up in the tables in this book). Also consider times when Mars is in a compatible sign (fire with air signs, or earth with water signs). You'll be sure to have planetary power on your side.

Mars Retrogrades in 2007

Mars turns retrograde on November 15 until January 30, 2008, from Cancer to Gemini.

When Other Planets Retrograde

The slower-moving planets stay retrograde for months at a time (Jupiter, Saturn, Neptune, Uranus, and Pluto).

When Saturn is retrograde, it's an uphill battle with self-discipline. You may not be in the mood for work. You may feel more like hanging out at the beach than getting things done.

Neptune retrograde promotes a dreamy escapism from reality, when you may feel you're in a fog (Pisces will feel this, especially).

Uranus retrograde may mean setbacks in areas where there have been sudden changes, when you may be forced to regroup or reevaluate the situation.

Pluto retrograde is a time to work on establishing proportion and balance in areas where there have been recent dramatic transformations.

When the planets move forward again, there's a shift in the atmosphere. Activities connected with each planet start moving ahead, plans that were stalled get rolling. Make a special note of those days on your calendar and proceed accordingly.

Other Retrogrades in 2007

The five slower-moving planets all go retrograde in 2007.

Jupiter retrogrades four months from April 5 to August 6 in Sagittarius.

Saturn turned retrograde on December 5, 2006, until

April 19, 2007. It turns retrograde again on December 19 for the duration of the year.

Uranus retrogrades from June 23 to November 24 in Pisces.

Neptune retrogrades from May 24 to October 31 in Aquarius.

Pluto retrogrades from March 31 to September 7 in Sagittarius.

CHAPTER 3

What Planets Could Rock Your World This Year

It's been said that knowledge is power, so why not use astrology's wisdom to ride with the tide this year and make the planets work for you?

Eclipses Clear the Air

Eclipses can bring on milestones in your life, if they aspect a key point in your horoscope. In general, they shake up the status quo, bringing hidden areas out into the open. During this time, problems you've been avoiding or have brushed aside can surface to demand your attention. A good coping strategy is to accept whatever comes up as a challenge that could make a positive difference in your life. And don't forget the power of your sense of humor. If you can laugh at something, you'll never be afraid of it.

What Is the Best Thing to Do During an Eclipse?

When the natural rhythms of the sun and moon are disturbed, it's best to postpone important activities. Be sure to mark eclipse days on your calendar, especially if the eclipse falls in your birth sign. This year, those born under Aries, Pisces, and Virgo should take special note of the feelings that arise. With lunar eclipses, some possibilities could be a break from attachments or the healing of an illness or substance abuse, which had been triggered by the subconscious. The temporary event could be a healing time, when you gain perspective. During solar eclipses, when you might be in a highly subjective state, pay attention to the hidden subconscious patterns that surface, the emotional truth that is revealed at this time.

The effect of the eclipse can reverberate for some time, often months after the event. But it is especially important to stay cool and make no major moves during the period known as the shadow of the eclipse, which begins about a week before and lasts until at least three days after the eclipse. After three days, the daily rhythms should return to normal, and you can proceed with business as usual.

This Year's Eclipse Dates

March 3: Lunar eclipse in Virgo
March 18: Solar eclipse in Pisces
August 28: Lunar eclipse in Pisces
September 11: Solar eclipse in Virgo

Saturn Gives You a Reality Check

When Saturn hits a critical point in your horoscope, you can count on an experience that will make you slow up, pull back, and reexamine your life. It is a call to eliminate what is not working, to shape up, to set priorities, to examine the boundaries and structures in your life (or lack of them) and set new ones. During this process, you may feel restricted, frustrated, or inhibited—not a fun time, but one that will serve you well in the long run. You may need to take on more responsibilities that will test your limits.

By the end of its twenty-eight-year trip around the zodiac, Saturn will have tested you in all areas of your life. The major tests happen in seven-year cycles, when Saturn passes over the angles of your chart, which means your rising sign, the top of your chart or midheaven, your descendant, and the nadir or bottom of your chart. This is when the real life-changing experiences happen. But you are also in for a testing period whenever Saturn passes a planet in your chart or stresses that planet from a distance. It is useful to check your planetary positions with the timetable of Saturn or prepare in advance, or at least to brace yourself.

When Saturn returns to its location at the time of your birth, at approximately age twenty-eight, you'll have your first Saturn return. At this time, a person usually takes stock or settles down to find his mission in life and assume full adult duties and responsibilities.

Another way Saturn helps us is to reveal the karmic lessons from previous lives and give us the chance to overcome them. So look at Saturn's challenges as much-needed opportunities for self-improvement.

Outwitting the Planets

Second-guessing Saturn and the eclipses this year is easy if you have a copy of your horoscope calculated by a computer. This enables you to pinpoint the area of your life that will be affected. However, you can make an educated guess, by setting up a rough diagram on your own. If you'd like to find out which area of your life this year's Saturn change is most likely to affect, follow these easy steps.

First, you must know the time of day you were born and look up your rising sign listed on the tables in this book (see chapter 7). Set up an estimated horoscope by drawing a circle, then dividing it into four parts by making a cross directly through the center. Continue to divide each of the parts into thirds, as if you were dividing a cake, until you have twelve slices. Write your rising sign on the middle left-hand slice, which would be the nine o'clock point, if you were looking at your watch. Then write the following signs on the dividing line of each slice, working counterclockwise, until you have listed all twelve signs of the zodiac.

You should now have a basic diagram of your horoscope chart (minus the planets, of course). Starting with your rising-sign slice, number each portion consecutively, again working counterclockwise.

Since this year's eclipses will fall in Pisces and Virgo, find the number of these slices, or houses, on the chart and read the following descriptions for the kinds of issues that are likely to be emphasized. On September 2, Saturn will move from Leo to Virgo, so check those houses in your chart for Saturn-related events.

If an eclipse or Saturn falls in your FIRST HOUSE:
Events cause you to examine the ways you are acting independently and push you to become more visible, to assert yourself. This is a time when you feel compelled to make your own decisions. You may want to change your physical appearance, body image, or style of dress in some way. Under affliction, there might be illness or physical harm.

If an eclipse or Saturn falls in your SECOND HOUSE:
This is the place where you consider all matters of security. You consolidate your resources, earn money, acquire property, and decide what you value and what you want to own. On a deeper level, this house reveals your sense of self-worth.

If an eclipse or Saturn falls in your THIRD HOUSE:
Here you reach out to others, express your ideas, and explore different courses of action. You may feel especially restless or have confrontations with neighbors or siblings. In your search for more knowledge, you may decide to improve your skills, get more education, or sign up for a course that interests you. Local transportation, especially your car, might be affected by an eclipse here.

If an eclipse or Saturn falls in your FOURTH HOUSE:
Here is where you put down roots and establish a base. You'll consider what home really means to you. Issues involving parents, the physical setup or location of your home, and your immediate family demand your attention. You may be especially concerned with parenting or relationships with your own mother. You may consider moving your home to a new location or leaving home.

25

If an eclipse or Saturn falls in your FIFTH HOUSE:

Here is where you express yourself, either through your personal talents or through procreating children. You are interested in making your special talents visible. This is also the house of love affairs and the romantic aspect of life, where you flirt, have fun, and enjoy the excitement of love. Hobbies and crafts fall in this area.

If an eclipse or Saturn falls in your SIXTH HOUSE:

How well are you doing your job? This is your mainte-nance department, where you take care of your health, or-ganize your life, and set up a daily routine. It is also the place where you perfect your skills and add polish to your life. The chores you do every day, the skills you learn, and the techniques you use fall here. If something doesn't work in your life, an eclipse is sure to bring this to light. If you've been neglecting your health, diet, and fitness, you'll proba-bly pay the consequences during an eclipse. Or you may be faced with work that requires much routine organization and steady effort, rather than creative ability. Or you may be required to perform services for others.

If an eclipse or Saturn falls in your SEVENTH HOUSE:

This is the area of committed relationships, of those which involve legal agreements, of working in a close rela-tionship with another. Here you'll be dealing with how you relate, what you'll be willing to give up for the sake of a marriage or partnership. Eclipses here can put extra pres-sure on a relationship and, if it's not working, precipitate a breakup. Lawsuits and open enemies also reside here.

If an eclipse or Saturn falls in your EIGHTH HOUSE:

This area is concerned with power and control. Consider what you are willing to give up in order that something might happen. Power struggles, intense relationships, and desires to penetrate deeper mysteries belong here. Debts, loans, finan-cial matters that involve another party, and wheeling and dealing also come into focus. So does sex, where you surren-der your individual power to create a new life together. Mat-ters involving birth and death are also involved here.

If an eclipse or Saturn falls in your NINTH HOUSE:

Here is where you look at the big picture. You'll seek information that helps you find meaning in life: higher education, religion, travel, global issues. Eclipses here can push you to get out of your rut, to explore something you've never done before, and to expand your horizons.

If an eclipse or Saturn falls in your TENTH HOUSE:

This is the high-profile point in your chart. Here is where you consider how society looks at you and your position in the outside world. You'll be concerned about whether you receive proper credit for your work and if you're recognized by higher-ups. Promotions, raises, and other forms of recognition can be given or denied. If you have worked hard, Saturn can give you well-deserved rewards here. Either your standing in your career or in your community can be challenged, or you'll be publicly acknowledged for achieving a goal. An eclipse here can make you famous or burst your balloon if you've been too ambitious or neglecting other areas of your life.

If an eclipse or Saturn falls in your ELEVENTH HOUSE:

Your relationship with groups of people comes under scrutiny during an eclipse: whom you are identified with, whom you socialize with, and how well you are accepted by other members of your team. Activities of clubs and political parties, networking, and other social interactions become important. You'll be concerned about what other people think.

If an eclipse or Saturn falls in your TWELFTH HOUSE:

This is the time when the focus turns to your inner life. An especially favorable eclipse here might bring you great insight and inspiration. On the other hand, events may happen that cause you to retreat from public life. Here is where we go to be alone or to work in retreats, hospitals, or religious institutions, or to explore psychotherapy. Here is where you deliver selfless service, through charitable acts. Good aspects from an eclipse could promote an ability to go with the flow or to rise above the competition to find an inner, almost mystical strength that enables you to connect with the deepest needs of others.

CHAPTER 4

The Moon and Your Emotions

How do you react to life's problems? What do you care about? What makes you feel comfortable, secure, or romantic? The answers are a few secrets revealed by the moon sign in your horoscope, where the moon represents your receptive, reflective, female, nurturing self. It also reflects who you were nurtured by—the mother or mother figure in your chart. In a man's chart, the moon position describes his receptive, emotional, yin side, as well as the woman in his life who will have the deepest effect, usually his mother. (Venus reveals the kind of woman who will attract him physically.)

It's well worth having an accurate chart cast to determine your moon sign or that of someone you'd like to know better, since this reveals much about your inner life. You can learn what appeals to a person subconsciously by knowing the person's moon sign, which reflects the instinctive emotional nature.

The moon is more at home in some signs than others. It rules maternal Cancer and is exalted in Taurus—both comforting, home-loving signs where the natural emotional energies of the moon are easily and productively expressed. But when the moon is in the opposite signs—Capricorn and Scorpio—it leaves the comfortable nest and deals with emotional issues of power and achievement in the outside world. Those of you with the moon in these signs are likely to find your emotional role more challenging in life.

Since detailed moon tables are too extensive for this book, check through the following listing to find the moon sign that feels most familiar.

Moon in Aries

This placement makes you both independent and ardent. An idealist, you tend to fall in and out of love easily. You love a challenge but could cool once your quarry is captured. Your emotional reactions are fast and fiery, quickly expressed and quickly forgotten. You may not think before expressing your feelings. It's not easy to hide how you feel. Channeling all your emotional energy could be one of your big challenges.

Moon in Taurus

A sentimental soul, you are very fond of the good life, and you gravitate toward solid, secure relationships. You like displays of affection and creature comforts—all the tangible trappings of a cozy, safe, calm atmosphere. You are sensual and steady emotionally, but very stubborn, possessive, and determined. You can't be pushed, and you tend to dislike changes. You should make an effort to broaden your horizons and to take a risk sometimes. You may become very attached to your home turf. You may also be a collector of objects that are meaningful to you.

Moon in Gemini

You crave mental stimulation and variety in life, which you usually get through either an ever-varied social life, the excitement of flirtation and/or multiple professional involvements. You may marry more than once and have a rather chaotic emotional life due to your difficulty with commitment and settling down, as well as your need to be constantly on the go. (Be sure to find a partner who is as outgoing as you are.) You will have to learn at some point to focus your energies because you tend to be somewhat fragmented—to do two things at once, to have two homes or even two lovers. If you can find a creative way to express your many-faceted nature, you'll be ahead of the game.

Moon in Cancer

This is the most powerful lunar position, which is sure to make a deep imprint on your character. Your needs are very much associated with your reaction to the needs of others. You are very sensitive, caring, and self-protective, though some of you may mask this with a hard shell, like the moon-sensitive crab. This placement also gives an excellent memory, keen intuition, and an uncanny ability to perceive the needs of others. All of the lunar phases will affect you, especially full moons and eclipses, so you would do well to mark them on your calendar. Because you're happiest at home, you may work at home or turn your office into a second home, where you can nurture and comfort people. (You may tend to mother the world.) With natural psychic, intuitive ability, you might be drawn to occult work in some way. Or you may get professionally involved with providing food and shelter to others.

Moon in Leo

This warm, passionate moon takes everything to heart. You are attracted to all that is noble, generous, and aristocratic in life (and may be a bit of a snob). You have an innate ability to take command emotionally, but you do need strong support, loyalty, and loud applause from those you love. You are possessive of your loved ones and your turf and will roar if anyone threatens to take over your territory.

Moon in Virgo

You are rather cool until you decide if others measure up. But once someone or something meets your ideal standards, you hold up your end of the arrangement perfectly. You may, in fact, drive yourself too hard to attain some notion of perfection. Try to be a bit easier on yourself and others. Don't always act the censor! You love to be the teacher and are drawn to situations where you can change others for the better, but sometimes you must learn to accept others for what they are—enjoy what you have!

Moon in Libra

Like other air-sign moons, you think before you feel. Therefore, you may not immediately recognize the emotional needs of others. However, you are relationship oriented and may find it difficult to be alone or to do things alone. After you have learned emotional balance by leaning on yourself first, you can have excellent partnerships. It is best for you to avoid extremes, which set your scales swinging and can make your love life precarious. You thrive in a rather conservative, traditional, romantic relationship, where you receive attention and flattery—but not possessiveness—from your partner. You'll be your most charming in an elegant, harmonious atmosphere.

Moon in Scorpio

This is a moon that enjoys and responds to intense, passionate feelings. You may go to extremes and have a very dramatic emotional life, full of ardor, suspicion, jealousy, and obsession. It would be much healthier to channel your need for power and control into meaningful work. This is a good position for anyone in the fields of medicine, police work, research, the occult, psychoanalysis, or intuitive work, because life-and-death situations don't faze you. However, you do take personal disappointments very hard.

Moon in Sagittarius

You take life's ups and downs with good humor and the proverbial grain of salt. You'll love 'em and leave 'em—take off on a great adventure at a moment's notice. Born free could be your slogan. Attracted by the exotic, you have wanderlust mentally and physically. You may be too much in search of new mental and spiritual stimulation to ever settle down.

Moon in Capricorn

Are you ever accused of being too cool and calculating? You have an earthy side, but you take prestige and position

very seriously. Your strong drive to succeed extends to your romantic life, where you will be devoted to improving your lifestyle, rising to the top. A structured situation where you can advance methodically makes you feel wonderfully secure. You may be attracted to someone older or very much younger or from a different social world. It may be difficult to look at the lighter side of emotional relationships. Though this moon is placed in the sign of its detriment, the good news is that you tend to be very dutiful and responsible to those you care for.

Moon in Aquarius

You are a people collector with many friends of all backgrounds. You are happiest surrounded by people and may feel uneasy when left alone. Though you usually stay friends with lovers, intense emotions and demanding one-on-one relationships turn you off. You don't like anything to be too rigid or scheduled. Though tolerant and understanding, you can be emotionally unpredictable and may opt for an unconventional love life. With plenty of space, you will be able to sustain relationships with liberal, freedom-loving types.

Moon in Pisces

You are very responsive and empathetic to others, especially if they have problems or are the underdog. (Be on guard against attracting too many people with sob stories.) You'll be happiest if you can express your creative imagination in the arts or in the spiritual or healing professions. Because you may tend to escape in fantasies or overreact to the moods of others, you need an emotional anchor to help you keep a firm foothold in reality. Steer clear of too much escapism (especially in alcohol) or reclusiveness. Places near water soothe your moods. Working in a field that gives you emotional variety will also help you be productive.

CHAPTER 5

Basic Astrology: Your Owner's Manual

You probably know your zodiac sign and those of your friends. But do you know the difference between a sign and a constellation? And what is a house? Is yours an earth sign or a water sign? If you'd like to venture around the zodiac into the deeper areas of astrology, this chapter can get you up and running. It's a quick owner's manual, your fast track to understanding the basic principles of this fascinating but often confusing subject.

Signs and Constellations: What's the Difference?

First, let's get our sign language straight, because for most readers, that's the starting point of astrology.

Signs are actually a type of celestial real estate, located on the zodiac, an imaginary 360-degree belt circling the earth. This belt is divided into twelve equal thirty-degree portions, which are the signs. There's a lot of confusion about the difference between the signs and the constellations of the zodiac. The latter are patterns of stars that originally marked the twelve divisions, like signposts. Though a sign is named after the constellation that once marked the same area, the constellations are no longer in the same place relative to the earth that they were many centuries ago. Over hundreds of years, the earth's orbit has shifted, so that from our point of view here on earth, the constellations seem to have moved. However, the signs remain in place. (Most Western astrology uses the twelve-equal-part division of the zodiac, though there are some other methods of astrology that still use the constellations instead of the signs.)

Most people think of themselves in terms of their sun sign. A sun sign refers to the sign the sun is orbiting through at a given moment (from our point of view here on earth). For instance, "I'm an Aries" means that the sun was passing through Aries when that person was born. However, there are nine other planets (plus asteroids, fixed stars, and sensitive points) that also form our total astrological personality, and some or many of these will be located in other signs. No one is completely Aries, with all astrological components in one sign! (Please note that, in astrology, the sun and moon are usually referred to as planets, though of course they're not.)

As we mentioned before, the sun signs are places on the zodiac. They do not do anything (the planets are the doers). However, they are associated with many things, depending on their location.

How We Define the Signs

The definitions of the signs evolved systematically from four components that interrelate. These four different criteria are a sign's element: its quality, its polarity or sex, and its order in the progression of the zodiac. All these factors work together to tell us what the sign is like.

The system is magically mathematical. The number 12—as in the twelve signs of the zodiac—is divisible by 4, by 3, and by 2. There are four elements, three qualities, and two polarities, which follow each other in sequence around the zodiac.

The four elements (earth, air, fire, and water) are the building blocks of astrology. The use of an element to describe a sign probably dates from man's first attempts to categorize what he saw. Ancient sages believed that all things were composed of combinations of these basic elements—earth, air, fire, and water. This included the human character, which was fiery/choleric, earthy/melancholy, airy/sanguine, or watery/phlegmatic. The elements also correspond to our emotional (water), physical (earth), mental (air) and spiritual (fire) natures. The energies of each of the elements were then observed to be related to the time of year when the sun was passing through a certain segment of the zodiac.

Those born with the sun in fire signs—Aries, Leo, Sagittarius—embody the characteristic of that element. Optimism, warmth, hot tempers, enthusiasm, and spirit are typical of these signs. Taurus, Virgo, and Capricorn are earthy—more grounded, physical, materialistic, organized and deliberate than fire-sign people. Air-sign people—Gemini, Libra, and Aquarius—are mentally oriented communicators. Water signs—Cancer, Scorpio, and Pisces—are emotional, sensitive, and creative.

Think of what each element does to the others. Water puts out fire or evaporates under heat. Air fans the flames or blows them out. Earth smothers fire, drifts and erodes with too much wind, becomes mud or fertile soil with water. Those are often perfect analogies for the relationships between people of different sun-sign elements. This astrochemistry was one of the first ways man described his relationships. Fortunately, no one is entirely air or fire. We all have a bit, or a lot, of each element in our horoscopes. It is this unique mix that defines each astrological personality.

Within each element, there are three qualities that describe types of behavior associated with the sign. Those of cardinal signs are activists, go-getters. These four signs—Aries, Cancer, Libra, and Capricorn—begin each season. Fixed signs, which happen in the middle of the season, are associated with builders, stabilizers. You'll find that sun signs Taurus, Leo, Scorpio, and Aquarius are usually gifted with concentration, stamina, and focus. Mutable signs—Gemini, Virgo, Sagittarius, and Pisces—fall at the end of each season and thus are considered catalysts for change. People born under mutable signs are flexible, adaptable.

The polarity of a sign is either its positive or negative charge. It can be masculine, active, positive, and yang like air or fire signs. Or feminine, reactive, negative, and yin like the water and earth signs.

Finally, we consider the sign's place in the order of the

zodiac. This is vital to the balance of all the forces and the transmission of energy moving through the signs. You may have noticed that your sign is quite different from your neighboring sign on either side. Yet each seems to grow out of its predecessor like links in a chain and transmits a synthesis of energy gathered along the chain to the following sign, beginning with the fire-powered, active, positive charge of Aries.

How the Signs Add Up

SIGN	ELEMENT	QUALITY	POLARITY	PLACE
Aries	fire	cardinal	masculine	first
Taurus	earth	fixed	feminine	second
Gemini	air	mutable	masculine	third
Cancer	water	cardinal	feminine	fourth
Leo	fire	fixed	masculine	fifth
Virgo	earth	mutable	feminine	sixth
Libra	air	cardinal	masculine	seventh
Scorpio	water	fixed	feminine	eighth
Sagittarius	fire	mutable	masculine	ninth
Capricorn	earth	cardinal	feminine	tenth
Aquarius	air	fixed	masculine	eleventh
Pisces	water	mutable	feminine	twelfth

Your Sign's Special Planet

Each sign has a ruling planet that is most compatible with its energies. Mars adds its fiery assertive characteristics to

Aries. The sensual beauty and comfort-loving side of Venus rules Taurus, whereas the idealistic side of Venus rules Libra. Quick-moving Mercury rules two mutable signs, Gemini and Virgo. Its mental agility belongs to Gemini while its analytical, critical side is best expressed in Virgo. The changeable emotional moon is associated with Cancer, while the outgoing Leo personality is ruled by the sun. Scorpio originally shared Mars, but when Pluto was discovered in this century, its powerful magnetic energies were deemed more suitable to the intense vibrations of the fixed water sign Scorpio. Disciplined Capricorn is ruled by Saturn, and expansive Sagittarius by Jupiter. Unpredictable Aquarius is ruled by Uranus and creative, imaginative Pisces by Neptune. In a horoscope, if a planet is placed in the sign it rules, it is sure to be especially powerful.

The Layout of a Horoscope Chart

A horoscope chart is a map of the heavens at a given moment in time. It looks like a wheel divided with twelve spokes. In between each of the spokes is a section called a house.

Each house deals with a different area of life and is influenced by a special sign and a planet. Astrologers look at the house to tell in what area of life an event is happening or about to happen.

The house is governed by the sign passing over the spoke (or cusp of the house) at that particular moment. Though the first house is naturally associated with Aries and Mars, it would also have an additional Capricorn influence if that sign was passing over the house cusp at the time the chart was cast. The sequence of the houses starts with the first house located at the left center spoke (or the number 9 position, if you were reading a clock). The houses are then read counterclockwise around the chart, with the fourth house at the bottom of the chart, the tenth house at the top or twelve o'clock position.

Where do the planets belong? Around the horoscope, planets are placed within the houses according to their location at the time of the chart. That is why it is so important to have an accurate time; with no specific time, the planets have no specific location in the houses and one cannot determine which area of life they will apply to. Since the signs move across the houses as the earth turns, planets in a house will naturally intensify the importance of that house. The house that contains the sun is naturally one of the most prominent.

The First House: Home of Aries and Mars

The sign passing over the first house at the time of your birth is known as your *ascendant,* or *rising sign.* The first house is the house of "firsts"—the first impression you make, how you initiate matters, the image you choose to project. This is where you advertise yourself, where you project your personality. Planets that fall here will intensify the way you come across to others.

The Second House: Home of Taurus and Venus

This house is where you experience the material world—what you value. Here are your attitudes about money, possessions, finances, whatever belongs to you, and what you own, as well as your earning and spending capacity. On a deeper level, this house reveals your sense of self-worth, the inner values that draw wealth in various forms.

The Third House: Home of Gemini and Mercury

This house describes how you communicate with others, how you reach out to others nearby, and how you interact with the immediate environment. It shows how your thinking process works and the way you express your thoughts. Are you articulate or tongue-tied? Can you think on your feet? This house also shows your first relationships, your experiences with brothers and sisters, and how you deal with people close to you such as your neighbors or pals. It's where you take short trips, write letters, or use the telephone. It shows how your mind works in terms of left-brain logical and analytical functions.

The Fourth House: Home of Cancer and the Moon

The fourth house shows the foundation of life, the psychological underpinnings. At the bottom of the chart, this house shows how you are nurtured and made to feel secure—your roots! It shows your early home environment and the circumstances at the end of your life (your final "home") as well as the place you call home now. Astrologers look here for information about the parental nurturers in your life.

The Fifth House: Home of Leo and the Sun

The fifth house is where the creative potential develops. Here you express yourself and procreate in the sense that children are outgrowths of your creative ability. But this house most represents your inner childlike self who delights in play. If your inner security has been established by the time you reach this house, you are now free to have fun, romance, and love affairs and to give of yourself. This is also the place astrologers look for playful love affairs, flirtations, and brief romantic encounters (rather than long-term commitments).

The Sixth House: Home of Virgo and Mercury

The sixth house has been called the "care and maintenance" department. This house shows how you take care of your body and organize yourself to perform efficiently in the world. Here is where you get things done, where you look after others, and fulfill service duties such as taking care of pets. Here is what you do to survive on a day-to-day basis. The sixth house demands order in your life; otherwise there would be chaos. This house is your "job" (as opposed to your career, which is the domain of the tenth house), your diet, and your health and fitness regimens.

The Seventh House: Home of Libra and Venus

This house shows your attitude toward partners and those with whom you enter into commitments, contracts, or agreements. Here is the way you relate to others, as well as your close, intimate, one-on-one relationships (including open enemies—those you "face off" with). Open hostilities, lawsuits, divorces, and marriages happen here. If the first house represents the "I," the seventh or opposite house is the "not-I"—the complementary partner you attract by the way you come across. If you are having trouble with partnerships, consider what you are attracting by the energies of your first and seventh houses.

The Eighth House: Home of Scorpio and Pluto (also Mars)

The eighth house refers to how you merge with something or someone, and how you handle power and control. This is one of the most mysterious and powerful houses, where your energy transforms itself from "I" to "we." As you give up power and control by uniting with something or someone, two kinds of energies merge and become something greater, leading to a regeneration of the self on a higher level. Here are your attitudes toward sex, shared resources, taxes (what you share with the government). Because this house involves what belongs to others, you face issues of control and power struggles, or undergo a deep psychological transformation as you bond with another. Here you transcend yourself with dreams, drugs, and occult or psychic experiences that reflect the collective unconscious.

The Ninth House: Home of Sagittarius and Jupiter

The ninth house shows your search for wisdom and higher knowledge—your belief system. As the third house represents the "lower mind," its opposite on the wheel, the ninth house, is the "higher mind"—the abstract, intuitive, spiritual mind that asks "big" questions like "Why are we here?" After the third house has explored what was close at hand, the ninth stretches out to broaden you mentally with higher education and travel. Here you stretch spiritually with religious activity. Since you are concerned with how everything is related, you tend to push boundaries, take risks. Here is where you express your ideas in a book or thesis, where you pontificate, philosophize, or preach.

The Tenth House: Home of Capricorn and Saturn

The tenth house is associated with your public life and high-profile activities. Located directly overhead at the "high noon" position on the horoscope wheel, this is the most "visible" house in the chart, the one where the world sees you. It deals with your career (but not your routine "job") and your reputation. Here is where you go public, take on responsibilities, (as opposed to the fourth house, where you stay home). This will affect the career you choose and your "public relations." This house is also associated with your father figure or the main authority figure in your life.

The Eleventh House: Home of Aquarius and Uranus

The eleventh house is where you extend yourself to a group, a goal, or a belief system. This house is where you define what you really want, the kinds of friends you have, your political affiliations, and the kind of groups you identify with as an equal. Here is where you become concerned with "what other people think" or where you rebel against social conventions. Here is where you could become a socially conscious humanitarian or a partygoing social butterfly. It's where you look to others to stimulate you and discover your kinship to the rest of humanity. The sign on this house can help you understand what you gain and lose from friendships.

The Twelfth House: Home of Pisces and Neptune

Old-fashioned astrologers used to put a rather negative spin on this house, calling it the house of self-undoing. When we undo ourselves, we surrender control, boundaries, limits, and rules. The twelfth house is where the boundaries between yourself and others become blurred and you become selfless. But instead of being self-undoing, the twelfth house can be a place of great creativity and talent. It is the place where you can tap into the collective unconscious, where your imagination is limitless.

In your trip around the zodiac, you've gone from the I of self-assertion in the first house to the final house, which symbolizes the dissolution that happens before rebirth. The twelfth house is where accumulated experiences are processed in the unconscious. Spiritually oriented astrologers look to this house for evidence of past lives and karma. Places where we go for solitude or to do spiritual or reparatory work belong here, such as retreats, religious institutions, or hospitals. Here is also where we withdraw from society voluntarily or involuntarily or are put in prison because of antisocial activity. Selfless giving through charitable acts is part of this house, as is dependence on charity.

In your daily life, the twelfth house reveals your deepest intimacies, your best-kept secrets, especially those you hide from yourself and keep repressed deep in the unconscious. It is where we surrender a sense of a separate self to a deep feeling of wholeness, such as selfless service in religion or any activity that involves merging with the greater whole. Many sports stars have important planets in the twelfth house that enable them to play in the zone, finding an inner, almost mystical, strength that transcends their limits.

Who's Home in Your Houses?

Houses are stronger or weaker depending on how many planets are inhabiting them. If there are many planets in a

42

given house, it follows that the activities of that house will be especially important in your life. If the planet that rules the house is also located there, this too adds power to the house.

CHAPTER 6

Your Planetary Recipe

Besides the sun and moon, there are eight planets in your horoscope. Each is an ingredient representing a basic force in life that interacts with the other planets to make up a recipe that is uniquely yours. The location of a planet in your horoscope can determine how strongly that planet will affect you. A planet that's close to your rising sign will be emphasized in your chart. If two or more planets are grouped together in one sign, they usually operate together, playing off each other, rather than expressing their energy singularly. A lone planet that stands far away from the others is usually outstanding and often calls the shots in a horoscope.

The sign of each planet also has a powerful influence. In some signs, the planetary energies are very much at home and can easily express themselves. In others, the planet has to work harder and is slightly out of sorts. The sign that most corresponds to the energies of a planet is said to be ruled by that planet and obviously is the best place for it to be. The next best place is in a sign where it is exalted, or especially harmonious. On the other hand, there are places in the horoscope where a planet has to work harder to play its role, such as the sign opposite a planet's rulership, which embodies the opposite area of life, and the sign opposite its exaltation. However, a planet that must work harder can actually be more complete, because it must stretch itself to meet the challenges of living in a more difficult sign. Like world leaders who've had to struggle for greatness, this planet may actually develop great strength and character.

Here's a list of the best places for each planet to be. Note that, as new planets were discovered, they replaced the traditional rulers of signs which best complemented their energies.

ARIES—Mars
TAURUS—Venus, in its most sensual form
GEMINI—Mercury, in its communicative role
CANCER—the moon
LEO—the sun
VIRGO—also Mercury, this time in its more critical capacity
LIBRA—also Venus, in its more aesthetic, judgmental form
SCORPIO—Pluto, replacing Mars, the sign's original ruler
SAGITTARIUS—Jupiter
CAPRICORN—Saturn
AQUARIUS—Uranus, replacing Saturn, its original ruler
PISCES—Neptune, replacing Jupiter, its original ruler

A person who has many planets in exalted signs is lucky indeed, for here is where the planet can accomplish the most and be its most influential and creative.

SUN—exalted in Aries, where its energy creates action
MOON—exalted in Taurus, where instincts and reactions operate on a highly creative level
MERCURY—exalted in Aquarius, where it can reach analytical heights
VENUS—exalted in Pisces, a sign whose sensitivity encourages love and creativity
MARS—exalted in Capricorn, a sign that puts energy to work productively
JUPITER—exalted in Cancer, where it encourages nurturing and growth
SATURN—at home in Libra, where it steadies the scales of justice and promotes balanced, responsible judgment
URANUS—powerful in Scorpio, where it promotes transformation
NEPTUNE—especially favored in Cancer, where it gains the security to transcend to a higher state
PLUTO—exalted in Pisces, where it dissolves the old cycle to make way for transition to the new

The Personal Planets: Mercury, Venus, and Mars

These planets work in your immediate personal life.

Mercury affects how you communicate and how your mental processes work. Are you a quick study who grasps information rapidly? Or do you learn more slowly and thoroughly? How is your concentration? Can you express yourself easily? Are you a good writer? All these questions can be answered by your Mercury placement.

Venus shows what you react to. What turns you on? What appeals to you aesthetically? Are you charming to others? Are you attractive to look at? Your taste, your refinement, your sense of balance and proportion are all Venus-ruled.

Mars is your outgoing energy, your drive and ambition. Do you reach out for new adventures? Are you assertive? Are you motivated? Self-confident? Hot-tempered? How you channel your energy and drive is revealed by your Mars placement.

Mercury Shows How Your Mind Works

In our cookbook analogy, Mercury would be the recipe instructions. Mercury shows how you think and speak, how logical you are. Since it stays close to the sun, read the description for Mercury in your sun sign, then the sign preceding and following it. Then decide which reflects the way you think.

Mercury in Aries

Your mind is very active and assertive. It approaches a plan aggressively. You never hesitate to say what you think, never shy away from a battle. In fact, you may relish a verbal confrontation. Tact is not your strong point, so you may have to learn not to trip over your tongue.

Mercury in Taurus

This is a cautious Mercury. Though you may be a slow learner, you have good concentration and mental stamina. You want to make your ideas really happen. You'll attack a problem methodically and consider every angle thoroughly, never jumping to conclusions. You'll stick with a subject until you master it.

Mercury in Gemini

You are a wonderful communicator with great facility for expressing yourself both verbally and in writing. You love gathering all kinds of information. You probably finish other people's sentences, and express yourself with eloquent hand gestures. You can talk to anybody anytime . . . and probably have phone and e-mail bills to prove it. You read anything from sci-fi to Shakespeare, and might need an extra room just for your book collection. Though you learn fast, you may lack focus and discipline. Watch a tendency to jump from subject to subject.

Mercury in Cancer

You rely on intuition more than logic. Your mental processes are usually colored by your emotions, so you may seem shy or hesitant to voice your opinions. However, this placement gives you the advantage of great imagination and empathy in the way you communicate with others.

Mercury in Leo

You are enthusiastic and very dramatic in the way you express yourself. You like to hold the attention of groups, and could be a great public speaker. Your mind thinks big, so you prefer to deal with the overall picture rather than with the details.

Mercury in Virgo

This is one of the best places for Mercury. It should give you critical ability, attention to details, and thorough analysis. Your mind focuses on the practical side of things. This type of thinking is very well suited to being a teacher or editor.

Mercury in Libra

You're either a born diplomat who smoothes over ruffled feathers or a talented debater. Many lawyers have this placement. However, since you're forever weighing the pros and cons of a situation, you may vacillate when making decisions.

Mercury in Scorpio

This is an investigative mind that stops at nothing to get the answers. You may have a sarcastic, stinging wit or a gift for the cutting remark. There's always a grain of truth to your verbal sallies, thanks to your penetrating insight.

Mercury in Sagittarius

You are a supersalesman with a tendency to expound. Though you are very broad-minded, you can be dogmatic when it comes to telling others what's good for them. You won't hesitate to tell the truth as you see it, so watch a tendency toward tactlessness. On the plus side, you have a great sense of humor. This position of Mercury is often considered by astrologers to be at a disadvantage because Sagittarius opposes Gemini, the sign Mercury rules, and squares off with Virgo, another Mercury-ruled sign. What often happens is that Mercury in Sagittarius oversteps its bounds and loses sight of the facts in a situation. Do a reality check before making promises you may not be able to deliver.

Mercury in Capricorn

This placement endows good mental discipline. You have a love of learning and a very orderly approach to your subjects. You will patiently plod through the facts and figures until you have mastered the tasks. You grasp structured situations easily, but may be short on creativity.

Mercury in Aquarius

An independent, original thinker, you'll have more cutting-edge ideas than the average person. You will be quick to check out any unusual opportunities. Your opinions are so well-researched and grounded that once your mind is made up, it is difficult to change.

Mercury in Pisces

You have the psychic and intuitive mind of a natural poet. Learn to make use of your creative imagination. You may think in terms of helping others, but check a tendency to be vague and forgetful of details.

Venus: The Sweet Things

In our recipe analogy, Venus would be dessert. Venus shows where you receive pleasure, what you love to do. Find your Venus placement from the charts at the end of this chapter by looking for the year of your birth in the left-hand column. Then follow the line of that year across the page until you reach the time period of your birthday. The sign heading that column will be your Venus. If you were born on a day when Venus was changing signs, check the signs preceding or following that day to determine if that sign feels more like your Venus nature.

Venus in Aries

You can't stand to be bored, confined, or ordered around. But a good challenge, maybe even a rousing row, turns you on. Confess—don't you pick a fight now and then just to get someone stirred up? You're attracted by the chase, not the catch, which could cause some problems in your love life if the object of your affection becomes too attainable. You like to wear red, and you can spot a trend before anyone else.

Venus in Taurus

All your senses work in high gear. You love to be surrounded by glorious tastes, smells, textures, sounds, and visuals. Austerity is not for you! Neither is being rushed. You like time to enjoy your pleasures. Soothing surroundings with plenty of creature comforts are your cup of tea. You like to feel secure in your nest, with no sudden jolts or surprises. You like familiar objects—in fact, you may hate to let anything or anyone go.

Venus in Gemini

You are a lively, sparkling personality who thrives in a situation that affords a constant variety and a frequent change of scenery. A varied social life is important to you, with plenty of stimulation and a chance to engage in some light flirtation. Commitment may be difficult, because playing the field is so much fun.

Venus in Cancer

An atmosphere where you feel protected, coddled, and mothered is best for you. You love to be surrounded by children in a cozy, homelike situation. You are attracted to those who are tender and nurturing, who make you feel secure and well provided for. You may be quite secretive about your emotional life, or attracted to clandestine relationships.

Venus in Leo

First-class attention in large doses turns you on, and so does the glitter of real gold and the flash of mirrors. You like to feel like a star at all times, surrounded by your admiring audience. The side effect is that you may be attracted to flatterers and tinsel, while the real gold requires some digging.

Venus in Virgo

Everything neatly in its place? On the surface, you are attracted to an atmosphere where everything is in perfect order, but underneath are some basic, earthy urges. You are attracted to those who appeal to your need to teach, to be of service, or to play out a Pygmalion fantasy. You are at your best when you are busy doing something useful.

Venus in Libra

Elegance and harmony are your key words. You can't abide an atmosphere of contention. Your taste tends toward the classic, with light harmonies of color—nothing clashing, trendy, or outrageous. You love doing things with a partner, and should be careful to pick one who is decisive but patient enough to let you weigh the pros and cons. And steer clear of argumentative types!

Venus in Scorpio

Hidden mysteries intrigue you. In fact, anything that is too open and aboveboard is a bit of a bore. You surely have a stack of whodunits by the bed, along with an erotic magazine or two. You like to solve puzzles, and may also be fascinated with the occult, crime, or scientific research. Intense, all-or-nothing situations add spice to your life, and you love to ferret out the secrets of others. But you could get burned by your flair for living dangerously. The color black, spicy food, dark wood furniture, and heady perfume all get you in the right mood.

Venus in Sagittarius

If you are not actually a world traveler, your surroundings are sure to reflect your love of faraway places. You like a casual outdoor atmosphere and a dog or two to pet. There should be plenty of room for athletic equipment and suitcases. You're attracted to kindred souls who love to travel and who share your freedom-loving philosophy of life. Athletics and spiritual or New Age pursuits could be other interests.

Venus in Capricorn

No fly-by-night relationships for you! You want substance in life, and you are attracted to whatever will help you get where you are going. Status objects turn you on. And so do those who have a serious, responsible, businesslike approach as well as those who remind you of a beloved parent. It is characteristic of this placement to be attracted to someone of a different generation. Antiques, traditional clothing, and dignified behavior are becoming to you.

Venus in Aquarius

This Venus wants to make friends, to be "cool." You like to be in a group, particularly one pushing a worthy cause. You feel quite at home surrounded by people, and could even court fame. Yet all the while you remain detached from any intense commitment. Original ideas and unpredictable people fascinate you. You don't like everything to be planned out in advance, preferring spontaneity and delightful surprises.

Venus in Pisces

This Venus loves to give of yourself, and you find plenty of takers. Stray animals and people appeal to your heart and your pocketbook, but be careful to look at their motives realistically once in a while. You are extremely vulnerable to sob stories of all kinds. Fantasy, the arts (especially film, dance, and theater), and psychic or spiritual activities also speak to you.

Mars: Hot and Spicy

In your cosmic recipe, Mars provides the heat and spice. It is the mover and shaker in your life. It shows how you pursue your goals, whether you have energy to burn or proceed at a slow, steady pace. It will also show how you get angry. Do you explode or do a slow burn or hold everything inside, then get revenge later?

To find your Mars, turn to the charts on pages 86–94. Then find your birth year in the left-hand column and trace the line across horizontally until you come to the column headed by the month of your birth. There you will find an abbreviation of your Mars sign. If the description of your Mars sign doesn't ring true, read the description of the sign preceding and following it. You may have been born on a day when Mars was changing signs, in which case your Mars might be in the adjacent sign.

Mars in Aries

In the sign it rules, Mars shows its brilliant fiery nature. You have an explosive temper and can be quite impatient. On the other hand, you have tremendous courage, energy, and drive. You'll let nothing stand in your way as you race to be first! Obstacles are met head-on and broken through by force. However, those that require patience and persistence can have you exploding in rage. You're a great starter, but not necessarily around for the finish.

Mars in Taurus

Slow, steady, concentrated energy gives you staying power to last until the finish line. You have great stamina, and you never give up. Your tactic is to wear away obstacles with your persistence. Often you come out a winner because you've had the patience to hang in there. When angered, you do a slow burn.

Mars in Gemini

You can't sit still for long. This Mars craves variety. You often have two or more things going on at once—it's all an amusing game to you. Your life can get very complicated, but that only adds spice and stimulation. What drives you into a nervous, hyper state? Boredom, sameness, routine, and confinement. You can do wonderful things with your hands, and you have a way with words.

Mars in Cancer

You rarely attack head-on. Instead, you'll keep things to yourself, make plans in secret, and always cover your actions. This might be interpreted by some as manipulative, but you are only being self-protective. You get furious when anyone knows too much about you. But you do like to know all about others. Your mothering and feeding instincts can be put to good use if you work in the food, hotel, or child-care business. You may have to overcome your fragile sense of security, which prompts you not to take risks and to get physically upset when criticized. Don't take things so personally!

Mars in Leo

You have a very dominant personality that takes center stage. Modesty is not one of your traits, nor is taking a backseat. You prefer giving the orders, and have been known to make a dramatic scene if they are not obeyed. Properly used, this Mars confers leadership ability, endurance, and courage.

Mars in Virgo

You are the faultfinder of the zodiac. You notice every detail. Mistakes of any kind make you very nervous. You may worry, even if everything is going smoothly. You may not express your anger directly, but you sure can nag. You have definite likes and dislikes, and you are sure you can do the job better than anyone else. You are certainly more industrious and detail-oriented than other signs. Your Mars energy is often most positively expressed in some kind of teaching role.

Mars in Libra

This Mars will have a passion for beauty, justice, and art. Generally, you will avoid confrontations at all costs. You prefer to spend your energy finding diplomatic solutions or weighing pros and cons. Your other techniques are passive aggression or exercising your well-known charm to get people to do what you want.

Mars in Scorpio

This is a powerful placement, so intense that it demands careful channeling into worthwhile activities. Otherwise, you could become obsessed with your sexuality or might use your need for power and control to manipulate others. You are strong-willed, shrewd, and very private about your affairs, and you'll usually have a secret agenda behind your actions. Your great stamina, focus, and discipline would be excellent assets for careers in the military or medical fields, especially research or surgery. When angry, you don't get mad—you get even!

Mars in Sagittarius

This expansive Mars often propels people into sales, travel, athletics, or philosophy. Your energies function well when you are on the move. You have a hot temper, and are inclined to say what you think before you consider the consequences. You shoot for high goals—and talk endlessly about them—but you may be weak on groundwork. This Mars needs a solid foundation. Watch a tendency to take unnecessary risks.

Mars in Capricorn

This is an ambitious Mars with an excellent sense of timing. You have an eye for those who can be of use to you, and you may dismiss people ruthlessly when you're angry, but you drive yourself hard and deliver full value. This is a good placement for an executive. You'll aim for status and a high material position in life, and you'll keep climbing despite the odds. A great Mars to have!

Mars in Aquarius

This is the most rebellious Mars. You seem to have a drive to assert yourself against the status quo. You may enjoy provoking people, shocking them out of traditional views. Or this placement could express itself in an offbeat sex life. Somehow you often find yourself in unconventional situations. You enjoy being a leader of an active group, which pursues forward-looking studies, politics, or goals.

Mars in Pisces

This Mars is a good actor who knows just how to appeal to the sympathies of others. You create and project wonderful fantasies, or you use your sensitive antennae to crusade for those less fortunate. You get what you want through creating a veil of illusion and glamour. This is a good Mars for someone in the creative and imaginative fields—a dancer, performer, photographer, actor. Many famous film stars have this placement. Watch a tendency to manipulate by making others feel sorry for you.

Jupiter Piles the Plate High

In our recipe analogy, Jupiter would be the high-carb dish that can add on pounds. This big, bright, swirling mass of gases is associated with abundance, prosperity, and the kind of windfall you get without too much hard work. You're optimistic under Jupiter's influence, when anything seems possible. You'll travel, expand your mind with higher education, and publish to share your knowledge widely. On the other hand, Jupiter's influence is neither discriminating nor disciplined. It represents the principle of growth without judgment, and therefore could result in extravagance, weight gain, laziness, and carelessness, if not kept in check.

Be sure to look up your Jupiter in the tables in this book. When the current position of Jupiter is favorable, you may get that lucky break. This is a great time to try new things, take risks, travel, or get more education. Opportunities seem to open up easily, so take advantage of them.

Once a year, Jupiter changes signs. That means you are due for an expansive time every twelve years, when Jupiter travels through your sun sign. You'll also have up periods every four years, when Jupiter is in the same element as your sun sign.

Jupiter in Aries

You are the soul of enthusiasm and optimism. Your luckiest times are when you are getting started on an exciting project or selling an idea that you really believe in. You may have to watch a tendency to be arrogant with those who do not share your enthusiasm. You follow your impulses, often ignoring budget or other commonsense limitations. To produce real, solid benefits, you'll need patience and follow-through wherever this Jupiter falls in your horoscope.

Jupiter in Taurus

You'll spend on beautiful material things, especially those that come from nature—items made of rare woods, natural fabrics, or precious gems, for instance. You can't have too much comfort or too many sensual pleasures. Watch a tendency to overindulge in good food, or to overpamper yourself with nothing but the best. Spartan living is not for you! You may be especially lucky in matters of real estate.

Jupiter in Gemini

You are the great talker of the zodiac, and you may be a great writer, too. But restlessness could be your weak point. You jump around, talk too much, and could be a jack-of-all-trades. Keeping a secret is especially difficult, so you'll have to watch a tendency to spill the beans. Since you love to be at the center of a beehive of activity, you'll have a vibrant social life. Your best opportunities will come through your talent for language—speaking, writing, communicating, and selling.

Jupiter in Cancer

You are luckiest in situations where you can find emotional closeness or deal with basic security needs such as food, nurturing, or shelter. You may be a great collector. Or you may simply love to accumulate things—you are the one who stashes things away for a rainy day. You probably have a very good memory and love children. In fact, you may have many children to care for. The food, hotel, child-care, and shipping businesses hold good opportunities for you.

Jupiter in Leo

You are a natural showman who loves to live in a larger-than-life way. Yours is a personality full of color that always finds its way into the limelight. You can't have too much attention or applause. Showbiz is a natural place for you, and so is any area where you can play to a crowd. Exercising your flair for drama, your natural playfulness, and your romantic nature brings you good fortune. But watch a tendency to be overly extravagant or to monopolize center stage.

Jupiter in Virgo

You actually love those minute details others find boring. To you, they make all the difference between the perfect and the ordinary. You are the fine craftsman who spots every flaw. You expand your awareness by finding the most efficient methods and by being of service to others. Many of you will be drawn to medical or teaching fields. You'll also have luck in publishing, crafts, nutrition, and service professions. Watch out for a tendency to overwork.

Jupiter in Libra

This is an other-directed Jupiter that develops best with a partner. The stimulation of others helps you grow. You are also most comfortable in harmonious, beautiful situations and you work well with artistic people. You have a great sense of fair play and an ability to evaluate the pros and cons of a situation. You usually prefer to play the role of diplomat rather than adversary.

Jupiter in Scorpio

You love the feeling of power and control, of taking things to their limit. You can't resist a mystery. Your shrewd, penetrating mind sees right through to the heart of most situations and people. You have luck in work that provides for solutions to matters of life and death. You may be drawn to undercover work, behind-the-scenes intrigue, psychotherapy, the occult, and sex-related ventures. Your challenge will be to develop a sense of moderation and tolerance for other beliefs. This Jupiter can be fanatical. You may have luck in handling other people's money—insurance, taxes, and inheritance can bring you a windfall.

Jupiter in Sagittarius

Independent, outgoing, and idealistic, you'll shoot for the stars. This Jupiter compels you to travel far and wide, both physically and mentally, via higher education. You may have luck while traveling in an exotic place. You also have luck with outdoor ventures, exercise, and animals, particularly horses. Since you tend to be very open about your opinions, watch a tendency to be tactless and to exaggerate. Instead, use your wonderful sense of humor to make your point.

Jupiter in Capricorn

Jupiter is much more restrained in Capricorn, the sign of rules and authority. Here, Jupiter can make you overwork and heighten any ambition or sense of duty you may have.

You'll expand in areas that advance your position, putting you farther up the social or corporate ladder. You are lucky working within the establishment in a very structured situation where you can show off your ability to organize and reap rewards for your hard work.

Jupiter in Aquarius

This is another freedom-loving Jupiter, with great tolerance and originality. You are at your best when you are working for a humanitarian cause and in the company of many supporters. This is a good Jupiter for a political career. You'll relate to all kinds of people on all social levels. You have an abundance of original ideas, but you are best off away from routine and any situation that imposes rigid rules. You need mental stimulation!

Jupiter in Pisces

You are a giver whose feelings and pocketbook are easily touched by others, so choose your companions with care. You could be the original sucker for a hard-luck story. Better find a worthy hospital or a charity that will appreciate your selfless support. You have a great creative imagination. You may attract good fortune in fields related to oil, perfume, pharmaceuticals, petroleum, dance, footwear, and alcohol. But beware of overindulgence in alcohol—focus on a creative outlet instead.

Saturn Is a Disciplined Diet

Jupiter speeds you up with *lucky breaks* and quick energy. Then along comes Saturn to slow you down with the *disciplinary brakes* and slow-burning energy. It is the part of your planetary diet that helps you achieve lasting goals. Saturn has unfairly been called a malefic planet, one of the bad guys of the zodiac. On the contrary, Saturn is one of our best friends, the kind who tells you what you need to hear even if it's not good news. Under a Saturn transit, we grow up, take responsibility for our lives, and emerge from whatever test this planet has in store as far wiser, more capable and mature human beings. It is when we are under pressure that we grow stronger.

Look up your natal Saturn in the tables in this book for clues on where you need work.

Saturn in Aries

Saturn here puts the brakes on Aries' natural drive and enthusiasm. There is often an angry side to this placement. You don't let anyone push you around, and you know what's best for yourself. Following orders is not your strong point, and neither is diplomacy. You tend to be quick to go on the offensive in relationships, attacking first, before anyone attacks you. Because no one quite lives up to your standards, you often wind up doing everything yourself. You'll have to learn to cooperate and tone down self-centeredness. Both Pat Buchanan and Saddam Hussein have this Saturn.

Saturn in Taurus

A big issue is getting control of the cash flow. There will be lean periods that can be frightening, but you have the patience and endurance to stick them out and the methodical drive to prosper in the end. Learn to take a philosophical attitude, like Ben Franklin, who also had this placement and who said, "A penny saved is a penny earned."

Saturn in Gemini

You are a serious student of life, but you may have difficulty communicating or sharing your knowledge. You may be shy, speak slowly, or have fears about communicating, like Eleanor Roosevelt. You dwell in the realms of science, theory, or abstract analysis—even when you are dealing with the emotions, like Sigmund Freud, who also had this placement.

Saturn in Cancer

Your tests come with establishing a secure emotional base. In doing so, you may have to deal with some very basic fears centering on your early home environment. Most of your Saturn tests will have emotional roots in those early childhood experiences. You may have difficulty remaining objective in terms of what you try to achieve. So it will be especially important for you to deal with negative feelings such as guilt, paranoia, jealousy, resentment, and suspicion. Galileo and Michelangelo also navigated these murky waters.

Saturn in Leo

This is an authoritarian Saturn—a strict, demanding parent who may deny the pleasure principle in your zeal to see that rules are followed. Though you may feel guilty about taking the spotlight, you are very ambitious and loyal. You have to watch a tendency toward rigidity, also toward over-work and holding back affection. Joseph Kennedy and Billy Graham share this placement.

Saturn in Virgo

This is a cautious, exacting Saturn. You are intensely hard on yourself. Most of all, you give yourself the roughest time with your constant worries about every little detail, often making yourself sick. You may have difficulties setting priorities and getting the job done. Your tests will come in learning tolerance and understanding of others. Charles de Gaulle, Mae West, and Nathaniel Hawthorne had this meticulous Saturn.

Saturn in Libra

Saturn is exalted here, which makes this planet an ally. You may choose very serious, older partners in life, perhaps stemming from a fear of dependency. You need to learn to stand solidly on your own before you commit to another. You are extremely cautious as you deliberate every involvement—with good reason. It is best that you find an occupation that makes good use of your sense of duty and honor. Steer clear of fly-by-night situations. Both Khrushchev and Mao Tse-tung had this placement.

Saturn in Scorpio

You have great staying power. This Saturn tests you in situations involving the control of others. You may feel drawn to some kind of intrigue or undercover work, like J. Edgar Hoover. Or there may be an air of mystery surrounding your life and death, like Marilyn Monroe and Robert Kennedy, who both had this placement. There are lessons to be learned from your sexual involvements. Often sex is used for manipulation or is somehow out of the ordinary. The Roman emperor Caligula and the transsexual Christine Jorgensen are extreme cases.

Saturn in Sagittarius

Your challenges and lessons will come from tests of your spiritual and philosophical values, as happened to Martin Luther King and Gandhi. You are high-minded and sincere with this reflective, moral placement. Uncompromising in your ethical standards, you could become a benevolent despot.

Saturn in Capricorn

With the help of Saturn at maximum strength, your judgment will improve with age. And like Spencer Tracy's screen image, you'll be the gray-haired hero with a strong sense of responsibility. You advance in life slowly but steadily, always with a strong hand at the helm and an eye for the advantageous situation. Like Pat Robertson, you're likely to stand for conservative values. Negatively, you may be a loner, prone to periods of melancholy.

Saturn in Aquarius

Your tests come from relationships with groups. Do you care too much about what others think? Do you feel like an outsider, like Greta Garbo? You may fear being different from others and therefore slight your own unique, forward-looking gifts. Or like Lord Byron and Howard Hughes, you may take the opposite tack and rebel in the extreme. You can apply discipline to accomplish great humanitarian goals, as Albert Schweitzer did.

Saturn in Pisces

Your fear of the unknown and the irrational may lead you to the safety and protection of an institution. You may go on the run like Jesse James, who had this placement, to avoid looking too deeply inside. Or you might go in the opposite, more positive direction and develop a disciplined psychoanalytic approach, which puts you more in control of your feelings. Some of you will take refuge in work with hospitals, charities, or religious institutions. Queen Victoria, who had this placement, symbolized an era when institutions of all kinds were sustained. Discipline applied to artistic work, especially poetry and dance, or to spiritual work, such as yoga or meditation, might be helpful.

How Uranus, Neptune, and Pluto Influence a Whole Generation

These three planets remain in signs such a long time that a whole generation bears the imprint of the sign. Mass movements, great sweeping changes, fads that characterize a generation, even the issues of the conflicts and wars of the time are influenced by these "outer three" planets. When one of those distant planets changes signs, there is a definite shift in the atmosphere, the feeling of the end of an era.

Since these planets are so far away from the sun—too distant to be seen by the naked eye—they pick up signals from the universe at large. These planetary receivers literally link the sun with distant energies, and then perform a similar function in your horoscope by linking your central character with intuitive, spiritual, transformative forces from the cosmos. Each planet has a special domain, and will reflect this in the area of your chart where it falls.

Uranus Is the Surprise Ingredient

In your cosmic recipe, Uranus is the unexpected ingredient that sets you and your generation apart. There is nothing ordinary about this quirky green planet that seems to be traveling on its side, surrounded by a swarm of moons. Is it any wonder that astrologers assigned it to Aquarius, the most eccentric and gregarious sign? Uranus seems to wend its way around the sun, marching to its own tune.

Significantly, Uranus follows Saturn, the planet of limitations and structures. Often we get caught up in the structures we have created to give ourselves a sense of security. However, if we lose contact with our spiritual roots, then Uranus is likely to jolt us out of our comfortable rut and wake us up.

Uranus energy is electrical, happening in sudden flashes. It is not influenced by karma or past events, nor does it regard tradition, sex, or sentiment. The Uranus key words are surprise and awakening. Suddenly, there's that flash of inspiration, that bright idea, that totally new approach to revolutionize whatever scheme you were undertaking. A Uranus event takes you by surprise; it happens from out of the blue, for better or for worse. The Uranus place in your life is where you awaken and become your own person, leaving the structures of Saturn behind. And it is probably the most unconventional place in your chart.

Look up the sign of Uranus at the time of your birth and see where you follow your own tune.

Uranus in Aries

Birth Dates:
    March 31, 1927–November 4, 1927

January 13, 1928–June 6, 1934
October 10, 1934–March 28, 1935

Your generation is original, creative, pioneering. It developed the computer, the airplane, and the cyclotron. You let nothing hold you back from exploring the unknown, and you have a powerful mixture of fire and electricity behind you. Women of your generation were among the first to be liberated. You were the unforgettable style setters. You have a surprise in store for everyone. Like Yoko Ono, Grace Kelly, and Jacqueline Onassis, your life may be jolted by sudden and violent changes.

Uranus in Taurus

Birth Dates:
June 6, 1934–October 10, 1934
March 28, 1935–August 7, 1941
October 5, 1941–May 15, 1942

The great territorial shake-ups of World War II began during your generation. You are independent, probably self-employed or would like to be. You have original ideas about making money, and you brace yourself for sudden changes of fortune. This Uranus can cause shake-ups, particularly in finances, but it can also make you a born entrepreneur.

Uranus in Gemini

Birth Dates:
August 7, 1941–October 5, 1941
May 15, 1942–August 30, 1948
November 12, 1948–June 10, 1949

You were the first children to be influenced by television. Now, in your adult years, your generation stocks up on answering machines, cell phones, computers, and fax machines—any new way you can communicate. You have an inquiring mind, but your interests may be rather short-lived. This Uranus can be easily fragmented if there is no structure and focus.

Uranus in Cancer

Birth Dates:
  August 30, 1948–November 12, 1948
  June 10, 1949–August 24, 1955
  January 28, 1956–June 10, 1956
  This generation came at a time when divorce was becoming commonplace, so your home image is unconventional. You may have an unusual relationship with your parents; you may have come from a broken home or an unconventional one. You'll have unorthodox ideas about parenting, intimacy, food, and shelter. You may also be interested in dreams, psychic phenomena, and memory work.

Uranus in Leo

Birth Dates:
  August 24, 1955–January 28, 1956
  June 10, 1956–November 1, 1961
  January 10, 1962–August 10, 1962
  This generation understood how to use electronic media. Many of your group are now leaders in the high-tech industries, and you also understand how to use the new media to promote yourself. Like Isadora Duncan, you may have a very eccentric kind of charisma and a life that is sparked by unusual love affairs. Your children, too, may have traits that are out of the ordinary. Where this planet falls in your chart, you'll have a love of freedom, be a bit of an egomaniac, and show the full force of your personality in a unique way, like tennis great Martina Navratilova.

Uranus in Virgo

Birth Dates:
  November 1, 1961–January 10, 1962
  August 10, 1962–September 28, 1968
  May 20, 1969–June 24, 1969
  You'll have highly individual work methods. Many of you will be finding newer, more practical ways to use computers. Like Einstein, who had this placement, you'll break the rules brilliantly. Your generation came at a time of student

rebellions, the civil rights movement, and the general acceptance of health foods. Chances are, you're concerned about pollution and cleaning up the environment. You may also be involved with nontraditional healing methods.

Uranus in Libra

Birth Dates:
   September 28, 1968–May 20, 1969
   June 24, 1969–November 21, 1974
   May 1, 1975–September 8, 1975
Your generation will be always changing partners. Born during the era of women's liberation, you may have come from a broken home and have no clear image of what a marriage entails. There will be many sudden splits and experiments before you settle down. Your generation will be much involved in legal and political reforms and in changing artistic and fashion looks.

Uranus in Scorpio

Birth Dates:
   November 21, 1974–May 1, 1975
   September 8, 1975–February 17, 1981
   March 20, 1981–November 16, 1981
Interest in transformation, meditation, and life after death signaled the beginning of New Age consciousness. Your generation recognizes no boundaries, no limits, and no external controls. You'll have new attitudes toward death and dying, psychic phenomena, and the occult. Like Mae West and Casanova, you'll shock 'em sexually, too.

Uranus in Sagittarius

Birth Dates:
   February 17, 1981–March 20, 1981
   November 16, 1981–February 15, 1988
   May 27, 1988–December 2, 1988
Could this generation be the first to travel in outer space? An earlier generation with this placement included Charles Lindbergh and a time when the first zeppelins and

the Wright Brothers were conquering the skies. Uranus here forecasts great discoveries, mind expansion, and long-distance travel. Like Galileo and Martin Luther, those born in these years will generate new theories about the cosmos and mankind's relation to it.

Uranus in Capricorn

Birth Dates:
  December 20, 1904–January 30, 1912
  September 4, 1912–November 12, 1912
  February 15, 1988–May 27, 1988
  December 2, 1988–April 1, 1995
  June 9, 1995–January 12, 1996

This generation, now growing up, will challenge traditions with the help of electronic gadgets. In these years, we got organized with the help of technology put to practical use. The Internet was born following the great economic boom of the 1990s. Great leaders who were movers and shakers of history, like Julius Caesar and Henry VIII, were born under this placement.

Uranus in Aquarius

Birth Dates:
  January 30, 1912–September 4, 1912
  November 12, 1912–April 1, 1919
  August 16, 1919–January 22, 1920
  April 1, 1995–June 9, 1995
  January 12, 1996–March 10, 2003
  September 15, 2003–December 30, 2003

Uranus in Aquarius is the strongest placement for this planet. Recently we've had the opportunity to witness the full force of its power of innovation, as well as its sudden wake-up calls and insistence on humanitarian values. This was a time of high-tech development, when home computers became as ubiquitous as television. It was a time of globalization, of surprise attacks (9/11), and underdeveloped countries demanding attention. The last generation with this placement produced great innovative minds such as Leonard Bernstein and Orson Welles. The next will become another radical breakthrough generation, much concerned with global issues that involve all humanity.

Uranus in Pisces

Birth Dates:
  April 1, 1919–August 16, 1919
  January 22, 1920–March 31, 1927
  November 4, 1927–January 12, 1928
  March 10, 2003–September 15, 2003
  December 20, 2003–May 28, 2010

Uranus is now in Pisces, ushering in a new generation. In the past century, Uranus in Pisces focused attention on the rise of electronic entertainment—radio and the cinema—and the secretiveness of Prohibition. This produced a generation of idealists exemplified by Judy Garland's theme "Somewhere over the Rainbow." Uranus in Pisces also hints at stealth activities, at hospital and prison reform, at high-tech drugs and medical experiments, at shake-ups and reforms in the Pisces-ruled petroleum industry. Issues regarding the water and oil supply, water-related storm damage, sudden hurricanes, and floods demand our attention.

Neptune Is the Magic Solvent

Neptune is the liquid in your horoscope recipe that dissolves other ingredients and creates a magical, inspired result. It is often maligned as the planet of illusions that dissolves reality, enabling you to escape the material world. Under Neptune's influence, you see what you want to see. But Neptune also encourages you to create. It embodies glamour, subtlety, mystery, and mysticism, and it governs anything that takes you beyond the mundane world, including out-of-body experiences.

Neptune acts to transcend your ordinary perceptions to take you to another level, where you experience either confusion or ecstasy. Its force can pull you off course only if you allow this to happen. Those who use Neptune wisely can translate their daydreams into poetry, theater, design, or inspired moves in the business world, avoiding the tricky "con artist" side of this planet.

Find your Neptune listed below.

Neptune in Cancer

Birth Dates:
    July 19, 1901–December 25, 1901
    May 21, 1902–September 23, 1914
    December 14, 1914–July 19, 1915
    March 19, 1916–May 2, 1916

Dreams of the homeland, idealistic patriotism, and glamorization of the nurturing assets of women characterized this time. You who were born here have unusual psychic ability and deep insights into basic needs of others.

Neptune in Leo

Birth Dates:
    September 23, 1914–December 14, 1914
    July 19, 1915–March 19, 1916
    May 2, 1916–September 21, 1928
    February 19, 1929–July 24, 1929

Neptune in Leo brought us the glamour and high living of the 1920s and the big spenders of that time. The Neptune temptations of gambling, seduction, theater, and lavish entertaining distracted from the realities of the age. Those born in that generation also made great advances in the arts.

Neptune in Virgo

Birth Dates:
    September 21, 1928–February 19, 1929
    July 24, 1929–October 3, 1942
    April 17, 1943–August 2, 1943

Neptune in Virgo encompassed the 1930s, the Great Depression, and the beginning of World War II, when a new order was born. There was a time of facing "what doesn't work." Many were unemployed and found solace at the movies, watching the great Virgo star Greta Garbo or the escapist dance films of Busby Berkeley. New public services were born. Those with Neptune in Virgo later spread the gospel of health and fitness. This generation's devotion to spending hours at the office inspired the term *workaholic*.

Neptune in Libra

Birth Dates:
  October 3, 1942–April 17, 1943
  August 2, 1943–December 24, 1955
  March 12, 1956–October 19, 1956
  June 15, 1957–August 6, 1957
This was the time of World War II and the postwar period, when the world regained balance and returned to relative stability. Neptune in Libra was the romantic generation who would later be concerned with relating. As this generation matured, there was a new trend toward marriage and commitment. Racial and sexual equality became important issues, as they redesigned traditional roles to suit modern times.

Neptune in Scorpio

Birth Dates:
  December 24, 1955–March 12, 1956
  October 19, 1956–June 15, 1957
  August 6, 1957–January 4, 1970
  May 3, 1970–November 6, 1970
Neptune in Scorpio brought in a generation that would become interested in transformative power. Born in an era that glamorized sex, drugs, rock and roll, and Eastern religion, they matured in a more sobering time of AIDS, cocaine abuse, and New Age spirituality. As they evolve, they will become active in healing the planet from the results of the abuse of power.

Neptune in Sagittarius

Birth Dates:
  January 4, 1970–May 3, 1970
  November 6, 1970–January 19, 1984

June 23, 1984–November 21, 1984

Neptune in Sagittarius was the time when space and astronaut travel became a reality. The Neptune influence glamorized new approaches to mysticism, religion, and mind expansion. This generation will take a new approach to spiritual life, with emphasis on visions, mysticism, and clairvoyance.

Neptune in Capricorn

Birth Dates:
  January 19, 1984–June 23, 1984
  November 21, 1984–January 29, 1998

Neptune in Capricorn brought a time when delusions about material power were glamorized in the mid–1980s and 1990s. There was a boom in the stock market, and the Internet era spawned young tycoons who later lost it all. It was also a time when the psychic and occult worlds spawned a new category of business enterprise, and sold services on television.

Neptune in Aquarius

Birth Dates:
  January 29, 1998–April 4, 2011

This should continue to be a time of breakthroughs. Here the creative influence of Neptune reaches a universal audience. This is a time of dissolving barriers, of globalization—when we truly become one world. During this transit of high-tech Aquarius, new kinds of entertainment media reach across cultural differences. However, the transit of Neptune has also raised boundary issues between cultures, especially in Middle Eastern countries with Neptune-ruled oil fields. As Neptune raises issues of social and political structures not being as solid as they seem, this could continue to produce rebellion and chaos in the environment. However, by using imagination (Neptune) in partnership with a global view (Aquarius) we could reach creative solutions.

Those born with this placement should be true citizens of the world with a remarkable creative ability to transcend social and cultural barriers.

Pluto Can Transform You

Add a small touch of Pluto to your recipe and it will change the dish completely! Though it is a tiny planet, its influence is great. When Pluto zaps a strategic point in your horoscope, your life changes dramatically.

This little planet is the power behind the scenes; it affects you at deep levels of consciousness, causing events to come to the surface that will transform you and your generation. Nothing escapes, or is sacred, with this probing planet. Its purpose is to wipe out the past so something new can happen.

The Pluto place in your horoscope is where you have invisible power (Mars governs the visible power), where you can transform, heal, and affect the unconscious needs of the masses. Pluto tells lots about how your generation projects power, what makes it seem cool to others. And when Pluto changes signs, there is a whole new concept of what's cool. Pluto's strange elliptical orbit occasionally runs inside the orbit of neighboring Neptune. Because of its eccentric path, the length of time Pluto stays in any given sign can vary from thirteen to thirty-two years. It covered only seven signs in the last century.

Pluto in Gemini

Birth Dates:
    Late 1800s–May 26, 1914
    This was a time of mass suggestion and breakthroughs in communications, a time when many brilliant writers such as Ernest Hemingway and F. Scott Fitzgerald were born. Henry Miller, D. H. Lawrence, and James Joyce scandalized society by using explicit sexual images and language in their literature. "Muckraking" journalists exposed corruption. Pluto-ruled Scorpio President Theodore Roosevelt said, "Speak softly, but carry a big stick." This generation had an intense need to communicate and made major breakthroughs in knowledge. A compulsive restlessness and a thirst for a variety of experiences characterized many of this generation.

Pluto in Cancer

Birth Dates:

May 26, 1914–June 14, 1939

Dictators and mass media arose to wield emotional power over the masses. Women's rights was a popular issue. Deep sentimental feelings, acquisitiveness, and possessiveness characterized these times and people. Most of the great stars of the Hollywood era that embodied the American image were born during this period: Grace Kelly, Esther Williams, Frank Sinatra, Lana Turner, to name a few.

Pluto in Leo

Birth Dates:

June 14, 1939–August, 19, 1957

The performing arts played on the emotions of the masses. Mick Jagger, John Lennon, and rock and roll were born at this time. So were "baby boomers" like Bill and Hillary Clinton. Those born here tend to be self-centered, powerful, and boisterous. This generation does its own thing, for better or for worse.

Pluto in Virgo

Birth Dates:

August 19, 1957–October 5, 1971
April 17, 1972–July 30, 1972

This is the "yuppie" generation that sparked a mass movement toward fitness, health, and career. It is a much more sober, serious, driven generation than the fun-loving Pluto in Leo. During this time, machines were invented to process detail work efficiently. Inventions took a practical turn with answering machines, fax machines, car phones, and home office equipment—all making the workplace far more efficient.

Pluto in Libra

Birth Dates:

October 5, 1971–April 17, 1972

July 30, 1972–November 5, 1983
May 18, 1984–August 27, 1984

A mellower generation, people born at this time are concerned with partnerships, working together, and finding diplomatic solutions to problems. Marriage is important to this generation, and they will define it by combining traditional values with equal partnership. This was a time of women's liberation, gay rights, ERA, and legal battles over abortion, all of which transformed our ideas about relationships.

Pluto in Scorpio

Birth Dates:
November 5, 1983–May 18, 1984
August 27, 1984–January 17, 1995

Pluto was in the sign it rules for a comparatively short period of time. However, this was a time of record achievements, destructive sexually transmitted diseases, nuclear power controversies, and explosive political issues. Pluto destroys in order to create new understanding—the phoenix rising from the ashes—which should be some consolation for those of you who felt Pluto's force before 1995. Sexual shockers were par for the course during these intense years when black clothing, transvestites, body piercing, tattoos, and sexually explicit advertising pushed the boundaries of good taste.

Pluto in Sagittarius

Birth Dates:
January 17, 1995–April 20, 1995
November 10, 1995–January 26, 2008

During our current Pluto transit, we are being pushed to expand our horizons, to find deeper spiritual meaning in life. Pluto's opposition with Saturn in 2001 brought an enormous conflict between traditional societies and the forces of change. It signals a time when religious convictions will exert more power in our political life as well.

Since Sagittarius is the sign that rules travel, there's a good possibility that Pluto, the planet of extremes, will make space travel a reality for some of us. Already, we are seeing wealthy adventurers paying for the privilege of travel on space shuttles. Discovery of life-forms on other planets could transform our ideas about where we came from.

New dimensions in electronic publishing, concern with animal rights and the environment, and an increasing emphasis on extreme forms of religion are other signs of these times. Look for charismatic religious leaders to arise now. Wc'll also be developing far-reaching philosophies designed to elevate our lives with a new sense of purpose.

VENUS SIGNS 1901–2007

	Aries	Taurus	Gemini	Cancer	Leo	Virgo
1901	3/29–4/22	4/22–5/17	5/17–6/10	6/10–7/5	7/5–7/29	7/29–8/23
1902	5/7–6/3	6/3–6/30	6/30–7/25	7/25–8/19	8/19–9/13	9/13–10/7
1903	2/28–3/24	3/24–4/18	4/18–5/13	5/13–6/9	6/9–7/7	7/7–8/17
						9/6–11/8
1904	3/13–5/7	5/7–6/1	6/1–6/25	6/25–7/19	7/19–8/13	8/13–9/6
1905	2/3–3/6	3/6–4/9	7/8–8/6	8/6–9/1	9/1–9/27	9/27–10/21
	4/9–5/28	5/28–7/8				
1906	3/1–4/7	4/7–5/2	5/2–5/26	5/26–6/20	6/20–7/16	7/16–8/11
1907	4/27–5/22	5/22–6/16	6/16–7/11	7/11–8/4	8/4–8/29	8/29–9/22
1908	2/14–3/10	3/10–4/5	4/5–5/5	5/5–9/8	9/8–10/8	10/8–11/3
1909	3/29–4/22	4/22–5/16	5/16–6/10	6/10–7/4	7/4–7/29	7/29–8/23
1910	5/7–6/3	6/4–6/29	6/30–7/24	7/25–8/18	8/19–9/12	9/13–10/6
1911	2/28–3/23	3/24–4/17	4/18–5/12	5/13–6/8	6/9–7/7	7/8–11/18
1912	4/13–5/6	5/7–5/31	6/1–6/24	6/24–7/18	7/19–8/12	8/13–9/5
1913	2/3–3/6	3/7–5/1	7/8–8/5	8/6–8/31	9/1–9/26	9/27–10/20
	5/2–5/30	5/31–7/7				
1914	3/14–4/6	4/7–5/1	5/2–5/25	5/26–6/19	6/20–7/15	7/16–8/10
1915	4/27–5/21	5/22–6/15	6/16–7/10	7/11–8/3	8/4–8/28	8/29–9/21
1916	2/14–3/9	3/10–4/5	4/6–5/5	5/6–9/8	9/9–10/7	10/8–11/2
1917	3/29–4/21	4/22–5/15	5/16–6/9	6/10–7/3	7/4–7/28	7/29–8/21
1918	5/7–6/2	6/3–6/28	6/29–7/24	7/25–8/18	8/19–9/11	9/12–10/5
1919	2/27–3/22	3/23–4/16	4/17–5/12	5/13–6/7	6/8–7/7	7/8–11/8
1920	4/12–5/6	5/7–5/30	5/31–6/23	6/24–7/18	7/19–8/11	8/12–9/4
1921	2/3–3/6	3/7–4/25	7/8–8/5	8/6–8/31	9/1–9/25	9/26–10/20
	4/26–6/1	6/2–7/7				
1922	3/13–4/6	4/7–4/30	5/1–5/25	5/26–6/19	6/20–7/14	7/15–8/9
1923	4/27–5/21	5/22–6/14	6/15–7/9	7/10–8/3	8/4–8/27	8/28–9/20
1924	2/13–3/8	3/9–4/4	4/5–5/5	5/6–9/8	9/9–10/7	10/8–11/12
1925	3/28–4/20	4/21–5/15	5/16–6/8	6/9–7/3	7/4–7/27	7/28–8/21

Libra	Scorpio	Sagittarius	Capricorn	Aquarius	Pisces
8/23–9/17	9/17–10/12	10/12–1/16	1/16–2/9	2/9–3/5	3/5–3/29
			11/7–12/5	12/5–1/11	
10/7–10/31	10/31–11/24	11/24–12/18	12/18–1/11	2/6–4/4	1/11–2/6
					4/4–5/7
8/17–9/6	12/9–1/5			1/11–2/4	2/4–2/28
11/8–12/9					
9/6–9/30	9/30–10/25	1/5–1/30	1/30–2/24	2/24–3/19	3/19–4/13
		10/25–11/18	11/18–12/13	12/13–1/7	
10/21–11/14	11/14–12/8	12/8–1/1/06			1/7–2/3
8/11–9/7	9/7–10/9	10/9–12/15	1/1–1/25	1/25–2/18	2/18–3/14
	12/15–12/25	12/25–2/6			
9/22–10/16	10/16–11/9	11/9–12/3	2/6–3/6	3/6–4/2	4/2–4/27
			12/3–12/27	12/27–1/20	
11/3–11/28	11/28–12/22	12/22–1/15			1/20–2/4
8/23–9/17	9/17–10/12	10/12–11/17	1/15–2/9	2/9–3/5	3/5–3/29
			11/17–12/5	12/5–1/15	
10/7–10/30	10/31–11/23	11/24–12/17	12/18–12/31	1/1–1/15	1/10–1/20
				1/29–4/4	4/5–5/6
11/19–12/8	12/9–12/31		1/1–1/10	1/11–2/2	2/3–2/27
9/6–9/30	1/1–1/4	1/5–1/29	1/30–2/23	2/24–3/18	3/19–4/12
	10/1–10/24	10/25–11/17	11/18–12/12	12/13–12/31	
10/21–11/13	11/14–12/7	12/8–12/31		1/1–1/6	1/7–2/2
8/11–9/6	9/7–10/9	10/10–12/5	1/1–1/24	1/25–2/17	2/18–3/13
	12/6–12/30	12/31			
9/22–10/15	10/16–11/8	1/1–2/6	2/7–3/6	3/7–4/1	4/2–4/26
		11/9–12/2	12/3–12/26	12/27–12/31	
11/3–11/27	11/28–12/21	12/22–12/31		1/1–1/19	1/20–2/13
8/22–9/16	9/17–10/11	1/1–1/14	1/15–2/7	2/8–3/4	3/5–3/28
		10/12–11/6	11/7–12/5	12/6–12/31	
10/6–10/29	10/30–11/22	11/23–12/16	12/17–12/31	1/1–4/5	4/6–5/6
11/9–12/8	12/9–12/31		1/1–1/9	1/10–2/2	2/3–2/26
9/5–9/30	1/1–1/3	1/4–1/28	1/29–2/22	2/23–3/10	3/10–4/11
	9/31–10/23	10/24–11/17	11/18–12/11	12/12–12/31	
10/21–11/13	11/14–12/7	12/8–12/31		1/1–1/6	1/7–2/2
8/10–9/6	9/7–10/10	10/11–11/28	1/1–1/24	1/25–2/16	2/17–3/12
	11/29–12/31				
9/21–10/14	1/1	1/2–2/6	2/7–3/5	3/6–3/31	4/1–4/26
	10/15–11/7	11/8–12/1	12/2–12/25	12/26–12/31	
11/13–11/26	11/27–12/21	12/22–12/31		1/1–1/19	1/20–2/12
8/22–9/15	9/16–10/11	1/1–1/14	1/15–2/7	2/8–3/3	3/4–3/27
		10/12–11/6	11/7–12/5	12/6–12/31	

VENUS SIGNS 1901–2007

	Aries	Taurus	Gemini	Cancer	Leo	Virgo
1926	5/7–6/2	6/3–6/28	6/29–7/23	7/24–8/17	8/18–9/11	9/12–10/5
1927	2/27–3/22	3/23–4/16	4/17–5/11	5/12–6/7	6/8–7/7	7/8–11/9
1928	4/12–5/5	5/6–5/29	5/30–6/23	6/24–7/17	7/18–8/11	8/12–9/4
1929	2/3–3/7 4/20–6/2	3/8–4/19 6/3–7/7	7/8–8/4	8/5–8/30	8/31–9/25	9/26–10/19
1930	3/13–4/5	4/6–4/30	5/1–5/24	5/25–6/18	6/19–7/14	7/15–8/9
1931	4/26–5/20	5/21–6/13	6/14–7/8	7/9–8/2	8/3–8/26	8/27–9/19
1932	2/12–3/8	3/9–4/3	4/4–5/5 7/13–7/27	5/6–7/12 7/28–9/8	9/9–10/6	10/7–11/1
1933	3/27–4/19	4/20–5/28	5/29–6/8	6/9–7/2	7/3–7/26	7/27–8/20
1934	5/6–6/1	6/2–6/27	6/28–7/22	7/23–8/16	8/17–9/10	9/11–10/4
1935	2/26–3/21	3/22–4/15	4/16–5/10	5/11–6/6	6/7–7/6	7/7–11/8
1936	4/11–5/4	5/5–5/28	5/29–6/22	6/23–7/16	7/17–8/10	8/11–9/4
1937	2/2–3/8 4/14–6/3	3/9–4/13 6/4–7/6	7/7–8/3	8/4–8/29	8/30–9/24	9/25–10/18
1938	3/12–4/4	4/5–4/28	4/29–5/23	5/24–6/18	6/19–7/13	7/14–8/8
1939	4/25–5/19	5/20–6/13	6/14–7/8	7/9–8/1	8/2–8/25	8/26–9/19
1940	2/12–3/7	3/8–4/3	4/4–5/5 7/5–7/31	5/6–7/4 8/1–9/8	9/9–10/5	10/6–10/31
1941	3/27–4/19	4/20–5/13	5/14–6/6	6/7–7/1	7/2–7/26	7/27–8/20
1942	5/6–6/1	6/2–6/26	6/27–7/22	7/23–8/16	8/17–9/9	9/10–10/3
1943	2/25–3/20	3/21–4/14	4/15–5/10	5/11–6/6	6/7–7/6	7/7–11/8
1944	4/10–5/3	5/4–5/28	5/29–6/21	6/22–7/16	7/17–8/9	8/10–9/2
1945	2/2–3/10 4/7–6/3	3/11–4/6 6/4–7/6	7/7–8/3	8/4–8/29	8/30–9/23	9/24–10/18
1946	3/11–4/4	4/5–4/28	4/29–5/23	5/24–6/17	6/18–7/12	7/13–8/8
1947	4/25–5/19	5/20–6/12	6/13–7/7	7/8–8/1	8/2–8/25	8/26–9/18
1948	2/11–3/7	3/8–4/3	4/4–5/6 6/29–8/2	5/7–6/28 8/3–9/7	9/8–10/5	10/6–10/31
1949	3/26–4/19	4/20–5/13	5/14–6/6	6/7–6/30	7/1–7/25	7/26–8/19
1950	5/5–5/31	6/1–6/26	6/27–7/21	7/22–8/15	8/16–9/9	9/10–10/3
1951	2/25–3/21	3/22–4/15	4/16–5/10	5/11–6/6	6/7–7/7	7/8–11/9

Libra	Scorpio	Sagittarius	Capricorn	Aquarius	Pisces
10/6–10/29	10/30–11/22	11/23–12/16	12/17–12/31	1/1–4/5	4/6–5/6
11/10–12/8	12/9–12/31	1/1–1/7	1/8	1/9–2/1	2/2–2/26
9/5–9/28	1/1–1/3	1/4–1/28	1/29–2/22	2/23–3/17	3/18–4/11
	9/29–10/23	10/24–11/16	11/17–12/11	12/12–12/31	
10/20–11/12	11/13–12/6	12/7–12/30	12/31	1/1–1/5	1/6–2/2
8/10–9/6	9/7–10/11	10/12–11/21	1/1–1/23	1/24–2/16	2/17–3/12
	11/22–12/31				
9/20–10/13	1/1–1/3	1/4 2/6	2/7–3/4	3/5–3/31	4/1–4/25
	10/14–11/6	11/7–11/30	12/1–12/24	12/25–12/31	
11/2–11/25	11/26–12/20	12/21–12/31		1/1–1/18	1/19–2/11
8/21–9/14	9/15–10/10	1/1–1/13	1/14–2/6	2/7–3/2	3/3–3/26
		10/11–11/5	11/6–12/4	12/5–12/31	
10/5–10/28	10/29–11/21	11/22–12/15	10/16–12/31	1/1–4/5	4/6–5/5
11/9–12/7	10/8 12/31		1/1–1/7	1/8–1/31	2/1–2/25
9/5–9/27	1/1–1/2	1/3–1/27	1/28–2/21	2/22–3/16	3/17–4/10
	9/28–10/22	10/23–11/15	11/16–12/10	12/11–12/31	
10/19–11/11	11/12–12/5	12/6–12/29	12/30–12/31	1/1–1/5	1/6–2/1
8/9–9/6	9/7–10/13	10/14–11/14	1/1–1/22	1/23–2/15	2/16–3/11
	11/15–12/31				
9/20–10/13	1/1–1/3	1/4–2/5	2/6–3/4	3/5–3/30	3/31–4/24
	10/14–11/6	11/7–11/30	12/1–12/24	12/25–12/31	
11/1–11/25	11/26–12/19	12/20–12/31		1/1–1/18	1/19–2/11
8/21–9/14	9/15–10/9	1/1–1/12	1/13–2/5	2/6–3/1	3/2–3/26
		10/10–11/5	11/6–12/4	12/5–12/31	
10/4–10/27	10/28–11/20	11/21–12/14	12/15–12/31	1/1 4/5	4/6–5/5
11/9–12/7	12/8–12/31		1/1–1/7	1/8–1/31	2/1–2/24
9/3–9/27	1/1–1/2	1/3–1/27	1/28–2/20	2/21–3/16	3/17–4/9
	9/28–10/21	10/22–11/15	11/16–12/10	12/11–12/31	
10/19–11/11	11/12–12/5	12/6–12/29	12/30–12/31	1/1–1/4	1/5–2/1
8/9–9/6	9/7–10/15	10/16–11/7	1/1–1/21	1/22–2/14	2/15–3/10
	11/8–12/31				
9/19–10/12	1/1–1/4	1/5–2/5	2/6–3/4	3/5–3/29	3/30–4/24
	10/13–11/5	11/6–11/29	11/30–12/23	12/24–12/31	
11/1–11/25	11/26–12/19	12/20–12/31		1/1–1/17	1/18–2/10
8/20–9/14	9/15–10/9	1/1–1/12	1/13–2/5	2/6–3/1	3/2–3/25
		10/10–11/5	11/6–12/5	12/6–12/31	
10/4–10/27	10/28–11/20	11/21–12/13	12/14–12/31	1/1–4/5	4/6–5/4
11/10–12/7	12/8–12/31		1/1–1/7	1/8–1/31	2/1–2/24

VENUS SIGNS 1901–2007

	Aries	Taurus	Gemini	Cancer	Leo	Virgo
1952	4/10–5/4	5/5–5/28	5/29–6/21	6/22–7/16	7/17–8/9	8/10–9/3
1953	2/2–3/3	3/4–3/31	7/8–8/3	8/4–8/29	8/30–9/24	9/25–10/18
	4/1–6/5	6/6–7/7				
1954	3/12–4/4	4/5–4/28	4/29–5/23	5/24–6/17	6/18–7/13	7/14–8/8
1955	4/25–5/19	5/20–6/13	6/14–7/7	7/8–8/1	8/2–8/25	8/26–9/18
1956	2/12–3/7	3/8–4/4	4/5–5/7	5/8–6/23	9/9–10/5	10/6–10/31
			6/24–8/4	8/5–9/8		
1957	3/26–4/19	4/20–5/13	5/14–6/6	6/7–7/1	7/2–7/26	7/27–8/19
1958	5/6–5/31	6/1–6/26	6/27–7/22	7/23–8/15	8/16–9/9	9/10–10/3
1959	2/25–3/20	3/21–4/14	4/15–5/10	5/11–6/6	6/7–7/8	7/9–9/20
					9/21–9/24	9/25–11/9
1960	4/10–5/3	5/4–5/28	5/29–6/21	6/22–7/15	7/16–8/9	8/10–9/2
1961	2/3–6/5	6/6–7/7	7/8–8/3	8/4–8/29	8/30–9/23	9/24–10/17
1962	3/11–4/3	4/4–4/28	4/29–5/22	5/23–6/17	6/18–7/12	7/13–8/8
1963	4/24–5/18	5/19–6/12	6/13–7/7	7/8–7/31	8/1–8/25	8/26–9/18
1964	2/11–3/7	3/8–4/4	4/5–5/9	5/10–6/17	9/9–10/5	10/6–10/31
			6/18–8/5	8/6–9/8		
1965	3/26–4/18	4/19–5/12	5/13–6/6	6/7–6/30	7/1–7/25	7/26–8/19
1966	5/6–5/31	6/1–6/26	6/27–7/21	7/22–8/15	8/16–9/8	9/9–10/2
1967	2/24–3/20	3/21–4/14	4/15–5/10	5/11–6/6	6/7–7/8	7/9–9/9
					9/10–10/1	10/2–11/9
1968	4/9–5/3	5/4–5/27	5/28–6/20	6/21–7/15	7/16–8/8	8/9–9/2
1969	2/3–6/6	6/7–7/6	7/7–8/3	8/4–8/28	8/29–9/22	9/23–10/17
1970	3/11–4/3	4/4–4/27	4/28–5/22	5/23–6/16	6/17–7/12	7/13–8/8
1971	4/24–5/18	5/19–6/12	6/13–7/6	7/7–7/31	8/1–8/24	8/25–9/17
1972	2/11–3/7	3/8–4/3	4/4–5/10	5/11–6/11		
			6/12–8/6	8/7–9/8	9/9–10/5	10/6–10/30
1973	3/25–4/18	4/18–5/12	5/13–6/5	6/6–6/29	7/1–7/25	7/26–8/19
1974	5/5–5/31	6/1–6/25	6/26–7/21	7/22–8/14	8/15–9/8	9/9–10/2
1975	2/24–3/20	3/21–4/13	4/14–5/9	5/10–6/6	6/7–7/9	7/10–9/2
					9/3–10/4	10/5–11/9

Libra	Scorpio	Sagittarius	Capricorn	Aquarius	Pisces
9/4–9/27	1/1–1/2	1/3–1/27	1/28–2/20	2/21–3/16	3/17–4/9
	9/28–10/21	10/22–11/15	11/16–12/10	12/11–12/31	
10/19–11/11	11/12–12/5	12/6–12/29	12/30–12/31	1/1–1/5	1/6–2/1
8/9–9/6	9/7–10/22	10/23–10/27	1/1–1/22	1/23–2/15	2/16–3/11
	10/28–12/31				
9/19–10/13	1/1–1/6	1/7–2/5	2/6–3/4	3/5–3/30	3/31–4/24
	10/14–11/5	11/6–11/30	12/1–12/24	12/25–12/31	
11/1–11/25	11/26–12/19	12/20–12/31		1/1–1/17	1/18–2/11
8/20–9/14	9/15–10/9	1/1–1/12	1/13–2/5	2/6–3/1	3/2–3/25
		10/10–11/5	11/6–12/6	12/7–12/31	
10/4–10/27	10/28–11/20	11/21–12/14	12/15–12/31	1/1–4/6	4/7–5/5
11/10–12/7	12/8–12/31		1/1–1/7	1/8–1/31	2/1–2/24
9/3–9/26	1/1–1/2	1/3–1/27	1/28–2/20	2/21–3/15	3/16–4/8
	9/27–10/21	10/22–11/15	11/16–12/10	12/11–12/31	
10/18–11/11	11/12–12/4	12/5–12/28	12/29–12/31	1/1–1/5	1/6–2/2
8/9–9/6	9/7–12/31		1/1–1/21	1/22–2/14	2/15–3/10
9/19–10/12	1/1–1/6	1/7–2/5	2/6–3/4	3/5–3/29	3/30–4/23
	10/13–11/5	11/6–11/29	11/30–12/23	12/24–12/31	
11/1–11/24	11/25–12/19	12/20–12/31		1/1–1/16	1/17–2/10
8/20–9/13	9/14–10/9	1/1–1/12	1/13–2/5	2/6–3/1	3/2–3/25
		10/10–11/5	11/6–12/7	12/8–12/31	
10/3–10/26	10/27–11/19	11/20–12/13	2/7–2/25	1/1–2/6	4/7–5/5
			12/14–12/31	2/26–4/6	
11/10–12/7	12/8–12/31		1/1–1/6	1/7–1/30	1/31–2/23
9/3–9/26	1/1	1/2–1/26	1/27–2/20	2/21–3/15	3/16–4/8
	9/27–10/21	10/22–11/14	11/15–12/0	12/10–12/31	
10/18–11/10	11/11–12/4	12/5–12/28	12/29–12/31	1/1–1/4	1/5–2/2
8/9–9/7	9/8–12/31		1/1–1/21	1/22–2/14	2/15–3/10
9/18–10/11	1/1–1/7	1/8–2/5	2/6–3/4	3/5–3/29	3/30–4/23
	10/12–11/5	11/6–11/29	11/30–12/23	12/24–12/31	
	11/25–12/18	12/19–12/31		1/1–1/16	1/17–2/10
10/31–11/24					
8/20–9/13	9/14–10/8	1/1–1/12	1/13–2/4	2/5–2/28	3/1–3/24
		10/9–11/5	11/6–12/7	12/0–12/31	
			1/30–2/28	1/1–1/29	
10/3–10/26	10/27–11/19	11/20–12/13	12/14–12/31	3/1–4/6	4/7–5/4
11/10–12/7	12/8–12/31		1/1–1/6	1/7–1/30	1/31–2/23

VENUS SIGNS 1901–2007

	Aries	Taurus	Gemini	Cancer	Leo	Virgo
1976	4/8–5/2	5/2–5/27	5/27–6/20	6/20–7/14	7/14–8/8	8/8–9/1
1977	2/2–6/6	6/6–7/6	7/6–8/2	8/2–8/28	8/28–9/22	9/22–10/17
1978	3/9–4/2	4/2–4/27	4/27–5/22	5/22–6/16	6/16–7/12	7/12–8/6
1979	4/23–5/18	5/18–6/11	6/11–7/6	7/6–7/30	7/30–8/24	8/24–9/17
1980	2/9–3/6	3/6–4/3	4/3–5/12 6/5–8/6	5/12–6/5 8/6–9/7	9/7–10/4	10/4–10/30
1981	3/24–4/17	4/17–5/11	5/11–6/5	6/5–6/29	6/29–7/24	7/24–8/18
1982	5/4–5/30	5/30–6/25	6/25–7/20	7/20–8/14	8/14–9/7	9/7–10/2
1983	2/22–3/19	3/19–4/13	4/13–5/9	5/9–6/6	6/6–7/10 8/27–10/5	7/10–8/27 10/5–11/9
1984	4/7–5/2	5/2–5/26	5/26–6/20	6/20–7/14	7/14–8/7	8/7–9/1
1985	2/2–6/6	6/7–7/6	7/6–8/2	8/2–8/28	8/28–9/22	9/22–10/16
1986	3/9–4/2	4/2–4/26	4/26–5/21	5/21–6/15	6/15–7/11	7/11–8/7
1987	4/22–5/17	5/17–6/11	6/11–7/5	7/5–7/30	7/30–8/23	8/23–9/16
1988	2/9–3/6	3/6–4/3	4/3–5/17 5/27–8/6	5/17–5/27 8/28–9/22	9/7–10/4 9/22–10/16	10/4–10/29
1989	3/23–4/16	4/16–5/11	5/11–6/4	6/4–6/29	6/29–7/24	7/24–8/18
1990	5/4–5/30	5/30–6/25	6/25–7/20	7/20–8/13	8/13–9/7	9/7–10/1
1991	2/22–3/18	3/18–4/13	4/13–5/9	5/9–6/6	6/6–7/11 8/21–10/6	7/11–8/21 10/6–11/9
1992	4/7–5/1	5/1–5/26	5/26–6/19	6/19–7/13	7/13–8/7	8/7–8/31
1993	2/2–6/6	6/6–7/6	7/6–8/1	8/1–8/27	8/27–9/21	9/21–10/16
1994	3/8–4/1	4/1–4/26	4/26–5/21	5/21–6/15	6/15–7/11	7/11–8/7
1995	4/22–5/16	5/16–6/10	6/10–7/5	7/5–7/29	7/29–8/23	8/23–9/16
1996	2/9–3/6	3/6–4/3	4/3–8/7	8/7–9/7	9/7–10/4	10/4–10/29
1997	3/23–4/16	4/16–5/10	5/10–6/4	6/4–6/28	6/28–7/23	7/23–8/17
1998	5/3–5/29	5/29–6/24	6/24–7/19	7/19–8/13	8/13–9/6	9/6–9/30
1999	2/21–3/18	3/18–4/12	4/12–5/8	5/8–6/5	6/5–7/12 8/15–10/7	7/12–8/15 10/7–11/9
2000	4/6–5/1	5/1–5/25	5/25–6/13	6/13–7/13	7/13–8/6	8/6–8/31
2001	2/2–6/6	6/6–7/5	7/5–8/1	8/1–8/26	8/26–9/20	9/20–10/15
2002	3/7–4/1	4/1–4/25	4/25–5/20	5/20–6/14	6/14–7/10	7/10–8/7
2003	4/21–5/16	5/16–6/9	6/9–7/4	7/4–7/29	7/29–8/22	8/22–9/15
2004	2/8–3/5	3/5–4/3	4/3–8/7	8/7–9/6	9/6–10/3	10/3–10/28
2005	3/22–4/15	4/15–5/10	5/10–6/3	6/3–6/28	6/28–7/23	7/23–8/17
2006	5/3–5/29	5/29–6/24	6/24–7/19	7/19–8/12	8/12–9/6	9/6–9/30
2007	2/21–3/16	3/17–4/10	4/11–5/7	5/8–6/4	6/5–7/13 8/8–10/6	7/14–8/7 10/7–11/7

Libra	Scorpio	Sagittarius	Capricorn	Aquarius	Pisces
9/1–9/26	9/26–10/20	1/1–1/26	1/26–2/19	2/19–3/15	3/15–4/8
10/17–11/10	11/10–12/4	12/4–12/27	12/27–1/20/78		1/4–2/2
8/6–9/7	9/7–1/7			1/20–2/13	2/13–3/9
9/17–10/11	10/11–11/4		2/5–3/3	3/3–3/29	3/29–4/23
		11/4–11/28	11/28–12/22	12/22–1/16/80	
10/30–11/24	11/24–12/18	12/18–1/11/81			1/16–2/9
8/18–9/12	9/12–10/9	10/9–11/5	1/11–2/4	2/4–2/28	2/28–3/24
			11/5–12/8	12/8–1/23/82	
10/2–10/26	10/26–11/18	11/18–12/12	1/23–3/2	3/2–4/6	4/6–5/4
			12/12–1/5/83		
11/9–12/6	12/6–1/1/84			1/5–1/29	1/29–2/22
9/1–9/25	9/25–10/20	1/1–1/25	1/25–2/19	2/19–3/14	3/14–4/7
		10/20–11/13	11/13–12/9	12/10–1/4	
10/16–11/9	11/9–12/3	12/3–12/27	12/28–1/19		1/4–2/2
8/7–9/7	9/7–1/7			1/20–2/13	2/13–3/9
9/16–10/10	10/10–11/3		2/5–3/3	3/3–3/28	3/28–4/22
		11/3–11/28	11/28–12/22	12/22–1/15	
10/29–11/23	11/23–12/17	12/17–1/10			1/15–2/9
8/18–9/12	9/12–10/8	10/8–11/5	1/10–2/3	2/3–2/27	2/27–3/23
			11/5–12/10	12/10–1/16/90	
10/1–10/25	10/25–11/18	11/18–12/12	1/16–3/3	3/3–4/6	4/6–5/4
			12/12–1/5		
11/9–12/6	12/6–12/31	12/31–1/25/92		1/5–1/29	1/29–2/22
8/31–9/25	9/25–10/19	10/19–11/13	1/25–2/18	2/18–3/13	3/13–4/7
			11/13–12/8	12/8–1/3/93	
10/16–11/9	11/9–12/2	12/2–12/26	12/26–1/19		1/3–2/2
8/7–9/7	9/7–1/7			1/19–2/12	2/12–3/8
9/16–10/10	10/10–11/13	1/7–2/4	2/4–3/2	3/2–3/28	3/28–4/22
		11/3–11/27	11/27–12/21	12/21–1/15	
10/29–11/23	11/23–12/17	12/17–1/10/97			1/15–2/9
8/17–9/12	9/12–10/8	10/8–11/5	1/10–2/3	2/3–2/27	2/27–3/23
			11/5–12/12	12/12–1/9	
9/30–10/24	10/24–11/17	11/17–12/11	1/9–3/4	3/4–4/6	4/6–5/3
11/9–12/5	12/5–12/31	12/31–1/24		1/4–1/28	1/28–2/21
8/31–9/24	9/24–10/19	10/19–11/13	1/24–2/18	2/18–3/12	3/13–4/6
			11/13–12/8	12/8	
10/15–11/8	11/8–12/2	12/2–12/26	12/26/01–1/18/02	12/0/00 1/3/01	1/3–2/2
8/7–9/7	9/7–1/7/03		12/26/01–1/18	1/18–2/11	2/11–3/7
9/15–10/9	10/9–11/2		2/4–3/2	3/2–3/27	3/27–4/21
		11/2–11/26	11/26–12/21	12/21–1/14/04	
10/28–11/22	11/22–12/16	12/16–1/9/05		1/1–1/14	1/14–2/8
8/17–9/11	9/11–10/8	10/8–11/15	1/9–2/2	2/2–2/26	2/26–3/22
			11/5–12/15	12/15–1/1/06	
9/30–10/24	10/24–11/17	11/17–12/11	1/1–3/5	3/5–4/6	4/6–5/3
11/8–12/4	12/5–12/29	12/30–1/24/08		1/3–1/26	1/27–2/20

How to Use the Mars, Jupiter, and Saturn Tables

Find the year of your birth on the left side of each column. The dates when the planet entered each sign are listed on the right side of each column. (Signs are abbreviated to three letters.) Your birthday should fall on or between each date listed, and your planetary placement should correspond to the earlier sign of that period.

All planet changes are calculated for the Greenwich Mean Time zone.

MARS SIGNS 1901–2007

1901	MAR	1	Leo		OCT	1	Vir
	MAY	11	Vir		NOV	20	Lib
	JUL	13	Lib	1905	JAN	13	Scp
	AUG	31	Scp		AUG	21	Sag
	OCT	14	Sag		OCT	8	Cap
	NOV	24	Cap		NOV	18	Aqu
1902	JAN	1	Aqu		DEC	27	Pic
	FEB	8	Pic	1906	FEB	4	Ari
	MAR	19	Ari		MAR	17	Tau
	APR	27	Tau		APR	28	Gem
	JUN	7	Gem		JUN	11	Can
	JUL	20	Can		JUL	27	Leo
	SEP	4	Leo		SEP	12	Vir
	OCT	23	Vir		OCT	30	Lib
	DEC	20	Lib		DEC	17	Scp
1903	APR	19	Vir	1907	FEB	5	Sag
	MAY	30	Lib		APR	1	Cap
	AUG	6	Scp		OCT	13	Aqu
	SEP	22	Sag		NOV	29	Pic
	NOV	3	Cap	1908	JAN	11	Ari
	DEC	12	Aqu		FEB	23	Tau
1904	JAN	19	Pic		APR	7	Gem
	FEB	27	Ari		MAY	22	Can
	APR	6	Tau		JUL	8	Leo
	MAY	18	Gem		AUG	24	Vir
	JUN	30	Can		OCT	10	Lib
	AUG	15	Leo		NOV	25	Scp

1909	JAN	10	Sag		MAR	9	Pic
	FEB	24	Cap		APR	16	Ari
	APR	9	Aqu		MAY	26	Tau
	MAY	25	Pic		JUL	6	Gem
	JUL	21	Ari		AUG	19	Can
	SEP	26	Pic		OCT	7	Leo
	NOV	20	Ari	1916	MAY	28	Vir
1910	JAN	23	Tau		JUL	23	Lib
	MAR	14	Gem		SEP	8	Scp
	MAY	1	Can		OCT	22	Sag
	JUN	19	Leo		DEC	1	Cap
	AUG	6	Vir	1917	JAN	9	Aqu
	SEP	22	Lib		FEB	16	Pic
	NOV	6	Scp		MAR	26	Ari
	DEC	20	Sag		MAY	4	Tau
1911	JAN	31	Cap		JUN	14	Gem
	MAR	14	Aqu		JUL	28	Can
	APR	23	Pic		SEP	12	Leo
	JUN	2	Ari		NOV	2	Vir
	JUL	15	Tau	1918	JAN	11	Lib
	SEP	5	Gem		FEB	25	Vir
	NOV	30	Tau		JUN	23	Lib
1912	JAN	30	Gem		AUG	17	Scp
	APR	5	Can		OCT	1	Sag
	MAY	28	Leo		NOV	11	Cap
	JUL	17	Vir		DEC	20	Aqu
	SEP	2	Lib	1919	JAN	27	Pic
	OCT	18	Scp		MAR	6	Ari
	NOV	30	Sag		APR	15	Tau
1913	JAN	10	Cap		MAY	26	Gem
	FEB	19	Aqu		JUL	8	Can
	MAR	30	Pic		AUG	23	Leo
	MAY	8	Ari		OCT	10	Vir
	JUN	17	Tau		NOV	30	Lib
	JUL	29	Gem	1920	JAN	31	Scp
	SEP	15	Can		APR	23	Lib
1914	MAY	1	Leo		JUL	10	Scp
	JUN	26	Vir		SEP	4	Sag
	AUG	14	Lib		OCT	18	Cap
	SEP	29	Scp		NOV	27	Aqu
	NOV	11	Sag	1921	JAN	5	Pic
	DEC	22	Cap		FEB	13	Ari
1915	JAN	30	Aqu		MAR	25	Tau

Year	Mon	Day	Sign		Year	Mon	Day	Sign
	MAY	6	Gem			OCT	26	Scp
	JUN	18	Can			DEC	8	Sag
	AUG	3	Leo		1928	JAN	19	Cap
	SEP	19	Vir			FEB	28	Aqu
	NOV	6	Lib			APR	7	Pic
	DEC	26	Scp			MAY	16	Ari
1922	FEB	18	Sag			JUN	26	Tau
	SEP	13	Cap			AUG	9	Gem
	OCT	30	Aqu			OCT	3	Can
	DEC	11	Pic			DEC	20	Gem
1923	JAN	21	Ari		1929	MAR	10	Can
	MAR	4	Tau			MAY	13	Leo
	APR	16	Gem			JUL	4	Vir
	MAY	30	Can			AUG	21	Lib
	JUL	16	Leo			OCT	6	Scp
	SEP	1	Vir			NOV	18	Sag
	OCT	18	Lib			DEC	29	Cap
	DEC	4	Scp		1930	FEB	6	Aqu
1924	JAN	19	Sag			MAR	17	Pic
	MAR	6	Cap			APR	24	Ari
	APR	24	Aqu			JUN	3	Tau
	JUN	24	Pic			JUL	14	Gem
	AUG	24	Aqu			AUG	28	Can
	OCT	19	Pic			OCT	20	Leo
	DEC	19	Ari		1931	FEB	16	Can
1925	FEB	5	Tau			MAR	30	Leo
	MAR	24	Gem			JUN	10	Vir
	MAY	9	Can			AUG	1	Lib
	JUN	26	Leo			SEP	17	Scp
	AUG	12	Vir			OCT	30	Sag
	SEP	28	Lib			DEC	10	Cap
	NOV	13	Scp		1932	JAN	18	Aqu
	DEC	28	Sag			FEB	25	Pic
1926	FEB	9	Cap			APR	3	Ari
	MAR	23	Aqu			MAY	12	Tau
	MAY	3	Pic			JUN	22	Gem
	JUN	15	Ari			AUG	4	Can
	AUG	1	Tau			SEP	20	Leo
1927	FEB	22	Gem			NOV	13	Vir
	APR	17	Can		1933	JUL	6	Lib
	JUN	6	Leo			AUG	26	Scp
	JUL	25	Vir			OCT	9	Sag
	SEP	10	Lib			NOV	19	Cap

	DEC	28	Aqu		FEB	17	Tau
1934	FEB	4	Pic		APR	1	Gem
	MAR	14	Ari		MAY	17	Can
	APR	22	Tau		JUL	3	Leo
	JUN	2	Gem		AUG	19	Vir
	JUL	15	Can		OCT	5	Lib
	AUG	30	Leo		NOV	20	Scp
	OCT	18	Vir	1941	JAN	4	Sag
	DEC	11	Lib		FEB	17	Cap
1935	JUL	29	Scp		APR	2	Aqu
	SEP	16	Sag		MAY	16	Pic
	OCT	28	Cap		JUL	2	Ari
	DEC	7	Aqu	1942	JAN	11	Tau
1936	JAN	14	Pic		MAR	7	Gem
	FEB	22	Ari		APR	26	Can
	APR	1	Tau		JUN	14	Leo
	MAY	13	Gem		AUG	1	Vir
	JUN	25	Can		SEP	17	Lib
	AUG	10	Leo		NOV	1	Scp
	SEP	26	Vir		DEC	15	Sag
	NOV	14	Lib	1943	JAN	26	Cap
1937	JAN	5	Scp		MAR	8	Aqu
	MAR	13	Sag		APR	17	Pic
	MAY	14	Scp		MAY	27	Ari
	AUG	8	Sag		JUL	7	Tau
	SEP	30	Cap		AUG	23	Gem
	NOV	11	Aqu	1944	MAR	28	Can
	DEC	21	Pic		MAY	22	Leo
1938	JAN	30	Ari		JUL	12	Vlr
	MAR	12	Tau		AUG	29	Lib
	APR	23	Gem		OCT	13	Scp
	JUN	7	Can		NOV	25	Sag
	JUL	22	Leo	1945	JAN	5	Cap
	SEP	7	Vir		FEB	14	Aqu
	OCT	25	Lib		MAR	25	Pic
	DEC	11	Scp		MAY	2	Ari
1939	JAN	29	Sag		JUN	11	Tau
	MAR	21	Cap		JUL	23	Gem
	MAY	25	Aqu		SEP	7	Can
	JUL	21	Cap		NOV	11	Leo
	SEP	24	Aqu		DEC	26	Can
	NOV	19	Pic	1946	APR	22	Leo
1940	JAN	4	Ari		JUN	20	Vir

	AUG	9	Lib		OCT	12	Cap
	SEP	24	Scp		NOV	21	Aqu
	NOV	6	Sag		DEC	30	Pic
	DEC	17	Cap	1953	FEB	8	Ari
1947	JAN	25	Aqu		MAR	20	Tau
	MAR	4	Pic		MAY	1	Gem
	APR	11	Ari		JUN	14	Can
	MAY	21	Tau		JUL	29	Leo
	JUL	1	Gem		SEP	14	Vir
	AUG	13	Can		NOV	1	Lib
	OCT	1	Leo		DEC	20	Scp
	DEC	1	Vir	1954	FEB	9	Sag
1948	FEB	12	Leo		APR	12	Cap
	MAY	18	Vir		JUL	3	Sag
	JUL	17	Lib		AUG	24	Cap
	SEP	3	Scp		OCT	21	Aqu
	OCT	17	Sag		DEC	4	Pic
	NOV	26	Cap	1955	JAN	15	Ari
1949	JAN	4	Aqu		FEB	26	Tau
	FEB	11	Pic		APR	10	Gem
	MAR	21	Ari		MAY	26	Can
	APR	30	Tau		JUL	11	Leo
	JUN	10	Gem		AUG	27	Vir
	JUL	23	Can		OCT	13	Lib
	SEP	7	Leo		NOV	29	Scp
	OCT	27	Vir	1956	JAN	14	Sag
	DEC	26	Lib		FEB	28	Cap
1950	MAR	28	Vir		APR	14	Aqu
	JUN	11	Lib		JUN	3	Pic
	AUG	10	Scp		DEC	6	Ari
	SEP	25	Sag	1957	JAN	28	Tau
	NOV	6	Cap		MAR	17	Gem
	DEC	15	Aqu		MAY	4	Can
1951	JAN	22	Pic		JUN	21	Leo
	MAR	1	Ari		AUG	8	Vir
	APR	10	Tau		SEP	24	Lib
	MAY	21	Gem		NOV	8	Scp
	JUL	3	Can		DEC	23	Sag
	AUG	18	Leo	1958	FEB	3	Cap
	OCT	5	Vir		MAR	17	Aqu
	NOV	24	Lib		APR	27	Pic
1952	JAN	20	Scp		JUN	7	Ari
	AUG	27	Sag		JUL	21	Tau

Year	Month	Day	Sign		Year	Month	Day	Sign
	SEP	21	Gem			NOV	6	Vir
	OCT	29	Tau		1965	JUN	29	Lib
1959	FEB	10	Gem			AUG	20	Scp
	APR	10	Can			OCT	4	Sag
	JUN	1	Leo			NOV	14	Cap
	JUL	20	Vir			DEC	23	Aqu
	SEP	5	Lib		1966	JAN	30	Pic
	OCT	21	Scp			MAR	9	Ari
	DEC	3	Sag			APR	17	Tau
1960	JAN	14	Cap			MAY	28	Gem
	FEB	23	Aqu			JUL	11	Can
	APR	2	Pic			AUG	25	Leo
	MAY	11	Ari			OCT	12	Vir
	JUN	20	Tau			DEC	4	Lib
	AUG	2	Gem		1967	FEB	12	Scp
	SEP	21	Can			MAR	31	Lib
1961	FEB	5	Gem			JUL	19	Scp
	FEB	7	Can			SEP	10	Sag
	MAY	6	Leo			OCT	23	Cap
	JUN	28	Vir			DEC	1	Aqu
	AUG	17	Lib		1968	JAN	9	Pic
	OCT	1	Scp			FEB	17	Ari
	NOV	13	Sag			MAR	27	Tau
	DEC	24	Cap			MAY	8	Gem
1962	FEB	1	Aqu			JUN	21	Can
	MAR	12	Pic			AUG	5	Leo
	APR	19	Ari			SEP	21	Vir
	MAY	28	Tau			NOV	9	Lib
	JUL	9	Gem			DEC	29	Scp
	AUG	22	Can		1969	FEB	25	Sag
	OCT	11	Leo			SEP	21	Cap
1963	JUN	3	Vir			NOV	4	Aqu
	JUL	27	Lib			DEC	15	Pic
	SEP	12	Scp		1970	JAN	24	Ari
	OCT	25	Sag			MAR	7	Tau
	DEC	5	Cap			APR	18	Gem
1964	JAN	13	Aqu			JUN	2	Can
	FEB	20	Pic			JUL	18	Leo
	MAR	29	Ari			SEP	3	Vir
	MAY	7	Tau			OCT	20	Lib
	JUN	17	Gem			DEC	6	Scp
	JUL	30	Can		1971	JAN	23	Sag
	SEP	15	Leo			MAR	12	Cap

Year	Month	Day	Sign		Year	Month	Day	Sign
	MAY	3	Aqu			JUN	6	Tau
	NOV	6	Pic			JUL	17	Gem
	DEC	26	Ari			SEP	1	Can
1972	FEB	10	Tau			OCT	26	Leo
	MAR	27	Gem		1978	JAN	26	Can
	MAY	12	Can			APR	10	Leo
	JUN	28	Leo			JUN	14	Vir
	AUG	15	Vir			AUG	4	Lib
	SEP	30	Lib			SEP	19	Scp
	NOV	15	Scp			NOV	2	Sag
	DEC	30	Sag			DEC	12	Cap
1973	FEB	12	Cap		1979	JAN	20	Aqu
	MAR	26	Aqu			FEB	27	Pic
	MAY	8	Pic			APR	7	Ari
	JUN	20	Ari			MAY	16	Tau
	AUG	12	Tau			JUN	26	Gem
	OCT	29	Ari			AUG	8	Can
	DEC	24	Tau			SEP	24	Leo
1974	FEB	27	Gem			NOV	19	Vir
	APR	20	Can		1980	MAR	11	Leo
	JUN	9	Leo			MAY	4	Vir
	JUL	27	Vir			JUL	10	Lib
	SEP	12	Lib			AUG	29	Scp
	OCT	28	Scp			OCT	12	Sag
	DEC	10	Sag			NOV	22	Cap
1975	JAN	21	Cap			DEC	30	Aqu
	MAR	3	Aqu		1981	FEB	6	Pic
	APR	11	Pic			MAR	17	Ari
	MAY	21	Ari			APR	25	Tau
	JUL	1	Tau			JUN	5	Gem
	AUG	14	Gem			JUL	18	Can
	OCT	17	Can			SEP	2	Leo
	NOV	25	Gem			OCT	21	Vir
1976	MAR	18	Can			DEC	16	Lib
	MAY	16	Leo		1982	AUG	3	Scp
	JUL	6	Vir			SEP	20	Sag
	AUG	24	Lib			OCT	31	Cap
	OCT	8	Scp			DEC	10	Aqu
	NOV	20	Sag		1983	JAN	17	Pic
1977	JAN	1	Cap			FEB	25	Ari
	FEB	9	Aqu			APR	5	Tau
	MAR	20	Pic			MAY	16	Gem
	APR	27	Ari			JUN	29	Can

Year	Month	Day	Sign		Year	Month	Day	Sign
	AUG	13	Leo		1990	JAN	29	Cap
	SEP	30	Vir			MAR	11	Aqu
	NOV	18	Lib			APR	20	Pic
1984	JAN	11	Scp			MAY	31	Ari
	AUG	17	Sag			JUL	12	Tau
	OCT	5	Cap			AUG	31	Gem
	NOV	15	Aqu			DEC	14	Tau
	DEC	25	Pic		1991	JAN	21	Gem
1985	FEB	2	Ari			APR	3	Can
	MAR	15	Tau			MAY	26	Leo
	APR	26	Gem			JUL	15	Vir
	JUN	9	Can			SEP	1	Lib
	JUL	25	Leo			OCT	16	Scp
	SEP	10	Vir			NOV	29	Sag
	OCT	27	Lib		1992	JAN	9	Cap
	DEC	14	Scp			FEB	18	Aqu
1986	FEB	2	Sag			MAR	28	Pic
	MAR	28	Cap			MAY	5	Ari
	OCT	9	Aqu			JUN	14	Tau
	NOV	26	Pic			JUL	26	Gem
1987	JAN	8	Ari			SEP	12	Can
	FEB	20	Tau		1993	APR	27	Leo
	APR	5	Gem			JUN	23	Vir
	MAY	21	Can			AUG	12	Lib
	JUL	6	Leo			SEP	27	Scp
	AUG	22	Vir			NOV	9	Sag
	OCT	8	Lib			DEC	20	Cap
	NOV	24	Scp		1994	JAN	28	Aqu
1988	JAN	8	Sag			MAR	7	Pic
	FEB	22	Cap			APR	14	Ari
	APR	6	Aqu			MAY	23	Tau
	MAY	22	Pic			JUL	3	Gem
	JUL	13	Ari			AUG	16	Can
	OCT	23	Pic			OCT	4	Leo
	NOV	1	Ari			DEC	12	Vir
1989	JAN	19	Tau		1995	JAN	22	Leo
	MAR	11	Gem			MAY	25	Vir
	APR	29	Can			JUL	21	Lib
	JUN	16	Leo			SEP	7	Scp
	AUG	3	Vir			OCT	20	Sag
	SEP	19	Lib			NOV	30	Cap
	NOV	4	Scp		1996	JAN	8	Aqu
	DEC	18	Sag			FEB	15	Pic

Year	Month	Day	Sign		Year	Month	Day	Sign
	MAR	24	Ari			MAR	1	Tau
	MAY	2	Tau			APR	13	Gem
	JUN	12	Gem			MAY	28	Can
	JUL	25	Can			JUL	13	Leo
	SEP	9	Leo			AUG	29	Vir
	OCT	30	Vir			OCT	15	Lib
1997	JAN	3	Lib			DEC	1	Scp
	MAR	8	Vir		2003	JAN	17	Sag
	JUN	19	Lib			MAR	4	Cap
	AUG	14	Scp			APR	21	Aqu
	SEP	28	Sag			JUN	17	Pic
	NOV	9	Cap			DEC	16	Ari
	DEC	18	Aqu		2004	FEB	3	Tau
1998	JAN	25	Pic			MAR	21	Gem
	MAR	4	Ari			MAY	7	Can
	APR	13	Tau			JUN	23	Leo
	MAY	24	Gem			AUG	10	Vir
	JUL	6	Can			SEP	26	Lib
	AUG	20	Leo			NOV	11	Sep
	OCT	7	Vir			DEC	25	Sag
	NOV	27	Lib		2005	FEB	6	Cap
1999	JAN	26	Scp			MAR	20	Aqu
	MAY	5	Lib			MAY	1	Pic
	JUL	5	Scp			JUN	12	Ari
	SEP	2	Sag			JUL	28	Tau
	OCT	17	Cap		2006	FEB	17	Gem
	NOV	26	Aqu			APR	14	Can
2000	JAN	4	Pic			JUN	3	Leo
	FEB	12	Ari			JUL	22	Vir
	MAR	23	Tau			SEP	8	Lib
	MAY	3	Gem			OCT	23	Scp
	JUN	16	Can			DEC	6	Sag
	AUG	1	Leo		2007	JAN	16	Cap
	SEP	17	Vir			FEB	25	Aqu
	NOV	4	Lib			APR	6	Pic
	DEC	23	Scp			MAY	15	Ari
2001	FEB	14	Sag			JUNE	24	Tau
	SEP	8	Cap			AUG	7	Gem
	OCT	27	Aqu			SEP	28	Can
	DEC	8	Pic			DEC	31	Gem*
2002	JAN	18	Ari					

*Repeat means planet is retrograde.

94

JUPITER SIGNS 1901–2007

1901	JAN	19	Cap
1902	FEB	6	Aqu
1903	FEB	20	Pic
1904	MAR	1	Ari
	AUG	8	Tau
	AUG	31	Ari
1905	MAR	7	Tau
	JUL	21	Gem
	DEC	4	Tau
1906	MAR	9	Gem
	JUL	30	Can
1907	AUG	18	Leo
1908	SEP	12	Vir
1909	OCT	11	Lib
1910	NOV	11	Scp
1911	DEC	10	Sag
1913	JAN	2	Cap
1914	JAN	21	Aqu
1915	FEB	4	Pic
1916	FEB	12	Ari
	JUN	26	Tau
	OCT	26	Ari
1917	FEB	12	Tau
	JUN	29	Gem
1918	JUL	13	Can
1919	AUG	2	Leo
1920	AUG	27	Vir
1921	SEP	25	Lib
1922	OCT	26	Scp
1923	NOV	24	Sag
1924	DEC	18	Cap
1926	JAN	6	Aqu
1927	JAN	18	Pic
	JUN	6	Ari
	SEP	11	Pic
1928	JAN	23	Ari
	JUN	4	Tau
1929	JUN	12	Gem

1930	JUN	26	Can
1931	JUL	17	Leo
1932	AUG	11	Vir
1933	SEP	10	Lib
1934	OCT	11	Scp
1935	NOV	9	Sag
1936	DEC	2	Cap
1937	DEC	20	Aqu
1938	MAY	14	Pic
	JUL	30	Aqu
	DEC	29	Pic
1939	MAY	11	Ari
	OCT	30	Pic
	DEC	20	Ari
1940	MAY	16	Tau
1941	MAY	26	Gem
1942	JUN	10	Can
1943	JUN	30	Leo
1944	JUL	26	Vir
1945	AUG	25	Lib
1946	SEP	25	Scp
1947	OCT	24	Sag
1948	NOV	15	Cap
1949	APR	12	Aqu
	JUN	27	Cap
	NOV	30	Aqu
1950	APR	15	Pic
	SEP	15	Aqu
	DEC	1	Pic
1951	APR	21	Ari
1952	APR	28	Tau
1953	MAY	9	Gem
1954	MAY	24	Can
1955	JUN	13	Leo
	NOV	17	Vir
1956	JAN	18	Leo
	JUL	7	Vir
	DEC	13	Lib

1957	FEB	19	Vir		1974	MAR	8	Pic
	AUG	7	Lib		1975	MAR	18	Ari
1958	JAN	13	Scp		1976	MAR	26	Tau
	MAR	20	Lib			AUG	23	Gem
	SEP	7	Scp			OCT	16	Tau
1959	FEB	10	Sag		1977	APR	3	Gem
	APR	24	Scp			AUG	20	Can
	OCT	5	Sag			DEC	30	Gem
1960	MAR	1	Cap		1978	APR	12	Can
	JUN	10	Sag			SEP	5	Leo
	OCT	26	Cap		1979	FEB	28	Can
1961	MAR	15	Aqu			APR	20	Leo
	AUG	12	Cap			SEP	29	Vir
	NOV	4	Aqu		1980	OCT	27	Lib
1962	MAR	25	Pic		1981	NOV	27	Scp
1963	APR	4	Ari		1982	DEC	26	Sag
1964	APR	12	Tau		1984	JAN	19	Cap
1965	APR	22	Gem		1985	FEB	6	Aqu
	SEP	21	Can		1986	FEB	20	Pic
	NOV	17	Gem		1987	MAR	2	Ari
1966	MAY	5	Can		1988	MAR	8	Tau
	SEP	27	Leo			JUL	22	Gem
1967	JAN	16	Can			NOV	30	Tau
	MAY	23	Leo		1989	MAR	11	Gem
	OCT	19	Vir			JUL	30	Can
1968	FEB	27	Leo		1990	AUG	18	Leo
	JUN	15	Vir		1991	SEP	12	Vir
	NOV	15	Lib		1992	OCT	10	Lib
1969	MAR	30	Vir		1993	NOV	10	Scp
	JUL	15	Lib		1994	DEC	9	Sag
	DEC	16	Scp		1996	JAN	3	Cap
1970	APR	30	Lib		1997	JAN	21	Aqu
	AUG	15	Scp		1998	FEB	4	Pic
1971	JAN	14	Sag		1999	FEB	13	Ari
	JUN	5	Scp			JUN	28	Tau
	SEP	11	Sag			OCT	23	Ari
1972	FEB	6	Cap		2000	FEB	14	Tau
	JUL	24	Sag			JUN	30	Gem
	SEP	25	Cap		2001	JUL	14	Can
1973	FEB	23	Aqu		2002	AUG	1	Leo

2003	AUG	27	Vir	2006	NOV	24	Sag
2004	SEP	24	Lib	2007	DEC	17	Cap
2005	OCT	26	Scp				

SATURN SIGNS 1903–2007

1903	JAN	19	Aqu		SEP	22	Ari
1905	APR	13	Pic	1940	MAR	20	Tau
	AUG	17	Aqu	1942	MAY	8	Gem
1906	JAN	8	Pic	1944	JUN	20	Can
1908	MAR	19	Ari	1946	AUG	2	Leo
1910	MAY	17	Tau	1948	SEP	19	Vir
	DEC	14	Ari	1949	APR	3	Leo
1911	JAN	20	Tau		MAY	29	Vir
1912	JUL	7	Gem	1950	NOV	20	Lib
	NOV	30	Tau	1951	MAR	7	Vir
1913	MAR	26	Gem		AUG	13	Lib
1914	AUG	24	Can	1953	OCT	22	Scp
	DEC	7	Gem	1956	JAN	12	Sag
1915	MAY	11	Can		MAY	14	Scp
1916	OCT	17	Leo		OCT	10	Sag
	DEC	7	Can	1959	JAN	5	Cap
1917	JUN	24	Leo	1962	JAN	3	Aqu
1919	AUG	12	Vir	1964	MAR	24	Pic
1921	OCT	7	Lib		SEP	16	Aqu
1923	DEC	20	Scp		DEC	16	Pic
1924	APR	6	Lib	1967	MAR	3	Ari
	SEP	13	Scp	1969	APR	29	Tau
1926	DEC	2	Sag	1971	JUN	18	Gem
1929	MAR	15	Cap	1972	JAN	10	Tau
	MAY	5	Sag		FEB	21	Gem
	NOV	30	Cap	1973	AUG	1	Can
1932	FEB	24	Aqu	1974	JAN	7	Gem
	AUG	13	Cap		APR	18	Can
	NOV	20	Aqu	1975	SEP	17	Leo
1935	FEB	14	Pic	1976	JAN	14	Can
1937	APR	25	Ari		JUN	5	Leo
	OCT	18	Pic	1977	NOV	17	Vir
1938	JAN	14	Ari	1978	JAN	5	Leo
1939	JUL	6	Tau		JUL	26	Vir

1980	SEP	21	Lib	1994	JAN	28	Pic
1982	NOV	29	Scp	1996	APR	7	Ari
1983	MAY	6	Lib	1998	JUN	9	Tau
	AUG	24	Scp		OCT	25	Ari
1985	NOV	17	Sag	1999	MAR	1	Tau
1988	FEB	13	Cap	2000	AUG	10	Gem
	JUN	10	Sag		OCT	16	Tau
	NOV	12	Cap	2001	APR	21	Gem
1991	FEB	6	Aqu	2003	JUN	3	Can
1993	MAY	21	Pic	2005	JUL	16	Leo
	JUN	30	Aqu	2007	SEP	2	Vir

CHAPTER 7

Your Rising Sign Tells Where the Action Is

You can learn much about a person by the signs and interactions of the sun, moon, and planets in the horoscope, but you can't tell where in that person's life the activity will take place. Knowing the rising sign, which is based on the exact moment in time of an event such as a birth, will provide information that enables the astrologer to make predictions. For example, you might know that a person has Mars in Aries, which will describe that person's dynamic fiery energy. But if you also know that the person has a Capricorn rising sign, this Mars will fall in the fourth house of home and family, so you know where that energy will operate.

Your rising sign is the degree of the zodiac ascending over the eastern horizon when you were born. (That's why it's often called the ascendant.) It marks the first point in the horoscope, the beginning of the first house, one of twelve divisions of the horoscope, each of which represents a different area of your life. After the rising sign sets up the first house, the other houses parade around the chart in sequence, with the following sign on the house cusp. Due to the earth's rotation, the rising sign changes every two hours, which means that other babies, who may have been born later or earlier on the same day in the same hospital as you were (and will be sure to have most planets in the same signs as you do) may not have the same rising sign and their planets may fall in different houses in the chart.

For instance, if Mars is in Gemini and your rising sign is Taurus, Mars will most likely be active in the second or financial house of your chart. Someone born later in the day when the rising sign is Virgo would have Mars positioned at the top of the chart, energizing the tenth house of career.

Most astrologers insist on knowing the exact time of a client's birth before analyzing a chart. The more accurate your birth time, the more accurately an astrologer can position the planets in your chart. Without a valid rising sign, your collection of planets would have no homes. One would have no idea which area of your life would be influenced by a particular planet.

How Your Rising Sign Can Influence Your Sun Sign

Your rising sign has an important relationship with your sun sign. Some will complement the sun sign; others hide it under a totally different mask, as if playing an entirely different role, making it difficult to guess the person's sun sign from outer appearances. This may be the reason why you might not look or act like your sun sign's archetype. For example, a Leo with a conservative Capricorn ascendant would come across as much more serious than a Leo with a fiery Aries or Sagittarius ascendant.

Though the rising sign usually creates the first impression you make, there are exceptions. When the sun sign is reinforced by other planets in the same sign, this might overpower the impression of the rising sign. For instance, a Leo sun plus a Leo Venus and Leo Jupiter would counteract the more conservative image that would otherwise be conveyed by the person's Capricorn ascendant.

Those born early in the morning when the sun was on the horizon will be most likely to project the image of their sun sign. These people are often called a "double Aries" or a "double Virgo" because the same sun sign and ascendant reinforce each other.

Find Your Rising Sign

Look up your rising sign from the chart at the end of this chapter. Since rising signs change every two hours, it is important to know your birth time as close to the minute as possible. Even a few minutes' difference could change the rising sign and therefore the setup of your chart. If you are unsure about the exact time, but know within a few hours, check the following descriptions to see which is most like the personality you project.

Aries Rising: Alpha Energy

You are the most aggressive version of your sun sign, with boundless energy that can be used productively if it's channeled in the right direction. Watch a tendency to overreact emotionally and blow your top. You come across as openly competitive, a positive asset in business or sports. Be on guard against impatience, which could lead to head injuries. Your walk and bearing could have the telltale head-forward Aries posture. You may wear more bright colors, especially red, than others of your sign. You may also have a tendency to drive your car faster.

Can you see the alpha Aries tendency in Barbra Streisand (a sun-sign Taurus) and Bette Midler (a sun-sign Sagittarius)?

Taurus Rising: Down to Earth

You're slow-moving, with a beautiful (or distinctive) speaking or singing voice that can be especially soothing or melodious. You probably surround yourself with comfort, good food, luxurious environments, and other sensual pleasures. You prefer welcoming others into your home to gadding about. You may have a talent for business, especially in trading, appraising, and real estate. A Taurus ascendant gives a well-padded physique that gains weight easily, like Liza Minnelli. This ascendant can also endow females with a curvaceous beauty.

Gemini Rising: A Way with Words

You're naturally sociable, with lighter, more ethereal mannerisms than others of your sign, especially if you're female.

You love to communicate with people, and express your ideas and feelings easily, like British prime minister Tony Blair. You may have a talent for writing or public speaking. You thrive on variety, a constantly changing scene, and a lively social life. However, you may relate to others at a deeper level than might be suspected. And you will be far more sympathetic and caring than you project. You will probably travel widely, changing partners and jobs several times (or juggle two at once). Physically, your nerves are quite sensitive. Occasionally, you would benefit from a calm, tranquil atmosphere away from your usual social scene.

Cancer Rising: Nurturing Instincts

You are naturally acquisitive, possessive, private, a moneymaker, like Bill Gates or Michael Bloomberg. You easily pick up on others' needs and feelings—a great gift in business, the arts, and personal relationships. But you must guard against overreacting or taking things too personally, especially during full moon periods. Find creative outlets for your natural nurturing gifts, such as helping the less fortunate, particularly children. Your insights would be helpful in psychology. Your desire to feed and care for others would be useful in the restaurant, hotel, or child-care industries. You may be especially fond of wearing romantic old clothes, collecting antiques, and, of course, dining on exquisite food. Since your body may retain fluids, pay attention to your diet. To relax, escape to places near water.

Leo Rising: Diva Dazzle

You may come across as more poised than you really feel. However, you play it to the hilt, projecting a proud royal presence. A Leo ascendant gives you a natural flair for drama, like Marilyn Monroe, and you might be accused of stealing the spotlight. You'll also project a much more outgoing, optimistic, sunny personality than others of your sign. You take care to please your public by always projecting your best star quality, probably tossing a luxuriant mane of hair, sporting a striking hairstyle, or dressing to impress. Females often dazzle with spectacular jewelry. Since you may have a strong parental nature, you could well be the regal family matriarch or patriarch, like George W. Bush.

Virgo Rising: High Standards

Virgo rising masks your inner nature with a practical, analytical outer image. You seem neat, orderly, more particular than others of your sign. Others in your life may feel they must live up to your high standards. Though at times you may be openly critical, this masks a well-meaning desire to have only the best for loved ones. Your sharp eye for details could be used in the financial world, or your literary skills could draw you to teaching or publishing. The healing arts, health care, and service-oriented professions attract many with a Virgo ascendant. You're likely to take good care of yourself, with great attention to health, diet, and exercise, like Madonna. You might even show some hypochondriac tendencies, like Woody Allen. Physically, you may have a very sensitive digestive system.

Libra Rising: The Charmer

Libra rising gives you a charming, social public persona, like Bill Clinton. You tend to avoid confrontations in relationships, preferring to smooth the way or negotiate diplomatically rather than give in to an emotional reaction. Because you are interested in all aspects of a situation, you may be slow to reach decisions. Physically, you'll have good proportions and symmetry. You will move with natural grace and balance. You're likely to have pleasing, if not beautiful, facial features, with a winning smile, like Cary Grant. You'll show natural good taste and harmony in your clothes and home decor. Legal, diplomatic, or public relations professions could draw your interest.

Scorpio Rising: An Air of Mystery

You project an intriguing air of mystery with this ascendant, as the Scorpio secretiveness and sense of underlying power combines with your sun sign. As with Jackie O, there's more to you than meets the eye. You seem like someone who is always in control and who can move comfortably in the world of power. Your physical look comes across as intense. Many of you have remarkable eyes, with a direct, penetrating gaze. But you'll never reveal your private agenda, and you tend to keep your true feelings under wraps (watch a tendency toward paranoia). You may have an interesting romantic history with secret love affairs, like Grace Kelly. Many of you heighten your air of mystery by wearing black. You're happiest near water and should provide yourself with a seaside retreat.

Sagittarius Rising: The Explorer

You travel with this ascendant. You may also be a more outdoor, sportive type, with an athletic, casual, outgoing air. Your moods are camouflaged with cheerful optimism or a philosophical attitude. Though you don't hesitate to speak your mind, like Ted Turner, who was called the Mouth of the South, you can also laugh at your troubles or crack a joke more easily than others of your sign. A Sagittarius ascendant can also draw you to the field of higher education or to spiritual life. You'll seem to have less attachment to things and people, and may explore the globe. Your strong, fast legs are a physical bonus.

Capricorn Rising: Serious Business

This rising sign makes you come across as serious, goal-oriented, disciplined, and careful with cash. You are not one of the zodiac's big spenders, though you might splurge occasionally on items with good investment value. You're the traditional, conservative type in dress and environment, and you might come across as quite normal and business-like, like Rupert Murdoch. You'll function well in a structured or corporate environment where you can climb to the top. (You are always aware of who's the boss.) In your personal life, you could be a loner or a single parent who is "father and mother" to your children.

Aquarius Rising: One of a Kind

You come across as less concerned about what others think and could even be a bit eccentric. You're more at ease with groups of people than others in your sign, and you may be attracted to public life, like Jay Leno. Your appearance may be unique, either unconventional or unimportant to you. Those of you whose sun is in a water sign (Cancer, Scorpio, Pisces) may exercise your nurturing qualities with a large group, an extended family, or a day-care or community center.

Pisces Rising: Romantic Roles

Your creative, nurturing talents are heightened and so is your ability to project emotional drama. And, like Antonio Banderas, your dreamy eyes and poetic air bring out the protective instinct in others. You could be attracted to the arts, especially theater, dance, film, and photography, or to psychology, spiritual practice, and charity work. You are happiest when you are using your creative ability to help others. Since you are vulnerable to mood swings, it is especially important for you to find interesting, creative work where you can express your talents and heighten your self-esteem. Accentuate the positive. Be wary of escapist tendencies, particularly involving alcohol or drugs to which you are supersensitive, like Whitney Houston.

RISING SIGNS—A.M. BIRTHS

	1 AM	2 AM	3 AM	4 AM	5 AM	6 AM	7 AM	8 AM	9 AM	10 AM	11 AM	12 NOON
Jan 1	Lib	Sc	Sc	Sc	Sag	Sag	Cap	Cap	Aq	Aq	Pis	Ar
Jan 9	Lib	Sc	Sc	Sc	Sag	Sag	Cap	Cap	Aq	Pis	Ar	Tau
Jan 17	Sc	Sc	Sc	Sag	Sag	Cap	Cap	Aq	Aq	Pis	Ar	Tau
Jan 25	Sc	Sc	Sag	Sag	Sag	Cap	Cap	Aq	Pis	Ar	Tau	Tau
Feb 2	Sc	Sc	Sag	Sag	Cap	Cap	Aq	Pis	Pis	Ar	Tau	Gem
Feb 10	Sc	Sag	Sag	Sag	Cap	Cap	Aq	Pis	Ar	Tau	Tau	Gem
Feb 18	Sc	Sag	Sag	Cap	Cap	Aq	Pis	Pis	Ar	Tau	Gem	Gem
Feb 26	Sag	Sag	Sag	Cap	Aq	Aq	Pis	Ar	Tau	Tau	Gem	Gem
Mar 6	Sag	Sag	Cap	Cap	Aq	Aq	Pis	Pis	Ar	Tau	Gem	Can
Mar 14	Sag	Cap	Cap	Aq	Aq	Pis	Ar	Tau	Tau	Gem	Gem	Can
Mar 22	Sag	Cap	Cap	Aq	Pis	Ar	Ar	Tau	Gem	Gem	Can	Can
Mar 30	Cap	Cap	Aq	Pis	Pis	Ar	Tau	Tau	Gem	Can	Can	Can
Apr 7	Cap	Cap	Aq	Pis	Ar	Ar	Tau	Gem	Gem	Can	Can	Leo
Apr 14	Cap	Aq	Aq	Pis	Ar	Tau	Tau	Gem	Gem	Can	Can	Leo
Apr 22	Cap	Aq	Pis	Ar	Ar	Tau	Gem	Gem	Gem	Can	Leo	Leo
Apr 30	Aq	Aq	Pis	Ar	Tau	Tau	Gem	Can	Can	Can	Leo	Leo
May 8	Aq	Pis	Ar	Ar	Tau	Gem	Gem	Can	Can	Leo	Leo	Leo
May 16	Aq	Pis	Ar	Tau	Gem	Gem	Can	Can	Can	Leo	Leo	Vir
May 24	Pis	Ar	Ar	Tau	Gem	Gem	Can	Can	Can	Leo	Leo	Vir
June 1	Pis	Ar	Tau	Gem	Gem	Can	Can	Can	Leo	Leo	Vir	Vir
June 9	Ar	Ar	Tau	Gem	Gem	Can	Can	Leo	Leo	Leo	Vir	Vir
June 17	Ar	Tau	Gem	Gem	Can	Can	Can	Leo	Leo	Vir	Vir	Vir
June 25	Ar	Tau	Gem	Gem	Can	Can	Leo	Leo	Leo	Vir	Vir	Lib
July 3	Tau	Gem	Gem	Can	Can	Can	Leo	Leo	Vir	Vir	Vir	Lib
July 11	Tau	Gem	Gem	Can	Can	Leo	Leo	Leo	Vir	Vir	Lib	Lib
July 18	Gem	Gem	Can	Can	Can	Leo	Leo	Vir	Vir	Vir	Lib	Lib
July 26	Gem	Gem	Can	Can	Leo	Leo	Vir	Vir	Vir	Lib	Lib	Lib
Aug 3	Gem	Can	Can	Can	Leo	Leo	Vir	Vir	Vir	Lib	Lib	Sc
Aug 11	Gem	Can	Can	Leo	Leo	Leo	Vir	Vir	Lib	Lib	Lib	Sc
Aug 18	Can	Can	Can	Leo	Leo	Vir	Vir	Vir	Lib	Lib	Sc	Sc
Aug 27	Can	Can	Leo	Leo	Leo	Vir	Vir	Lib	Lib	Lib	Sc	Sc
Sept 4	Can	Can	Leo	Leo	Leo	Vir	Vir	Vir	Lib	Sc	Sc	Sc
Sept 12	Can	Leo	Leo	Leo	Vir	Vir	Lib	Lib	Lib	Sc	Sc	Sag
Sept 20	Leo	Leo	Leo	Vir	Vir	Vir	Lib	Lib	Sc	Sc	Sc	Sag
Sept 28	Leo	Leo	Leo	Vir	Vir	Lib	Lib	Lib	Sc	Sc	Sag	Sag
Oct 6	Leo	Leo	Vir	Vir	Vir	Lib	Lib	Sc	Sc	Sc	Sag	Sag
Oct 14	Leo	Vir	Vir	Vir	Lib	Lib	Lib	Sc	Sc	Sag	Sag	Cap
Oct 22	Leo	Vir	Vir	Lib	Lib	Lib	Sc	Sc	Sc	Sag	Sag	Cap
Oct 30	Vir	Vir	Vir	Lib	Lib	Sc	Sc	Sc	Sag	Sag	Cap	Cap
Nov 7	Vir	Vir	Lib	Lib	Lib	Sc	Sc	Sc	Sag	Sag	Cap	Cap
Nov 15	Vir	Vir	Lib	Lib	Lib	Sc	Sc	Sag	Sag	Cap	Cap	Aq
Nov 23	Vir	Lib	Lib	Lib	Sc	Sc	Sag	Sag	Sag	Cap	Cap	Aq
Dec 1	Vir	Lib	Lib	Sc	Sc	Sc	Sag	Sag	Cap	Cap	Aq	Aq
Dec 9	Lib	Lib	Lib	Sc	Sc	Sag	Sag	Sag	Cap	Cap	Aq	Pis
Dec 18	Lib	Lib	Sc	Sc	Sc	Sag	Sag	Cap	Cap	Aq	Aq	Pis
Dec 28	Lib	Lib	Sc	Sc	Sag	Sag	Sag	Cap	Aq	Aq	Pis	Ar

RISING SIGNS—P.M. BIRTHS

	1 PM	2 PM	3 PM	4 PM	5 PM	6 PM	7 PM	8 PM	9 PM	10 PM	11 PM	12 MID-NIGHT
Jan 1	Tau	Gem	Gem	Can	Can	Can	Leo	Leo	Vir	Vir	Vir	Lib
Jan 9	Tau	Gem	Gem	Can	Can	Leo	Leo	Leo	Vir	Vir	Vir	Lib
Jan 17	Gem	Gem	Gem	Can	Can	Can	Leo	Leo	Vir	Vir	Lib	Lib
Jan 25	Gem	Gem	Can	Can	Leo	Leo	Leo	Vir	Vir	Lib	Lib	Lib
Feb 2	Gem	Can	Can	Can	Leo	Leo	Vir	Vir	Vir	Lib	Lib	Sc
Feb 10	Gem	Can	Can	Leo	Leo	Leo	Vir	Vir	Lib	Lib	Lib	Sc
Feb 18	Can	Can	Can	Leo	Leo	Vir	Vir	Vir	Lib	Lib	Sc	Sc
Feb 26	Can	Can	Leo	Leo	Leo	Vir	Vir	Lib	Lib	Lib	Sc	Sc
Mar 6	Can	Leo	Leo	Leo	Vir	Vir	Vir	Lib	Lib	Sc	Sc	Sc
Mar 14	Can	Leo	Leo	Vir	Vir	Vir	Lib	Lib	Lib	Sc	Sc	Sag
Mar 22	Leo	Leo	Leo	Vir	Vir	Lib	Lib	Lib	Sc	Sc	Sc	Sag
Mar 30	Leo	Leo	Vir	Vir	Vir	Lib	Lib	Sc	Sc	Sc	Sag	Sag
Apr 7	Leo	Leo	Vir	Vir	Lib	Lib	Lib	Sc	Sc	Sc	Sag	Sag
Apr 14	Leo	Vir	Vir	Vir	Lib	Lib	Sc	Sc	Sc	Sc	Sag	Cap
Apr 22	Leo	Vir	Vir	Lib	Lib	Lib	Sc	Sc	Sc	Sag	Sag	Cap
Apr 30	Vir	Vir	Vir	Lib	Lib	Sc	Sc	Sc	Sag	Sag	Cap	Cap
May 8	Vir	Vir	Lib	Lib	Lib	Sc	Sc	Sag	Sag	Cap	Cap	Cap
May 16	Vir	Vir	Lib	Lib	Sc	Sc	Sc	Sag	Sag	Cap	Cap	Aq
May 24	Vir	Lib	Lib	Lib	Sc	Sc	Sag	Sag	Cap	Cap	Aq	
June 1	Vir	Lib	Lib	Sc	Sc	Sc	Sag	Sag	Cap	Cap	Aq	Aq
June 9	Lib	Lib	Lib	Sc	Sc	Sag	Sag	Sag	Cap	Cap	Aq	Pis
June 17	Lib	Lib	Sc	Sc	Sc	Sag	Sag	Cap	Cap	Aq	Aq	Pis
June 25	Lib	Lib	Sc	Sc	Sag	Sag	Sag	Cap	Cap	Aq	Pis	Ar
July 3	Lib	Sc	Sc	Sc	Sag	Cap	Cap	Aq	Aq	Pis	Ar	
July 11	Lib	Sc	Sc	Sag	Sag	Sag	Cap	Cap	Aq	Pis	Ar	Tau
July 18	Sc	Sc	Sc	Sag	Sag	Cap	Cap	Aq	Aq	Pis	Ar	Tau
July 26	Sc	Sc	Sag	Sag	Sag	Cap	Cap	Aq	Pis	Ar	Tau	Tau
Aug 3	Sc	Sc	Sag	Sag	Cap	Cap	Aq	Aq	Pis	Ar	Tau	Gem
Aug 11	Sc	Sag	Sag	Sag	Cap	Cap	Aq	Pis	Ar	Tau	Tau	Gem
Aug 18	Sc	Sag	Sag	Cap	Cap	Aq	Pis	Pis	Ar	Tau	Gem	Gem
Aug 27	Sag	Sag	Sag	Cap	Cap	Aq	Pis	Ar	Tau	Tau	Gem	Gem
Sept 4	Sag	Sag	Cap	Cap	Aq	Pis	Pis	Ar	Tau	Gem	Gem	Can
Sept 12	Sag	Sag	Cap	Aq	Aq	Pis	Ar	Tau	Tau	Gem	Gem	Can
Sept 20	Sag	Cap	Cap	Aq	Pis	Pis	Ar	Tau	Gem	Gem	Can	Can
Sept 28	Cap	Cap	Aq	Aq	Pis	Ar	Tau	Tau	Gem	Gem	Can	Can
Oct 6	Cap	Cap	Aq	Pis	Ar	Ar	Tau	Gem	Gem	Can	Can	Leo
Oct 14	Cap	Aq	Aq	Pis	Ar	Tau	Tau	Gem	Gem	Can	Can	Leo
Oct 22	Cap	Aq	Pis	Ar	Ar	Tau	Gem	Gem	Can	Can	Leo	Leo
Oct 30	Aq	Aq	Pis	Ar	Tau	Tau	Gem	Can	Can	Can	Leo	Leo
Nov 7	Aq	Aq	Pis	Ar	Tau	Tau	Gem	Can	Can	Can	Leo	Leo
Nov 15	Aq	Pis	Ar	Tau	Gem	Gem	Can	Can	Can	Leo	Leo	Vir
Nov 23	Pis	Ar	Ar	Tau	Gem	Can	Can	Can	Leo	Leo	Leo	Vir
Dec 1	Pis	Ar	Tau	Gem	Gem	Can	Can	Can	Leo	Leo	Vir	Vir
Dec 9	Ar	Tau	Tau	Gem	Gem	Can	Can	Leo	Leo	Leo	Vir	Vir
Dec 18	Ar	Tau	Gem	Gem	Can	Can	Can	Leo	Leo	Vir	Vir	Vir
Dec 28	Tau	Tau	Gem	Gem	Can	Can	Leo	Leo	Vir	Vir	Vir	Lib

CHAPTER 8

Learn the Glyphs and Read Your Own Chart!

If you get to a certain point in astrology, you'll want to read your own chart (or someone else's). Or perhaps you'll have a reading and be given a copy of your chart by an astrologer. In either case, you'll be confronted by a circular chart covered with mysterious symbols—unreadable except by someone who has learned these glyphs.

Breaking into astrology requires cracking the ancient code that is a type of picture writing universally understood by astrologers. It's well worth the effort to learn these symbols. You'll not only be able to read a chart, but you will be able to make use of free charts available on any number of Internet sites and astrology software programs. This year, you can even take astrology with you on your PDA and read a chart on the go. But almost none of these programs show the planetary positions written in plain English, so you'll miss out if you don't learn the glyphs.

Each little symbol has built-in clues to help you decipher not only which sign or planet it represents, but what the object means in a more esoteric sense. Actually the physical act of writing the symbol is a mystical experience in itself, a way to invoke the deeper meaning of the sign or planet through age-old visual elements that have been with us since time began.

Since there are only twelve signs and ten planets (not counting a few asteroids and other space objects some astrologers use), it's a lot easier than learning to read a foreign language. Here's a code cracker for the glyphs, beginning with the glyphs for the planets. To those who already know their glyphs, don't just skim over the chapter.

These familiar graphics have hidden meanings you will discover!

The Glyphs for the Planets

The glyphs for the planets are easy to learn. They're simple combinations of the most basic visual elements: the circle, the semicircle or arc, and the cross. However, each component of a glyph has a special meaning in relation to the other parts of the symbol.

The circle, which has no beginning or end, is one of the oldest symbols of spirit or spiritual forces. Early diagrams of the heavens—spiritual territory—are shown in circular form. The never-ending line of the circle is the perfect symbol for eternity. The semicircle or arc is an incomplete circle, symbolizing the receptive, finite soul, which contains spiritual potential in the curving line.

The vertical line of the cross symbolizes movement from heaven to earth. The horizontal line describes temporal movement, here and now, in time and space. Combined in a cross, the vertical and horizontal planes symbolize manifestation in the material world.

The Sun Glyph ☉

The sun is always shown by this powerful solar symbol, a circle with a point in the center. The center point is you, your spiritual center, and the symbol represents your infinite personality incarnating (the point) into the finite cycles of birth and death.

The sun has been represented by a circle or disk since ancient Egyptian times when the solar disk represented the sun god, Ra. Some archaeologists believe the great stone circles found in England were centers of sun worship. This particular version of the symbol was brought into common use in the sixteenth century after German occultist and scholar Cornelius Agrippa (1486–1535) wrote a book called *Die Occulta Philosophia*, which became accepted as the authority in the field. Agrippa collected many medieval astro-

109

logical and magical symbols in this book, which have been used by astrologers since then.

The Moon Glyph ☽

The moon glyph is the most recognizable symbol on a chart, a left-facing arc stylized into the crescent moon. As part of a circle, the arc symbolizes the potential fulfillment of the entire circle, the life force that is still incomplete. Therefore, it is the ideal representation of the reactive, receptive, emotional nature of the moon.

The Mercury Glyph ☿

Mercury contains all three elemental symbols: the crescent, the circle, and the cross in vertical order. This is the "Venus with a hat" glyph (compare with the symbol of Venus). With another stretch of the imagination, can't you see the winged cap of Mercury the messenger? Think of the upturned crescent as antennae that tune in and transmit messages from the sun, reminding you that Mercury is the way you communicate, the way your mind works. The upturned arc is receiving energy into the spirit or solar circle, which will later be translated into action on the material plane, symbolized by the cross. All the elements are equally sized because Mercury is neutral; it doesn't play favorites! This planet symbolizes objective, detached, unemotional thinking.

The Venus Glyph ♀

Here the relationship is between two components: the circle of spirit and the cross of matter. Spirit is elevated over matter, pulling it upward. Venus asks, "What is beautiful? What do you like best? What do you love to have done to you?" Consequently, Venus determines both your ideal of beauty and what feels good sensually. It governs your own allure and power to attract, as well as what attracts and pleases you.

The Mars Glyph ♂

In this glyph, the cross of matter is stylized into an arrowhead pointed up and outward, propelled by the circle of spirit. With a little imagination, you can visualize it as the shield and spear of Mars, the ancient god of war. You can deduce that Mars embodies your spiritual energy projected into the outer world. It's your assertiveness, your initiative, your aggressive drive, what you like to do to others, your temper. If you know someone's Mars, you know whether they'll blow up when angry or do a slow burn. Your task is to use your outgoing Mars energy wisely and well.

The Jupiter Glyph ♃

Jupiter is the basic cross of matter, with a large stylized crescent perched on the left side of the horizontal, temporal plane. You might think of the crescent as an open hand, because one meaning of Jupiter is "luck," what's handed to you. You don't have to work for what you get from Jupiter; it comes to you, if you're open to it.

The Jupiter glyph might also remind you of a jumbo jet plane, with a huge tail fin, about to take off. This is the planet of travel, mental and spiritual, of expanding your horizons via new ideas, new spiritual dimensions, and new places. Jupiter embodies the optimism and enthusiasm of the traveler about to embark on an exciting adventure.

The Saturn Glyph ♄

Flip Jupiter over, and you've got Saturn. This might not be immediately apparent because Saturn is usually stylized into an "h" form like the one shown here. The principle it expresses is the opposite of Jupiter's expansive tendencies. Saturn pulls you back to earth: the receptive arc is pushed down underneath the cross of matter. Before there are any rewards or expansion, the duties and obligations of the material world must be considered. Saturn says, "Stop, wait, finish your chores before you take off!"

Saturn's glyph also resembles the sickle of old "Father Time." Saturn was first known as Chronos, the Greek god of time, for time brings all matter to an end. When it was the most distant planet (before the discovery of Uranus), Saturn was believed to be the place where time stopped. After the soul departed from earth, it journeyed back to the outer reaches of the universe and finally stopped at Saturn, or at "the end of time."

The Uranus Glyph ♅

The glyph for Uranus is often stylized to form a capital *H* after Sir William Herschel, who discovered the planet. But the more esoteric version curves the two pillars of the H into crescent antennae, or "ears," like satellite disks receiving signals from space. These are perched on the horizontal material line of the cross of matter and pushed from below by the circle of the spirit. To many sci-fi fans, Uranus looks like an orbiting satellite.

Uranus channels the highest energy of all, the white electrical light of the universal spiritual force that holds the cosmos together. This pure electrical energy is gathered from all over the universe. Because Uranus energy doesn't follow any ordinary celestial drumbeat, it can't be controlled or predicted (which is also true of those who are strongly influenced by this eccentric planet). In the symbol, this energy is manifested through the balance of polarities (the two opposite arms of the glyph) like the two polarized wires of a lightbulb.

The Neptune Glyph ♆

Neptune's glyph is usually stylized to look like a trident, the weapon of the Roman god Neptune. However, on a more esoteric level, it shows the large upturned crescent of the soul pierced through by the cross of matter. Neptune nails down, or materializes, soul energy, bringing impulses from the soul level into manifestation. That is why Neptune is associated with imagination or "imagining in," making an image of the soul. Neptune works through feelings, sensitivity, and the mystical capacity to bring the divine into the earthly realm.

The Pluto Glyph ♀

Pluto is written two ways. One is a composite of the letters *PL,* the first two letters of the word Pluto and coincidentally the initials of Percival Lowell, one of the planet's discovers. The other, more esoteric symbol is a small circle above a large open crescent that surmounts the cross of matter. This depicts Pluto's power to regenerate. Imagine a new little spirit emerging from the sheltering cup of the soul. Pluto rules the forces of life and death. After this planet has passed a sensitive point in your chart, you are transformed, reborn in some way.

Sci-fi fans might visualize this glyph as a small satellite (the circle) being launched. It was shortly after Pluto's discovery that we learned how to harness the nuclear forces that made space exploration possible. Pluto rules the transformative power of atomic energy, which totally changed our lives and from which there is no turning back.

The Glyphs for the Signs

On an astrology chart, the glyph for the sign will appear after that of the planet. For example, when you see the moon glyph followed first by a number and then by another glyph representing the sign, this means that the moon was passing over a certain degree of that astrological sign at the time of the chart. On the dividing lines between the houses on your chart, you'll find the symbol for the sign that rules the house.

Because sun sign symbols do not contain the same basic geometric components of the planetary glyphs, we must look elsewhere for clues to their meanings. Many have been passed down from ancient Egyptian and Chaldean civilizations with few modifications. Others have been adapted over the centuries.

In deciphering many of the glyphs, you'll often find that the symbols reveal a dual nature of the sign, which is not always apparent in the usual sun sign descriptions. For instance, the Gemini glyph is similar to the Roman numeral for two, and reveals this sign's longing to discover a twin soul. The Cancer glyph may be interpreted as resembling either the nurturing breasts or the self-protective claws of a crab, both symbols associated with the contrasting qualities of this sign. Libra's glyph embodies the duality of the spirit balanced with material reality. The Sagittarius glyph shows that the aspirant must also carry along the earthly animal nature in his quest. The Capricorn sea goat is another symbol with dual emphasis. The goat climbs high, yet is always pulled back by the deep waters of the unconscious. Aquarius embodies the double waves of mental detachment, balanced by the desire for connection with others, in a friendly way. Finally, the two fishes of Pisces, which are forever tied together, show the duality of the soul and the spirit that must be reconciled.

The Aries Glyph ♈

Since the symbol for Aries is the Ram, this glyph is obviously associated with a ram's horns, which characterize one aspect of the Aries personality—an aggressive, me-first, leaping-headfirst attitude. But the symbol can be interpreted in other ways as well. Some astrologers liken it to a fountain of energy, which Aries people also embody. The first sign of the zodiac bursts on the scene eagerly, ready to go. Another analogy is to the eyebrows and nose of the human head, which Aries rules, and the thinking power that is initiated by the brain.

One theory of this symbol links it to the Egyptian god Amun, represented by a ram in ancient times. As Amun-Ra, this god was believed to embody the creator of the universe, the leader of all the other gods. This relates easily to the position of Aries as the leader (or first sign) of the zodiac, which begins at the spring equinox, a time of the year when nature is renewed.

The Taurus Glyph ♉

This is another easy glyph to draw and identify. It takes little imagination to decipher the bull's head with long curving horns. Like its symbol the Bull, the archetypal Taurus is slow to anger but ferocious when provoked, as well as stubborn, steady, and sensual. Another association is the larynx (and thyroid) of the throat area (ruled by Taurus) and the eustachian tubes running up to the ears, which coincides with the relationship of Taurus to the voice, song, and music. Many famous singers, musicians, and composers have prominent Taurus influences.

Many ancient religions involved a bull as the central figure in fertility rites or initiations, usually symbolizing the victory of man over his animal nature. Another possible origin is in the sacred bull of Egypt, who embodied the incarnate form of Osiris, god of death and resurrection. In early Christian imagery, the Taurus Bull represented St. Luke.

The Gemini Glyph ♊

The standard glyph immediately calls to mind the Roman numeral for two (II) and the Twins symbol, as it is called, for Gemini. In almost all drawings and images used for this sign, the relationship between two persons is emphasized. Usually one twin will be touching the other, which signifies communication, human contact, the desire to share.

The top line of the Gemini glyph indicates mental communication, while the bottom line indicates shared physical space.

The most famous Gemini legend is that of the twin sons, Castor and Pollux, one of whom had a mortal father while the other was the son of Zeus, king of the gods. When it came time for the mortal twin to die, his grief-stricken brother pleaded with Zeus, who agreed to let them spend half the year on earth in mortal form and half in immortal life, with the gods on Mount Olympus. This reflects a basic duality of humankind, which possesses an immortal soul yet is also subject to the limits of mortality.

The Cancer Glyph ♋

Two convenient images relate to the Cancer glyph. It is easiest to decode the curving claws of the Cancer symbol, the Crab. Like the crab's, Cancer's element is water. This sensitive sign also has a hard protective shell to protect its tender interior. The crab must be wily to escape predators, scampering sideways and hiding under rocks. The crab also responds to the cycles of the moon, as do all shellfish. The other image is that of two female breasts, which Cancer rules, showing that this is a sign that nurtures and protects others as well as itself.

In ancient Egypt, Cancer was also represented by the scarab beetle, a symbol of regeneration and eternal life.

The Leo Glyph ♌

Notice that the Leo glyph seems to be an extension of Cancer's glyph, with a significant difference. In the Cancer glyph, the lines curve inward protectively. The Leo glyph expresses energy outwardly. And there is no duality in the symbol, the Lion, or in Leo, the sign.

Lions have belonged to the sign of Leo since earliest times. It is not difficult to imagine the king of beasts with his sweeping mane and curling tail from this glyph. The upward sweep of the glyph easily describes the positive energy of Leo: the flourishing tail, their flamboyant qualities. Anther analogy, perhaps a stretch of the imagination, is that of a heart leaping up with joy and enthusiasm, also very typical of Leo, which also rules the heart. In early Christian imagery, the Leo Lion represented St. Mark.

The Virgo Glyph ♍

You can read much into this mysterious glyph. For instance, it could represent the initials of "Mary Virgin," or a young woman holding a staff of wheat, or stylized female genitalia, all common interpretations. The M shape might also remind you that Virgo is ruled by Mercury. The cross beneath the symbol reveals the grounded, practical nature of this earth sign.

The earliest zodiacs link Virgo with the Egyptian goddess Isis, who gave birth to the god Horus after her husband Osiris had been killed, in the archetype of a miraculous conception. There are many ancient statues of Isis nursing her baby son, which are reminiscent of medieval Virgin and Child motifs. This sign has also been associated with the image of the Holy Grail, when the Virgo symbol was substituted with a chalice.

The Libra Glyph ♎

It is not difficult to read the standard image for Libra, the Scales, into this glyph. There is another meaning, however, that is equally relevant: the setting sun as it descends over the horizon. Libra's natural position on the zodiac wheel is the descendant, or sunset position (as the Aries natural position is the ascendant, or rising sign). Both images relate to Libra's personality. Libra is always weighing pros and cons for a balanced decision. In the sunset image, the sun (male) hovers over the horizontal earth (female) before setting. Libra is the space between these lines, harmonizing yin and yang, spiritual and material, male and female, ideal and real worlds. The glyph has also been linked to the kidneys, which are ruled by Libra.

The Scorpio Glyph ♏

With its barbed tail, this glyph is easy to identify as the Scorpion for the sign of Scorpio. It also represents the male sexual parts, over which the sign rules. From the arrowhead, you can draw the conclusion that Mars was once its ruler. Some earlier Egyptian glyphs for Scorpio represent it as an erect serpent, so the Serpent is an alternate symbol.

Another symbol for Scorpio, which is not identifiable in this glyph, is the Eagle. Scorpios can go to extremes, either in soaring like the eagle or self-destructing like the scorpion. In early Christian imagery, which often used zodiacal symbols, the Scorpio Eagle was chosen to symbolize the intense apostle St. John the Evangelist.

The Sagittarius Glyph ♐

This is one of the easiest to spot and draw: an upward pointing arrow lifting up a cross. The arrow is pointing skyward, while the cross represents the four elements of the material world, which the arrow must convey. Elevating materiality into spirituality is an important Sagittarius quality, which explains why this sign is associated with higher learning, religion, philosophy, travel—the aspiring professions. Sagittarius can also send barbed arrows of frankness in the pursuit of truth, so the Archer symbol for Sagittarius is apt. (Sagittarius is also the sign of the supersalesman.)

Sagittarius is symbolically represented by the centaur, a mythological creature who is half man, half horse, aiming his arrow toward the skies. Though Sagittarius is motivated by spiritual aspiration, it also must balance the powerful appetites of the animal nature. The centaur Chiron, a figure in Greek mythology, became a wise teacher who, after many adventures and world travels, was killed by a poisoned arrow.

The Capricorn Glyph ♑

One of the most difficult symbols to draw, this glyph may take some practice. It is a representation of the sea goat: a mythical animal that is a goat with a curving fish's tail. The goat part of Capricorn wants to leave the waters of the emotions and climb to the elevated areas of life. But the fish tail is the unconscious, the deep chaotic psychic level that draws the goat back. Capricorn is often trying to escape the deep, feeling part of life by submerging himself in work, steadily ascending to the top. To some people, the glyph represents a seated figure with a bent knee, a reminder that Capricorn governs the knee area of the body.

An interesting aspect of this glyph is the contrast of the sharp pointed horns—which represent the penetrating, shrewd, conscious side of Capricorn—with the swishing tail—which represents its serpentine, unconscious, emotional force. One Capricorn legend, which dates from Roman times, tells of the earthy fertility god, Pan, who tried to save himself from uncontrollable sexual desires by jumping into the Nile. His upper body then turned into a goat, while the lower part became a fish. Later, Jupiter gave him a safe haven as a constellation in the skies.

The Aquarius Glyph ♒

This ancient water symbol can be traced back to an Egyptian hieroglyph representing streams of life force. Symbolized by the Water Bearer, Aquarius is distributor of the waters of life—the magic liquid of regeneration. The two waves can also be linked to the positive and negative charges of the electrical energy that Aquarius rules, a sort of universal wavelength. Aquarius is tuned in intuitively to higher forces via this electrical force. The duality of the glyph could also refer to the dual nature of Aquarius, a sign that runs hot and cold and that is friendly but also detached in the mental world of air signs.

In Greek legends, Aquarius is represented by Ganymede, who was carried to heaven by an eagle in order to become the cupbearer of Zeus and to supervise the annual flooding of the Nile. The sign later became associated with aviation and notions of flight.

The Pisces Glyph)(

Here is an abstraction of the familiar image of Pisces, two Fishes swimming in opposite directions yet bound together by a cord. The Fishes represent the spirit—which yearns for the freedom of heaven—and the soul—which remains attached to the desires of the temporal world. During life on earth, the spirit and the soul are bound together. When they complement each other, instead of pulling in opposite directions, they facilitate the Pisces creativity. The ancient version of this glyph, taken from the Egyptians, had no connecting line, which was added in the fourteenth century.

In another interpretation, it is said that the left fish indicates the direction of involution or the beginning of a cycle, while the right fish signifies the direction of evolution, the way to completion of a cycle. It's an appropriate grand finale for Pisces, the last sign of the zodiac.

CHAPTER 9

Astrology on Your Computer: Where to Find Software That Suits Your Budget and Ability

Once you've learned the basics of astrology, you'll be ready to practice reading charts. It's great fun to start out by analyzing the charts of friends and family so you can see how the planets manifest in real life. If you have a computer, there's no easier way than to use astrology software, which can calculate a chart in seconds and even help you interpret it.

When it comes to astrology software, there are endless options. How do you make the right choice? First, define your goals. Do you want to do charts of friends and family, study celebrity charts, or check the aspects every day on your Palm Pilot? Do you want to invest in a more comprehensive program that adapts to your changing needs as you learn astrology?

The good news is that there's a program for every level of interest in all price points—starting with free. For the dabbler, there are the affordable Winstar Express and the Astroscan shareware. For the serious student, there are Astrolog (free), Solar Fire, Kepler, Winstar Plus—software that does every technique on planets and gives you beautiful chart printouts. You can do a chart of someone you've just met on your PDA with Astracadabra. If you're a Mac user, you'll be satisfied with the wonderful IO and Time Passages software.

However, since all the programs use the astrology symbols, or glyphs, for planets and signs, rather than written words, you should learn the glyphs before you purchase your software. Our chapter on the glyphs in this book will help you do just that. Here are some software options for you to explore.

Easy for Beginners

Time Passages

Designed for either a Macintosh or Windows computer, Time Passages is straightforward and easy to use. It allows you to generate charts and interpretation reports for yourself or friends and loved ones at the touch of a button. If you haven't yet learned the astrology symbols, this might be the program for you; just roll your mouse over any symbol of the planets, signs, or house cusps, and you'll be shown a description in plain English below the chart. Then click on the planet, sign, or house cusp and up pops a detailed interpretation. It couldn't be easier. A new basic edition, under fifty dollars at this writing, is bargain priced and ideal for beginners.

Time Passages
(866) 772-7876 (866-77-ASTRO)
Web site: www.astrograph.com

Growth Opportunities

Astrolabe

Astrolabe is one of the top astrology software resources. Check out the latest version of their powerful Solar Fire software for Windows. A breeze to use, it will grow with your increasing knowledge of astrology to the most sophisticated levels. This company also markets a variety of programs for all levels of expertise and a wide selection of computer-generated astrology readings. This is a good resource for innovative software as well as applications for older computers.

The Astrolabe Web site is a great place to start your astrology tour of the Internet. Visitors to the site are greeted with a chart of the time you log on. And you can get your chart calculated, also free, with an interpretation e-mailed to you.

Astrolabe
Box 1750-R
Brewster, MA 02631
Phone: (800) 843-6682
Web site: www.alabe.com

Matrix Software

You'll find a wide variety of software at student and advanced levels in all price ranges, demo disks, and lots of interesting readings. Check out Winstar Express, a powerful but reasonably priced program suitable for all skill levels. The Matrix Web site offers lots of fun activities for Web surfers, such as free readings from the *I Ching,* the runes, and the tarot. There are many free desktop backgrounds with astrology themes. Go here to connect with news groups and online discussions. Their online almanac helps you schedule the best day to sign on the dotted line, ask for a raise, or plant your tomatoes.

Matrix Software
126 South Michigan Ave.
Big Rapids, MI 49307
Phone: (800) 752-6387
Web site: www.astrologysoftware.com

Astro Communications Services (ACS)

Books, software for Mac and IBM compatibles, individual charts, and telephone readings are offered by this California company. Their freebies include astrology greeting cards and new moon reports. Find technical astrology materials here, such as *The American Ephemeris* and PC atlases. ACS will calculate and send charts to you, a valuable service if you do not have a computer.

ACS Publications
P.O. box 1646
El Cajon, CA 72022-1646
Phone: (800) 514-5070
Fax: (619) 631-0185
Web site: www.astrocom.com

Air Software

Here you'll find powerful, creative astrology software, and current stock market analysis. Financial astrology programs for stock market traders are a specialty. There are some interesting freebies at this site; check out the maps of eclipse paths for any year and a free astrology clock program.

Air Software
115 Caya Avenue
West Hartford, CT 06110
Phone: (800) 659-1247
Web site: www.alphee.com

Kepler: State of the Art

Here's a program that has everything. Gorgeous graphic images, audio-visual effects, and myriad sophisticated chart options are built into this fascinating software. It's even got an astrological encyclopedia, plus diagrams and images to help you understand advanced concepts. This program is expensive, but if you're serious about learning astrology, it's an investment that will grow with you! There's a cheaper scaled-down version called Pegasus for those who don't want all the features. Check out its features at www.astrologysoftwareshop.com.

Time Cycles Research: For Mac Users

Here's where Mac users can find astrology software that's as sophisticated as it gets. If you have a Mac, you'll love their beautiful graphic IO Series programs.

Time Cycles Research
P.O. Box 797
Waterford, CT 06385
Web site: www.timecycles.com

Shareware and Freeware: The Price Is Right!

Halloran Software: A Super Shareware Program

Check out Halloran Software's Web site (www.halloran. com), which offers several levels of Windows astrology software. Beginners should consider their Astrology for Windows shareware program, which is available in unregistered demo form as a free download and in registered form for a very reasonable price.

Astrolog

If you're computer-savvy, you can't go wrong with Walter Pullen's amazingly complete Astrolog program, which is offered absolutely free at the site. The Web address is www.astrolog.org/astrolog.htm.

Astrolog is an ultrasophisticated program with all the features of much more expensive programs. It comes in versions for all formats—DOS, Windows, Mac, UNIX—and has some cool features, such as a revolving globe and a constellation map. If you are looking for astrology software with bells and whistles that doesn't cost big bucks, this program has it all!

Astroscan

Surf to www.astroscan.ca for a free program called Astroscan. Stunning graphics and ease of use make this basic program a winner. Astroscan has a fun list of celebrity charts you can call up with a few clicks.

Programs for the Pocket PDA and Palm Pilot

Would you like to have astrology at your fingertips everywhere you go? No need to drag along your laptop. You can check the chart of the moment or of someone you've just met on your pocket PDA or Palm Pilot. As with most other programs, you'll need to know the astrological symbols in order to read the charts.

For the pocket PC that has the Microsoft Pocket PC 2002 or the Microsoft Windows Mobile 2003 operating system, there is the versatile Astracadabra, which can interchange charts with the popular Solar Fire software. It can be ordered at www.leelehman.com or www.astrologysoftwareshop.com.

For the Palm OS5 and compatible handheld devices, there is Astropocket from www.yves.robert.org/features.html. This is a shareware program, which allows you to use all the features free. However, you cannot store more than one chart at a time until you pay a mere twenty-eight-dollar registration fee for the complete version.

CHAPTER 10

How to Connect with Astrology Fans Around the Globe

Are you interested in connecting with other astrology fans? How about expanding your knowledge by studying with a famous astrologer or by attending international lectures and conferences, even astrological workshops in exotic places? The astrological community is ready to welcome you.

You need only type the word astrology into any Internet search engine and watch hundreds of listings of astrology-related sites pop up. There are local meetings and international conferences where you can connect with other astrologers, and books and tapes to help you study at home.

To help you sort out the variety of options available, here are our top picks of the Internet and the astrological community at large.

Nationwide Astrology Organizations and Conferences

National Council for Geocosmic Research (NCGR)

Whether you'd like to know more about such specialties as financial astrology or techniques for timing events, or if you'd prefer the psychological or mythological approach, you'll meet the top astrologers at conferences sponsored by the National Council for Geocosmic Research. NCGR is dedicated to providing quality education, bringing astrologers and astrology fans together at conferences, and promoting fellowship. Their course structure provides a systematized study of the many facets of astrology. The organization sponsors educational workshops, taped lectures, conferences, and a directory of professional astrologers. For an annual membership fee, you get their excellent publications and newsletters, plus the opportunity to network with other astrology buffs at local chapter events. (At this writing there are chapters in twenty-six states and four countries.)

To join NCGR for the latest information on upcoming events and chapters in your city, consult their Web site: www.geocosmic.org.

American Federation of Astrologers (AFA)

Established in 1938, this is one of the oldest astrological organizations in the United States. AFA offers conferences, conventions, and a thorough correspondence course. If you are looking for a reading, their interesting Web site will refer you to an accredited AFA astrologer.

AFA
P.O. Box 22040
Tempe, AZ 85285-2040
Phone: (888) 301-7630 or (480) 838-1751
Fax: (480) 838-8293
Web site: www.astrologers.com

Association for Astrological Networking (AFAN)

Did you know that astrologers are still being harassed for practicing astrology? AFAN provides support and legal information and works toward improving the public image of astrology. AFAN's network of local astrologers links with the international astrological community. Here are the people who will go to bat for astrology when it is attacked in the media. Everyone who cares about astrology should join!

AFAN
8306 Wilshire Boulevard
PMB 537
Beverly Hills, CA 90211
Phone: (800) 578-2326
E-mail: info@afan.org
Web site: www.afan.org

International Society for Astrology Research (ISAR)

An international organization of professional astrologers dedicated to encouraging the highest standards of quality in the field of astrology with an emphasis on research. Among ISAR's benefits are a quarterly journal, a weekly e-mail newsletter, frequent conferences, and a free membership directory.

ISAR
P.O. Box 38613
Los Angeles, CA 90038
Fax: (805) 933-0301
Web site: www.isarastrology.com

Astrology Magazines

In addition to articles by top astrologers, most of these have listings of astrology conferences, events, and local happenings.

Horoscope Guide
Kappa Publishing Group
Dept. 4
P.O. Box 2085
Marion, OH 43306-8121

Dell Horoscope
P.O. Box 54097
Boulder, CO 80322-4907

The Mountain Astrologer

A favorite magazine of astrology fans! *The Mountain Astrologer* also has an interesting Web site featuring the latest news from an astrological point of view, plus feature articles from the magazine.

The Mountain Astrologer
P.O. Box 970
Cedar Ridge, CA 95924
Phone: (800) 247-4828
Web site: www.mountainastrologer.com

Astrology College

Kepler College of Astrological Arts and Sciences

A degree-granting college, which is also a center of astrology, has long been the dream of the astrological community and is a giant step forward in providing credibility to the profession. Therefore, the opening of Kepler College in 2000 was a historical event for astrology. It is the only college in the western hemisphere authorized to issue B.A. and M.A. degrees in Astrological Studies. Here is where to study with the best scholars, teachers, and communicators in the field. A long-distance study program is available for those interested.

For more information, contact:

Kepler College of Astrological Arts and Sciences
4630 200th Street SW
Suite A-1
Lynnwood, WA 98036
Phone: (425) 673-4292
Fax: (425) 673-4983
Web site: www.kepler.edu

Our Favorite Web Sites

Of the thousands of astrological Web sites that come and go on the Internet, these have stood the test of time and are likely to still be operating when this book is published.

Astrodienst (www.astro.com)

Don't miss this fabulous international site that has long been one of the best astrology resources on the Internet. It's also a great place to view and download your own astrology chart. The world atlas on this site will give you the accurate longitude and latitude of your birthplace for setting up your horoscope. Then you can print out your free chart in a range of easy-to-read formats. Other attractions: a list of famous people born on your birth date, a feature that helps you choose the best vacation spot, plus articles by world-famous astrologers.

AstroDatabank (www.astrodatabank.com)

When the news is breaking, you can bet this site will be the first to get accurate birthdays of the headliners. The late astrologer Lois Rodden was a stickler for factual information and her meticulous research is being continued, much to the benefit of the astrological community. The Web site specializes in charts of current newsmakers, political figures, and international celebrities. You can also participate in discussions and analysis of the charts and see what some of the world's best astrologers have to say about them. Their AstroDatabank program, which you can purchase at the site, provides thousands of verified birthdays sorted into categories. It's an excellent research tool.

StarIQ (www.stariq.com)

Find out how top astrologers view the latest headlines at the must-see StarIQ site. Many of the best minds in astrology comment on the latest news, stock market ups and downs, political contenders. You can sign up to receive e-mail forecasts at the most important times keyed to your individual chart. (This is one of the best of the many on-line forecasts.)

Astrology Books (www.astroamerica.com)

The Astrology Center of America sells a wide selection of books on all aspects of astrology, from the basics to the most advanced, at this online bookstore. Also available are many hard-to-find and recycled books.

Astrology Scholars' Sites

See what one of astrology's great teachers, Robert Hand, has to offer on his site: www.robhand.com. A leading expert on the history of astrology, he's on the cutting edge of the latest research.

The Project Hindsight group of astrologers is devoted to restoring the astrology of the Hellenistic period, the primary source for all later Western astrology. There are fascinating articles for astrology fans on this site, www.project hindsight.com.

Financial Astrology Sites

Financial astrology is a hot specialty, with many tipsters, players, and theorists. There are online columns, newsletters, specialized financial astrology software, and mutual funds run by astrology seers. One of the more respected financial astrologers is Ray Merriman, whose column on www.stariq.com is a must read for those following the bulls and bears. Other top financial astrologers offer tips and forecasts at the www.afund.com and www.alphee.com sites.

CHAPTER 11

Got a Big Question? A Personal Reading Might Give You the Answer

Life can sometimes leave you feeling bewitched, bothered, and bewildered, as the song goes. Whether you're faced with a seemingly insurmountable problem or would simply like an objective opinion, it might be helpful to consult a professional astrologer who will take all the facets of your astrological chart into consideration. A good reading can give you peace of mind by confirming those mysterious intuitive feelings that you can't quite identify. It can give you insights on your situation that will lead you to better choices, perhaps ones that have been blocked by a blind spot.

A reading can answer some very practical questions as well, such as setting the perfect date for a wedding, a crucial job interview, or a real estate closing. If a partnership is turning sour, insights from a reading might help you put the relationship back on track. Or, after a reading, you might understand the compromises and adjustments needed to make it work. For example, one astrologically minded business team has charts done to help them work well together. Charts for family members might be done to help improve home life or figure out some complicated family dynamics.

Another good reason for a reading is to improve your personal knowledge of astrology by consulting someone who has years of experience analyzing charts. You might choose someone with a special technique that intrigues you. Armed with the knowledge of your chart that you have acquired so far, you can learn to interpret subtle nuances or gain perspective on your talents and abilities.

But what kind of reading should you have? Besides one-on-one readings with a professional astrologer, there are personal readings by mail, telephone, Internet, and tape. Well-advertised computer-generated reports and celebrity-sponsored readings are sure to attract your attention.

Done by a qualified astrologer, the personal reading can be an empowering experience if you want to reach your full potential, size up a lover or business situation, or find out what the future has in store. There are astrologers who are specialists in certain areas such as finance or medical astrology. And, unfortunately, there are many questionable practitioners who range from streetwise gypsy fortune-tellers to unscrupulous scam artists.

The following basic guidelines can help you sort out your options to find the reading that's right for you.

One-on-One Consultations with a Professional Astrologer

Nothing compares to a one-on-one consultation with a professional astrologer who has analyzed thousands of charts and can pinpoint the potential in yours. During your reading, you can get your specific questions answered. For instance, how to get along better with your mate or coworker. There are many astrologers who now combine their skills with training in psychology and are well-suited to help you examine your alternatives.

To give you an accurate reading, an astrologer needs certain information from you: the date, time, and place where you were born. (A horoscope can be cast about anyone or anything that has a specific time and place.) Most astrologers will then enter this information into a computer, which will calculate a chart in seconds. From the resulting chart, the astrologer will do an interpretation.

If you don't know your exact birth time, you can usually locate it at the Bureau of Vital Statistics at the city hall or county seat of the state where you were born. If you still have no success in getting your time of birth, some astrologers can estimate an approximate birth time by using past events in your life to determine the chart. This technique is called *rectification*.

How to Find an Astrologer

Choose your astrologer with the same care as you would any trusted adviser such as a doctor, lawyer, or banker. Unfortunately, anyone can claim to be an astrologer—to date, there is no licensing of astrologers or universally established professional criteria. However, there are nationwide organizations of serious, committed astrologers that can help you in your search.

Good places to start your investigation are organizations such as the American Federation of Astrologers (AFA) or the National Council for Geocosmic Research (NCGR), which offer a program of study and certification. If you live near a major city, there is sure to be an active NCGR chapter or astrology club in your area; many are listed in astrology magazines available at your local newsstand. In response to many requests for referrals, both the AFA and the NCGR have directories of professional astrologers listed on their Web sites; these directories include a glossary of terms and an explanation of specialties within the astrological field. Contact the NCGR and AFA headquarters for information (see chapter 10 in this book).

Warning Signals

As a potentially lucrative freelance business, astrology has always attracted self-styled experts who may not have the knowledge or the counseling experience to give a helpful reading. These astrologers can range from the well-meaning amateur to the charlatan or street-corner gypsy who has for many years given astrology a bad name. Be very wary of astrologers who claim to have occult powers or who make pretentious claims of celebrated clients or miraculous achievements. You can often tell from the initial phone conversation if the astrologer is legitimate. He or she should ask for your birthday time and place, then conduct the conversation in a professional manner. Any astrologer who gives a reading based only on your sun sign is highly suspect.

When you arrive at the reading, the astrologer should be prepared. The consultation should be conducted in a private, quiet place. The astrologer should be interested in your problems of the moment. A good reading involves feedback on your part. So if the reading is not relating to your concerns, you should let the astrologer know. You should feel free to ask questions and get clarifications of technical terms. The more you actively participate, rather than expecting the astrologer to carry the reading or come forth with oracular predictions, the more meaningful your experience will be. An astrologer should help you validate your current experience and be frank about possible negative happenings, but also suggest a positive course of action.

In their approach to a reading, some astrologers may be more literal, others more intuitive. Those who have had counseling training may take a more psychological approach. Though some astrologers may seem to have an almost psychic ability, extrasensory perception or any other parapsychological talent is not essential. A very accurate picture can be drawn from the data in your horoscope chart.

An astrologer may do several charts for each client, including one for the time of birth and a *progressed chart,* showing the evolution from birth to the present time. According to your individual needs, there are many other possibilities, such as a chart for a different location if you are contemplating a change of place. Relationships between any two people, things, or events can be interpreted with a chart that compares one partner's horoscope with the other's. A composite chart, which uses the midpoint between planets in two individual charts to describe the relationship, is another commonly used device.

An astrologer will be particularly interested in transits, those times when cycling planets activate the planets or sensitive points in your birth chart. These indicate important events in your life.

Many astrologers offer tape-recorded readings, another option to consider, especially if the astrologer you choose lives at a distance. In this case, you'll be mailed a taped reading based on your birth chart. This type of reading is more personal than a computer printout and can give you valuable insights, though it is not equivalent to a live dialogue with the astrologer when you can discuss your specific interests and issues of the moment.

The Telephone Reading

Telephone readings come in two varieties: a dial-in taped reading, usually recorded in advance by an astrologer, or a live consultation with an "astrologer" on the other end of the line. The taped readings are general daily or weekly forecasts, applied to all members of your sign and charged by the minute. The quality depends on the astrologer. One caution: Be aware that these readings can run up quite a telephone bill, especially if you get into the habit of calling every day. Be sure that you are aware of the per-minute cost of each call beforehand.

Live telephone readings also vary with the expertise of the astrologer. Ideally, the astrologer at the other end of the line enters your birth date into a computer, which then quickly calculates your chart. This chart will be referred to during the consultation. The advantage of a live telephone reading is that your individual chart is used and you can ask about a specific problem. However, before you invest in any reading, be sure that your astrologer is qualified and that you fully understand in advance how much you will be charged. There should be no unpleasant financial surprises later.

Computer-Generated Reports

Companies that offer computer programs (such as ACS, Matrix, Astrolabe) also offer a variety of computer-generated horoscope readings. These can be quite comprehensive, offering a beautiful printout of the chart plus many pages of detailed information about each planet and aspect of the chart. You can then study it at your convenience. Of course, the interpretations will be general, since there is no personal input from you, and may not cover your immediate concerns. Since computer-generated horoscopes are much lower in cost than live consultations, you might consider one as either a supplement or a preparation for an eventual live reading. You'll then be more familiar with your chart and able to plan specific questions in advance. They also make terrific gifts for astrology fans. There are several companies, listed in chapter 9, that offer computerized readings prepared by reputable astrologers.

Whichever option you decide to pursue, may your reading be an empowering one!

CHAPTER 12

Your Pet-scope for 2007: How to Choose Your Best Friend for Life

With both Jupiter, the planet of luck and expansion, and powerful Pluto in the animal-loving sign of Sagittarius, this is sure to be a year of pets and a great time to bring joy into your life by adopting an animal friend. At this writing, 63 percent of all American households have at least one pet, according to a recent survey by the American Pet Product Manufacturers Association. And we spend billions of dollars on the care and feeding of our beloved pets. Our pets are counted as part of the family, often sharing our beds and accompanying us on trips.

Whether you choose to adopt an animal from a local shelter or buy a thoroughbred from a breeder, try for an optimal time of adoption and the sun sign of your new friend. If you're rescuing an animal, however, it's difficult to know the sun sign of the animal, but you can adopt on a day when the moon is compatible with yours, which should bless the emotional relationship. Using the moon signs listed in the daily forecasts in this book, choose a day when the moon is in your sign, a sign of the same element, or a compatible element. This means fire and air signs should go for a day when the moon is in fire signs—Aries, Leo, Sagittarius—or air signs—Gemini, Libra, or Aquarius. Water and earth signs should choose a day when the moon is in water signs—Cancer, Scorpio or Pisces—or earth signs—Taurus, Virgo, or Capricorn. If possible, aim for a new moon, good for beginning a new relationship.

Here are some sign-specific tips for adopting an animal that will become your best friend for life.

Aries: The Rescuer

Aries gets special pleasure from rescuing animals in distress and rehabing them, so check your local shelters if you're thinking of adopting an animal. As an active fire sign, you'd be happiest with a lively animal, and you might do well with a rescue animal, such as a German shepherd or Labrador retriever. You'd also enjoy training such an animal. Otherwise look for intelligence, alertness, playfulness, and obedience in your friend. Since Aries tend to have an active life, look for a sleek, low-maintenance coat on your dog or cat. Cat lovers would enjoy the more active breeds such as the Siamese or Abyssinian.

An Aries sun-sign dog or cat would be ideal. Aries animals have a brave, energetic, rather combative nature. They can be mischievous, so the kittens and puppies should be monitored for safety. They'll dare to jump higher, run faster, and chase more animals than their peers. They may require stronger words and more obedience training than other signs. Give them plenty of toys and play active games with them often.

Taurus: The Toucher

Taurus is a touchy-feely sign; this tendency extends to your animal relationships. Look for a dog or cat that enjoys being petted and groomed, is affectionate, and adapts well to family life. As one of the great animal-loving signs, Taurus is likely to have several pets, so it is important that they all get along together. Give each one its own special safe space to minimize turf wars.

Taurus animals are calm and even tempered, but do not like being teased and could retaliate, so be sure to instruct children how to handle and play with their pet. Since this sign has strong appetites and tends to put on weight easily, be careful not to overindulge the animals in high-calorie treats and table snacks.

Taurus female animals are excellent mothers and make good breeders. They tend to be clean and less destructive of home furnishings than other animals.

Gemini: The Companion

A bright, quick-witted sign like yours requires an equally interesting and communicative pet. Choose a social animal that adapts well to different environments, since you may travel or have homes in different locations.

Gemini animals can put up with noise, telephones, music, and people coming and going. They'll want to be part of the action, so place a pillow or roost in a public place. They do not like being left alone. If you will be away for long periods, find them an animal companion to play with. You might consider adopting two Gemini pets from the same litter.

Animals born under this sign are easy to teach and some enjoy doing tricks or retrieving. They may be more vocal than other animals, especially if they are confined without companionship.

Cancer: The Nurturer

Cancer enjoys a devoted, obedient animal who demonstrates loyalty to its master. An affectionate home-loving dog or cat that welcomes you and sits on your lap would be ideal. The emotional connection with your pet is most important; therefore, you may depend on your powerful psychic powers when choosing an animal. Wait until you feel a strong bond of psychic communication. The moon sign of the day you adopt is very important for moon-ruled Cancer, so choose a water sign, if possible.

Cancer animals need a feeling of security; they don't like changes of environment or too much chaos at home. If you intend to breed your animal, the Cancer pet makes a wonderful and fertile mother.

Leo: The Prideful Owner

The Leo owner may choose a pet that reminds you of your own physical characteristics, such as similar coloring or build. You will be proud of your pet, will keep the animal groomed to perfection, and will choose the most spectacular example of the breed. Noble animals with a regal attitude, beautiful fur, or striking markings are often preferred, such as the Himalayan or the red tabby Persian cat, the standard poodle or the chow chow. An attention getter is a must.

Under the sign of the king of beasts, Leo-born animals have proud noble natures. They usually have a cheerful, magnanimous disposition and rule their domains regardless of their breed, holding their heads with pride and walking with great authority. They enjoy being groomed, like to show off, and enjoy the attention of fans. Leo animals thrive in the spotlight.

Virgo: The Caregiver

Virgo owners will be very particular about their pets, paying special attention to requirements for care and maintenance. You need a pet who is clean, obedient, intelligent, yet rather quiet. A highly active, barking or meowing pet that might get on your nerves is a no-no.

Cats are usually very good pets for Virgo. Choose one of the calm breeds, such as a Persian. Though this is a high-maintenance cat, its beauty and personality will be rewarding. You are compassionate with animals in need, and you might find it rewarding to volunteer at a local shelter or veterinary clinic or to train service dogs.

Virgo animals can be fussy eaters and very particular about their environment. They are gentle and intelligent; they respond to kind words and quiet commands, never harsh treatment. Virgo is an excellent sign for dogs that are trained to do service work, since they seem to enjoy being useful and are intelligent enough to be easily trained.

Libra: The Beautifier

The Libra owner responds to beauty and elegance in your pet. You require a well-mannered, but social companion, who can be displayed in all of nature's finery. An exotic variety such as a graceful curly-haired Devon Rex cat would be a show stopper. Libra often prefers the smaller varieties, such as a miniature schnauzer, a mini greyhound, or a teacup poodle.

Pets born under Libra are usually charming and well-mannered. They tend to be more careful than those of other signs. They'll avoid confrontations and harsh sounds, but respond to words of love and gentle corrections.

Scorpio: The Powerful

Scorpios enjoy a powerful animal with a strong character. They enjoy training animals and do well with service dogs, guard dogs, or police animals. Some Scorpios enjoy exotic, edgy pets, such as hairless Sphynx cats or Chinese Chin dogs. Rescuing animals in dire circumstances and finding them new homes are especially rewarding for Scorpios, as Matthew McConaughey did during Hurricane Katrina.

Animals born under this sign tend to be one-person pets, very strongly attached to their owners and extremely loyal and possessive. They are natural guard animals that will take extreme risks to protect their owners. They are best ruled by love and with consistent behavior training. They need to respect their owners and will return their love with great devotion.

Sagittarius: The Jovial Freedom Lover

Sagittarius is a traveler and one of the great animal lovers of the zodiac. The horse is especially associated with your sign, and you could well be a horse whisperer. You generally respond most to large, active animals. If a small animal, like a chihuahua, steals your heart, be sure it's one that travels well or tolerates your absence. Outdoor dogs like hunting dogs, retrievers, and border collies would be good companions on your outdoor adventures.

Sagittarius animals are freedom-loving, jovial, happy-go-lucky types. They may be wanderers, however, so be sure they have the proper identification tags and consider embedded microchip identification. These animals tend to be openly affectionate, companionable, and untemperamental. They enjoy socializing and playing with humans and other animals and are especially good with active children.

Capricorn: The Thoroughbred

Capricorn is a discriminating owner, with a great sense of responsibility toward your animal. You will be concerned with maintenance and care; you will rarely neglect or overlook any health issues with your pet. You will also discipline your pet wisely, not tolerating any destructive or outrageous antics. You will be attracted to good breeding, good manners, and deep loyalty from your pet.

The Capricorn pet tends to be more quiet and serious than other pets, perhaps a lone wolf who prefers the company of its owner rather than a sociable or mischievous type. This is another good sign for a working dog, such as a herder, because Capricorn animals enjoy this outlet for their energy.

Aquarius: The Independent Original

Aquarius owners tend to lead active, busy lives and need an animal who can either accompany them cheerfully or who won't make waves. Demanding or high-maintenance dogs are not for you. You might prefer unusual or oddball pets, such as dressed-up chihuahuas that travel in your tote bag or scene-stealing, rather shocking hairless cats. Or you will acquire a group of animals that can play with one another when you are pursuing outside activities. You can relate to the independence of cats.

Aquarius animals are not loners. They enjoy the companionship of humans or groups of other animals. They tend to be more independent and may require more training to follow the house rules.

Pisces: The Soul-Mate

This is the sign that can talk to the animals. Pisces owners enjoy deep communication with their pets, love having their animals accompany them, sleep with them, and show affection. Pisces will often rescue an animal in distress or adopt an animal from a shelter. Tropical fish are often recommended as a Pisces pet, and they seem to have a natural tranquilizing effect on this sign. However, Pisces may require an animal that shows more affection than do their fish friends.

Pisces animals are creative types; they can be sensually seductive and mysterious, mischievous and theatrical. They make fine house pets, do not usually like to roam far from their owners, and have winning personalities, especially with the adults in the home. Naturally sensitive and seldom vicious, they should be treated gently and given much praise and encouragement.

CHAPTER 13

Your Baby-scope: Children Born in 2007

Will the babies born this year be easy to raise or will they require a time-out mat or supernanny? Astrology answers these questions by looking beyond sun signs to the planets that describe a whole generation.

Children born this year will belong to one of the most spiritual generations in history. The three outer planets—Uranus, Neptune, and Pluto, which stay in a sign for at least seven years—are the ones that most affect each generation. Now passing through Pisces, Aquarius, and Sagittarius respectively, the three most visionary signs are sure to imprint the children of 2007.

In the past century, Uranus in Pisces coincided with enormous creativity, which should impact this year's children. Neptune in Aquarius and Pluto in Sagittarius are bringing a time of dissolving barriers, of globalization, of interest in religion and spirituality . . . breaking away from the materialism of the last century. In contrast, the members of this generation will truly be children of the world, searching for deeper meanings to existence.

Astrology can be an especially helpful tool that can be used to design an environment that will enhance and encourage each child's positive qualities. Some parents start before conception, planning the birth of their child as far as possible to harmonize with the signs of other family members. However, each baby has its own schedule, so if yours arrives a week early or late, or elects a different sign than you'd planned, recognize that the new sign may be more in line with the mission your child is here to accomplish. In other words, if you were hoping for a Libra child and he arrives during Virgo, that Virgo energy may be just what is needed to stimulate or complement your family. Remember that there are many astrological elements besides the sun sign that indicate strong family ties. Usually each child will share a particular planetary placement, an emphasis on a particular sign or house, or a certain chart configuration with his parents and other family members. Often there is a significant planetary angle that will define the parent-child relationship, such as family sun signs that form a T-square or a triangle.

One important thing you can do is to be sure the exact moment of birth is recorded. This will be essential in calculating an accurate astrological chart. The following descriptions can be applied to the sun or moon sign (if known) of a child—the sun sign will describe basic personality and the moon sign indicates the child's emotional needs.

The Aries Child

Baby Aries is quite a handful! This energetic child will walk—and run—as soon as possible and perform daring feats of exploration. Caregivers should be vigilant. Little Aries seems to know no fear (and is especially vulnerable to head injuries). Many Aries children, in their rush to get on with life, seem hyperactive and are easily frustrated when they can't get their own way. Violent temper tantrums and dramatic physical displays are par for the course with these children, necessitating a time-out chair.

The very young Aries should be monitored carefully, since he is prone to take risks and may injure himself. An Aries loves to take things apart and may break toys easily, but with encouragement, the child will develop formidable coordination. Aries's bossy tendencies should be molded into leadership qualities, rather than bullying. Otherwise, the me-first Aries will have many clashes with other strong-willed youngsters. Encourage these children to take out aggressions and frustrations in active, competitive sports, where they usually excel. When a young Aries learns to focus his energies long enough to master a subject and learns consideration for others, the indomitable Aries spirit will rise to the head of the class.

Aries born in 2007 will benefit from the jovial rays of Jupiter in Sagittarius until December of that year, which should give this child a sunny, optimistic personality.

The Taurus Child

This is a cuddly, affectionate child who eagerly explores the world of the senses, especially the senses of taste and touch. The Taurus child can be a big eater and will put on weight easily if not encouraged to exercise. Since this child likes comfort and gravitates to beauty, try coaxing little Taurus to exercise to music or take him outdoors for hikes or long walks. Though Taurus may be a slow learner, this sign has an excellent retentive memory and generally masters a subject thoroughly. Taurus is interested in results and will see each project patiently through to completion, continuing long after others have given up.

Choose Taurus toys carefully to help develop innate talents. Construction toys, such as blocks or erector sets, appeal to their love of building. Paints or crayons develop their sense of color. Many Taurus have musical talents and love to sing, which is apparent at a young age.

This year's Taurus will want a pet or two and a few plants of his own. Give little Taurus a minigarden and watch the natural green thumb develop. This child has a strong sense of acquisition and an early grasp of material value. After filling a piggy bank, Taurus graduates to a savings account, before other children have started to learn the value of money. Jupiter in their house of joint ventures this year should give Taurus another edge in financial matters.

The Gemini Child

Little Gemini will talk as soon as possible, filing the air with questions and chatter. This is a friendly child who enjoys social contact, seems to require company, and adapts quickly to different surroundings. Geminis have quick minds that easily grasp the use of words, books, and telephones and will probably learn to talk and read at an earlier age than most. Though they are fast learners, Gemini may have a short attention span, darting from subject to subject. Projects and games that help focus the mind could be used to help them concentrate. Musical instruments, typewriters, and computers help older Gemini children combine mental with manual dexterity. Geminis should be encouraged to finish what they start before they go on to another project. Otherwise, they can become jack-of-all-trade types who have trouble completing anything they do. Their dispositions are usually cheerful and witty, making these children popular with their peers and delightful company at home.

This year's Gemini baby should go to the head of the class. Uranus in Pisces could inspire Gemini to make an unusual career choice, perhaps in a high-tech field. When he grows up, this year's Gemini may change fields several times before he finds a job that satisfies his need for stimulation and variety.

The Cancer Child

This emotional, sensitive child is especially influenced by patterns set early in life. Young Cancers cling to their first memories as well as their childhood possessions. They thrive in calm emotional waters, with a loving, protective mother, and usually remain close to her (even if their relationship with her was difficult) throughout their lives. Divorce, death—anything that disturbs the safe family unit—are devastating to Cancers, who may need extra support and reassurance during a family crisis.

They sometimes need a firm hand to push the positive, creative side of their personality and discourage them from getting swept away by emotional moods or resorting to emotional manipulation to get their way. Praised and encouraged to find creative expression, Cancer will be able to express his positive side consistently on a firm, secure foundation.

This year's Cancer child should be more grounded and practical, thanks to Jupiter in Sagittarius. This also brings the blessing of good health!

The Leo Child

Leo children love the limelight and will plot to get the lion's share of attention. These children assert themselves with flair and drama and can behave like tiny tyrants to get their way. But in general, they have sunny, positive dispositions and are rarely subject to blue moods. At school, they're the ones who are voted most popular, head cheerleader, or homecoming queen. Leo is sure to be noticed for personality, if not for stunning looks or academic work; the homely Leo will be a class clown and the unhappy Leo may be the class bully.

Above all, a Leo child cannot tolerate being ignored for long. Drama or performing-arts classes, sports, and school politics are healthy ways for Leo to be a star. But Leos must learn to take lesser roles occasionally, or they will have some painful put-downs in store. Usually, the popularity of Leos is well earned; they are hard workers who try to measure up to their own high standards—and usually succeed.

The Leo baby born this year is likely to be more serious than the typical Leo, thanks to the taskmaster planet Saturn finishing up its two-year stay in Leo. This endows the child with self-discipline and the ability to function well in structured situations. With enhanced focusing ability, little Leo can be a high achiever.

The Virgo Child

The young Virgo can be a quiet, rather serious child, with a quick, intelligent mind. Early on, little Virgo shows far more attention to detail and concern with small things than other children do. Little Virgo has a built-in sense of order and a fascination with how things work. It is important for these children to have a place of their own, which they can order as they wish and where they can read or busy themselves with crafts and hobbies.

This child's personality can be very sensitive. Little Virgo may get hyper and overreact to seemingly small irritations, which can take the form of stomach upsets or delicate digestive systems. But this child will flourish where there is mental stimulation and a sense of order. Virgos thrive in school, especially in writing or language skills, and seem truly happy when buried in books. Chances are, young Virgo will learn to read ahead of classmates. Hobbies that involve detail work or that develop fine craftsmanship are especially suited to young Virgos.

Baby Virgo of 2007 is likely to be an especially active, intelligent child, since there are at least five planets in mutable signs during this period. With Saturn, also in Virgo beginning on September 2, he should respond to discipline. However, there should be plenty of mental and social stimulation in his environment to tame his restless nature.

The Libra Child

The Libra child learns early about the power of charm and appearance. This is often a very physically appealing child with an enchanting dimpled smile, who is naturally sociable and enjoys the company of both children and adults. It is a rare Libra child who is a discipline problem, but when their behavior is unacceptable, they respond better to calm discussion than displays of emotion, especially if the discussion revolves around fairness. Because young Libras without a strong direction tend to drift with the mood of the group, these children should be encouraged to develop their unique talents and powers of discrimination so they can later stand on their own.

In school, this child is usually popular and will often have to choose between social invitations and studies. In the teen years, social pressures mount as the young Libra begins to look for a partner. This is the sign of best friends, so Libra's choice of companions can have a strong effect on his future direction. Beautiful Libra girls may be tempted to go steady or have an unwise early marriage. Chances are, both sexes will fall in and out of love several times in their search for the ideal partner.

Little Libra of 2007 should have a way with words, thanks to Jupiter and Pluto in Sagittarius, which will enhance verbal and communications skills. This is an especially social, talkative child, who gets along well with siblings and classmates. Later in life, this Libra could choose a career in writing or the communication field.

The Scorpio Child

The Scorpio child may seem quiet and shy, but will surprise others with intense feelings and formidable willpower. Scorpio children are single-minded when they want something and intensely passionate about whatever they do. One of a caregiver's tasks is to teach this child to balance activities and emotions, yet at the same time to make the most of his or her great concentration and intense commitment.

Since young Scorpios do not show their depth of feelings easily, parents will have to learn to read almost imperceptible signs that troubles are brewing beneath the surface. Both Scorpio boys and girls enjoy games of power and control on or off the playground. Scorpio girls may take an early interest in the opposite sex, masquerading as tomboys, while Scorpio boys may be intensely competitive and loners. When their powerful energies are directed into work, sports, or challenging studies, Scorpio is a superachiever, focused on a goal. With trusted friends, young Scorpio is devoted and caring—the proverbial friend through thick and thin, loyal for life.

Jupiter and Pluto in Sagittarius should give this year's baby Scorpio a more carefree personality plus a flair for finance. There's lots of water in their horoscope, with Pisces and Cancer planets endowing these babies with plenty of imagination and creativity to be developed. Mars in Cancer will ignite a spirit of adventure and a love of water sports. Long journeys could be in the future.

The Sagittarius Child

This restless, athletic child will be out of the playpen and off on adventures as soon as possible. Little Sagittarius is remarkably well-coordinated, attempting daredevil feats on any wheeled vehicle from scooters to skateboards. These natural athletes need little encouragement to channel their energies into sports. Their cheerful, friendly dispositions earn them popularity in school, and once they have found a subject where their talent and imagination can soar, they will do well academically. They love animals, especially horses, and will be sure to have a pet or two, if not a home zoo. When they are old enough to take care of themselves, they'll clamor to be off on adventures of their own, away from home, if possible.

This child loves to travel, will not get homesick at summer camp, and may sign up to be a foreign-exchange student or spend summers abroad. Outdoor adventure appeals to little Sagittarius, especially if it involves an active sport, such as skiing, cycling, or mountain climbing. Give them enough space and encouragement, and their fiery spirit will propel them to achieve high goals.

Baby Sagittarius of 2007 is a freedom-loving child with a bonanza of luck and charisma, thanks to potent Pluto and lucky Jupiter in Sagittarius. This child has a natural generosity of spirit and an optimistic, expansive nature. He may need reality checks from time to time, since he may also be a big risk taker. He will also demand a great deal of freedom.

The Capricorn Child

These purposeful, goal-oriented children will work to capacity if they feel this will bring results. They're not ones who enjoy work for its own sake—there must be an end in sight. Authority figures can do much to motivate these children, but once set on an upward path, young Capricorns will mobilize energy and talent and work harder, and with more perseverance, then any other sign. Capricorn has built-in self-discipline that can achieve remarkable results, even if lacking the flashy personality, quick brain power, or penetrating insight of others. Once involved, young Capricorn will stick to a task until it is mastered. These children also know how to use others to their advantage and may well become team captains or class presidents.

A wise parent will set realistic goals for the Capricorn child, paving the way for the early thrill of achievement. Youngsters should be encouraged to express their caring, feeling side to others, as well as their natural aptitude for leadership. Capricorn children may be especially fond of grandparents and older relatives and will enjoy spending time with them and learning from them. It is not uncommon for young Capricorns to have an older mentor or teacher who guides them. With their great respect for authority, Capricorn children will take this influence very much to heart.

The Capricorn born in 2007 will have serious and responsible alliances, thanks to Saturn in the house of mutual ventures. This placement also hints at financial savvy—so give the child a savings account early on. Jupiter in Sagittarius promises a deep inner life and a generous nature.

The Aquarius Child

The Aquarius child has an innovative, well-focused mind that often streaks so far ahead of those of peers that this child seems like an oddball. Routine studies never hold the restless youngster for long; he will look for another, more experimental place to try out his ideas and develop his inventions. Life is a laboratory to the inquiring Aquarius mind. School politics, sports, science, and the arts offer scope for such talents. But if there is no room for expression within approved social limits, Aquarius is sure to rebel. Questioning institutions and religions comes naturally, so these children may find an outlet elsewhere, becoming rebels with a cause. It is better not to force this child to conform, but rather to channel forward-thinking young minds into constructive group activities.

This year's Aquarius will have far-out glamour as well as

charisma, thanks to his ruler, Uranus, in a friendly bond with Neptune. This child could be a rock star, a statesman, or a scientist.

The Pisces Child

Give young Pisces praise, applause, and a gentle, but firm, push in the right direction. Lovable Pisces children may be abundantly talented, but may be hesitant to express themselves, because they are quite sensitive and easily hurt. It is a parent's challenge to help them gain self-esteem and self-confidence. However, this same sensitivity makes them trusted friends who'll have many confidants as they develop socially. It also endows many Pisces with spectacular creative talent.

Pisces adores drama and theatrics of all sorts; therefore, encourage them to channel their creativity into art forms rather than indulging in emotional dramas. Understand that they may need more solitude than other children, as they develop their creative ideas. But though daydreaming can be creative, it is important that these natural dreamers not dwell too long in the world of fantasy. Teach them practical coping skills for the real world. Since Pisces are physically sensitive, parents should help them build strong bodies with proper diet and regular exercise. Young Pisces may gravitate to more individual sports, such as swimming, sailing, and skiing, rather than to team sports. Or they may prefer more artistic physical activities like dance or ice skating.

Born givers, these children are often drawn to the underdog (they fall quickly for sob stories) and attract those who might take advantage of their emphatic nature. Teach them to choose friends wisely and to set boundaries in relationships, to protect their emotional vulnerability—invaluable lessons in later life.

With the planet Uranus now in Pisces, the 2007 baby belongs to a generation of Pisces movers and shakers. This child may have a rebellious streak that rattles the status quo. But this generation also has a visionary nature, which will be much concerned with the welfare of the world at large.

CHAPTER 14

Is This the Right Time to Fall in Love?

Astrology gives you a power tool for discovering why you are attracted to a certain person and how that person might act or react toward you. It also gives you the times when you are at your most attractive to the opposite sex. Although astrology can't guarantee that you'll have a problem-free relationship, it can give you a romantic timetable and road map to guide you over the rough spots and reveal what you might expect in the future with your partner, after the initial glow has given way to day-to-day reality. Working in your favor is the fact that no one totally embodies any one sign; we're a combination of all the signs in different proportions. So there will always be some naturally compatible (as well as incompatible) aspects between two people's charts.

The Right Time to Reunite with an Old Lover or Reignite Passion in Your Current Relationship

An old love might resurface in your life when the planet Mercury, which rules communications, is in retrograde motion, about three times each year. (Check this information in chapter 2.) This planet often brings back people from the past, as well as old issues that should be resolved. It's an ideal time to troubleshoot existing relationships in which passion has cooled and to take action to reignite the flame of love. Heart-to-heart talks about what went wrong could help you understand each other better. Retrograde Venus is another good time to set a relationship back on course; it happens briefly in Virgo this year, from July 27 until September 8, when it turns direct in Leo. Those especially affected will have the sun or moon in Leo or Virgo. It is not a good idea to begin a new romantic relationship when either Venus or Mercury is retrograding.

Take a Chance on Love

Jupiter, the planet of risk, is in the risk-taking sign Sagittarius, which it rules this year. This could inspire fire signs (Aries, Leo, Sagittarius), in particular, to take a chance on love, perhaps choosing someone from a distant land or different culture. The mood of love is adventurous, exciting, daring, flirtatious. You could be swept off your feet, but this is not necessarily a time for long-term monogamous relationships. Jupiter encourages exploration in all areas!

Make the First Move

Venus is the planet that makes others respond favorably to you. When it's in your sun sign or a favorable sign, you have a terrific opportunity to attract the opposite sex, so turn on the charm. Ideally both the sun and Venus in your sun sign make you catnip to others.

Go Out and Meet Someone New

New activities of all kinds are favored during the new moon, especially if it's the new moon in your sun sign (or a sign in the same or complementary element). You'll also want a favorable Mercury (not retrograde) to give you the right words and a good Venus so that hot new prospect gets your message.

When to Break Up

Breaking up may be easier to do during a waning moon, in the last quarter, when we're gearing up for a new cycle. However, some planetary aspects such as eclipses could force emotional issues out into the open and thus cause a breakup. As Mars transits your sun sign, you may become impatient with long-standing irritations in a relationship and be tempted to move on. Check the Mars tables after chapter 6 and the new and full moon list in chapter 2.

Is This Person the Right One?

Here's a three-step technique for determining if your lover is the right one for a lasting relationship.

How to Predict Your Romantic Success

Consider the other planets in your lover's chart, not just the sun sign (you can look up most of them using the charts in this book). Venus will tell what attracts you both. Mars reveals your temper and sex drive, Mercury how you'll communicate, and the moon your emotional nature. (For the moon and Mercury signs, consult one of the free charts available on the Internet. See chapter 10.)

Step One: Size Up the Overall Relationship

To do an instant take on your relationship, compare the elements of the sun, moon, Mercury, Mars, and Venus—each a key planet in compatibility, in both charts. The interaction of elements (earth, air, fire, water) is the fastest way to size up a relationship. Planets of the same element will have the smoothest chemistry.

Earth element: Taurus Virgo, Capricorn
Air element: Gemini, Libra, Aquarius

Fire element: Aries, Leo, Sagittarius
Water element: Cancer, Scorpio, Pisces

When your partner has the same planet in the same element as your planet in question, the energy will flow freely. Complementary elements (fire signs with air signs or earth signs with water signs) also get along easily.

What if many planets are in other combinations? That's where you'll probably have to work at the relationship. There is tension and possible combustion between fire and water signs or earth and air signs. Take the analogies literally. Fire brings water to a boil; earth and air create a dust storm or tornado. If both your Venus signs are clashing, you will probably have very different tastes, something that could adversely affect a long-term relationship. However, challenges can be stimulating as well, adding spice to a relationship, especially when planets of sexual attraction—Mars relating to Venus—are involved.

Step Two: Find Out How the Individual Planets Relate

Find out and compare how each planet operates in both your horoscopes (sun, moon, Mercury, Venus, and Mars) by comparing its quality or mode. Planets in cardinal signs are active, assertive; planets in fixed signs are tenacious, stubborn; planets in mutable signs are adaptable, easily changeable. Two planets of the same quality (but different signs) do not easily relate—there is usually a conflict of interests—but they can challenge each other to be more flexible or they can open up new areas in each other's lives. This is where you have to make compromises to reconcile different points of view. You'll have to be flexible or give in often.

Cardinal signs (active): Aries, Cancer, Libra, Capricorn
Fixed signs (static): Taurus, Leo, Scorpio, Aquarius
Mutable signs (changeable): Gemini, Virgo, Pisces, Sagittarius

Step Three: Rate Your Overall Compatibility

The planets closest to the earth (sun, moon, Mercury, Mars, Venus) are those most likely to affect close relationships. Where possible, look up your planets and those of your partner in this book and grade them as follows. (The more A's and B's, the better! Y's and Z's indicate where you'll have to compromise to work things out.)

Grade A: for the same element (earth, air, fire, water)
Grade B: for complementary elements (air with fire, earth with water)
Grade Y: for challenging elements (air with water, earth with fire)
Grade Z: for the same quality, but different signs

By now, you should have a good idea where your relationship stands astrologically. A further check of the individual planets can answer some all-important questions.

Here's what the individual planets in your charts can reveal about your relationship:

Are you basically attracted? Compare sun signs.

The sun sign gives the big picture. Though it is not the whole story, and can be modified by other factors, the sun sign will always have an overall effect.

Are you emotionally compatible? Check your moon signs.

Emotional compatibility is strong enough to offset many other stressful factors in your horoscopes. Compare moon and sun signs too. There is an especially strong bond if your partner's moon is in your sun sign or vice versa.

How well do you communicate? Check Mercury.

Mercury in the same quality (cardinal, fixed, or mutable) could give you mental stimulation or irritation. Mercury in the same sign or element could be a meeting of minds.

Do you have similar tastes? Check Venus.

An incompatible Venus relationship can be very difficult over the long run, if other factors do not balance this out, because it has so much to do with the kind of atmosphere that makes you happy. One of you likes modern; the other likes traditional. One of you has an elegant style; the other is casual. It can be difficult to find the middle ground where you both win. Sometimes you just don't want to compromise that much.

Sexually sizzling or fizzling? Check Mars.

It is also useful to compare both Mars and Venus signs. Mars and Venus in the same sign or element is strong chemistry. Your partner's Mars or Venus in your sun sign is another big plus. Sometimes if Mars and Venus are in different modes, it can add sizzle to the relationship.

Will your partner be faithful?

Some sun signs tend to more monogamous than others. Fixed signs like a steady relationship and tend not to have multiple lovers. However, if a person with a fixed sign is unhappy, he will tend to have lovers on the side. The chief culprit here is Leo, which needs to be treated like royalty or else it will exercise royal rights elsewhere. Mutable signs tend to be the least monogamous. Gemini, Sagittarius, and Pisces are difficult to tie down and more difficult to hold. Sharing common interests and providing a stable home base can be a big help here, especially with Gemini.

Where can you meet the sign of your dreams?

If you have a sun sign in mind, here are places where they are likely to be (and like to go):

Aries: Try a sports event, martial arts display, action movie, cooking school, adventure sports vacation, the trendy new hot spot in town, the jogging or bike path.

Taurus: Meet them at a gourmet restaurant, auction house, farm or place where there are animals, flower show, garden shop, art classes, stores—especially food or jewelry stores.

Gemini: Meet them working for a newspaper or radio station, at parties or social events, writing courses, lectures, watering holes where there's good talk.

Cancer: Family dinners, boating or boat shows, cruises, on the beach, at seafood dinners, fishing, cooking schools, gourmet food stores, photography classes, art exhibits.

Leo: Big parties, country clubs, golfing, tanning salons, acting classes, theatrical events, movies, dancing, nightclubs, fine department stores, classy restaurants, VIP lounges at the airport, first-class hotels and travel.

Virgo: Craft stores, craft shows, flea markets, adult education courses, your local college, libraries, book stores, health food stores, doctors' offices, your local hospital or medical centers, health lectures, concerts, fine art events.

Libra: Art shows, fine restaurants, shopping centers, tennis matches, social events, parties and entertainment, the most fashionable stores, exhibits of beautiful objects, antique shows, decorating centers, ballet and the theater.

Scorpio: In banks, tax-preparation offices, police stations, sports events, motorcycle rallies, at the beach or swimming pool, doing water sports, at the gym, at action movies or mysteries, psychic fairs, ghostbusting.

Sagittarius: At a comedy club or laugh-a-minute film, at horse races or horse shows, pet stores or animal breeders, walking your dog, taking night courses at your local college, at a political debate, traveling to an exotic place, at a car show, mountain climbing, jogging, skiing, discussion group.

Capricorn: At a country music show, decorator show house, investment seminar, prestigious country club, exclusive resort, mountain climbing, party for a worthy cause, self-improvement course.

Aquarius: At a political rally, sci-fi convention, restaurant off the beaten path, union meeting, working for a worthy cause, campaigning for your candidate, fund-raising, flying lessons or airport.

Pisces: At any waterside place, at the theater or acting class, arts class, dancing, ballet, swimming pool, seafood restaurant, psychic event, church or other spiritual gathering, visiting at a hospital, at your local watering hole.

For your sun sign's compatibility with every other sign, see chapter 21.

How to Keep Your Relationship Sizzling

The Aries Lover

To keep your Aries mate red-hot, be sure to maintain your own energy level. This is one sign that shows little sympathy for aches, pains, and physical complaints. Curb any tendency toward self-pity—whining is one sure Aries turnoff (water signs take note). This is an open, direct sign. Don't expect your lover to probe your innermost needs. Intense psychological discussions that would thrill a Cancer or Scorpio only make Aries restless. Aries is not the stay-at-home type. This sign is sure to have plenty of activities going on at once. Share them (or they'll find someone else who will)!

Always be a bit of a challenge to your Aries mate—this sign loves the chase almost as much as the conquest. So don't be too easy or accommodating—let them feel a sense of accomplishment when they've won your heart.

Stay up-to-date in your interests and appearance. You

can wear the latest style off the fashion show runway with an Aries, especially if it's bright red. Aries is a pioneer, an adventurer, always ahead of the pack. Play up your frontier spirit. Present the image of the two of you as an unbeatable team that can conquer the world, and you'll keep this courageous sign at your side.

Since they tend to idealize their lovers, Aries partners are especially disillusioned when their mates flirt. So tone down your roving eye to make sure they always feel like number one in your life.

The Taurus Lover

Taurus is an extremely sensual, affectionate, nurturing lover, but can be quite possessive. Taurus likes to own you. Don't hold back with them or play power games. If you need more space in the relationship, be sure to set clear boundaries, letting them know exactly where they stand. When ambiguity in a relationship makes Taurus uneasy, they may go searching for someone more solid and substantial. A Taurus romance works best where the limits are clearly spelled out.

Taurus needs physical demonstrations of affection—don't hold back on hugs. Together you should create an atmosphere of comfort, good food, and beautiful surroundings. In fact, Taurus is often seduced by surface physical beauty alone. Their five senses are highly susceptible, so find ways to appeal to all of them! Your home should be a restful haven from the outside world. Get a great sound system and some comfortable furniture to sink into and keep the refrigerator stocked with treats. Most Taurus would rather entertain on their own turf than gad about town, so it helps if you're a good host or hostess.

Taurus likes a calm, contented, committed relationship. This is not a sign to trifle with. Don't flirt or tease if you want to please. Don't rock the boat or try to make this sign jealous. Instead, create a steady, secure environment with lots of shared pleasures.

The Gemini Lover

Keeping Gemini faithful is like walking a tightrope. This sign needs stability and a strong home base to accomplish their goals. But they also require a great deal of personal freedom.

A great role model is Barbara Bush, a Gemini married to another Gemini. This is a sign that loves to communicate. Sit down and talk things over. Don't interfere: Be interested in your partner's doings, but have a life of your own and ideas to contribute. Since this is a social sign, don't insist on quiet nights at home when your Gemini is in a party mood.

Gemini needs plenty of rope but a steady hand. Focus on common goals and abstract ideals. Gemini likes to share—be a twin soul and do things together. Keep up on their latest interests. Stay in touch mentally and physically. Use both your mind and your hands to communicate.

Variety is the spice of life to this flirtatious sign. Guard against jealousy—it is rarely justified. Provide a stimulating sex life—this is a very experimental sign—to keep them interested. Be a bit unpredictable. Don't let lovemaking become a routine. Most of all, sharing lots of laughs can make Gemini take your relationship very seriously.

The Cancer Lover

This is probably the water sign that requires the most TLC. Cancers tend to be very private people who may take time to open up. They are extremely self-protective and will rarely tell you what is truly bothering them. They operate indirectly, like the movements of the crab. You may have to divine problems by following subtle clues. Draw them out gently and try to voice any criticism in the most tactful, supportive way possible.

Family ties are especially strong for Cancer. They will rarely break a strong family bond. Create an intimate family atmosphere, with an emphasis on food and family get-togethers. You can get valuable clues to Cancer appeal from their mothers and their family situation. Whatever you do, don't compete with a mother! Get her to teach you the favorite family recipes; take her out to dinner. If your lover's early life was unhappy, it's important that Cancer feels there is a close family with you.

Encouraging creativity can counter Cancer's moodiness,

which is also a sure sign of emotional insecurity. Find ways to distract them from negative moods. Calm them with a good meal or a trip to the seashore. Cancers are usually quite nostalgic and attached to the past. So be careful not to throw out their old treasures or photos.

The Leo Lover

Whether the Leo is a sunny, upbeat partner or reveals cat-like claws could depend on how you handle the royal Leo pride. A relationship is for two people—a fact that ego-centered Leo can forget. You must gently remind them. Appearances are important to Leo, so try to always look your best.

Leo thinks big—so don't you be petty or miserly—and likes to live like a king. Remember special occasions with a beautifully wrapped gift or flowers. Make an extra effort to treat them royally. Keep a sense of fun and playfulness and loudly applaud Leo's creative efforts. React, respond, and be a good audience! If Leo's ignored, this sign will seek a more appreciative audience fast! Cheating Leos are almost always looking for an ego boost.

Be generous with compliments. You can't possibly overdo here. Always accentuate the positive. Make them feel important by asking for advice and consulting them often. Leo enjoys a charming sociable companion, but be sure to make them the center of attention in your life. If you have a demanding job or outside schedule, make a point to pull out all the stops once in a while, to create special events that keep romance alive.

The Virgo Lover

Virgo may seem cool and conservative on the surface, but underneath, you'll find a sensual romantic. Think of Raquel Welch, Sophia Loren, Jacqueline Bisset, and Garbo! It's amazing how seductive this practical sign can be!

They are idealists, however, looking for someone who meets their high standards. If you've measured up, they'll do anything to serve and please you. Virgos love to feel needed, so give them a job to do in your life. They are great fixer-uppers. Take their criticism as a form of love and caring, of noticing what you do. Bring them out socially—they're often very shy. Calm their nerves with good food, a healthy environment, and trips to the country.

Mental stimulation is a turn-on to this Mercury-ruled sign. An intellectual discussion could lead to romantic action, so stay on your toes and keep well-informed. This sign often mixes business with pleasure, so it helps if you share the same professional interests—you'll get to see more of your busy mate. With Virgo, the couple who works as well as plays together stays together.

The Libra Lover

Libra enjoys life with a mate and needs the harmony of a steady relationship. Outside affairs can throw them off balance. However, members of this sign are natural charmers who love to surround themselves with admirers, and this can cause a very possessive partner to feel insecure. Most of the time, Libras, who love to be the belles of the ball, are only testing their allure with harmless flirtations and will rarely follow through, unless they are not getting enough attention or there is an unattractive atmosphere at home.

Mental compatibility is what keeps Libra in tune. Unfortunately this sign, like Taurus, often falls for physical beauty or someone who provides an elegant lifestyle, rather than someone who shares their ideals and activities, which is the kind of sharing that will keep you together in the long run.

Do not underestimate Libra's need for beauty and harmony. To keep them happy, avoid scenes. Opt for calm, impersonal discussion of problems (or a well-reasoned debate) over an elegant dinner. Pay attention to the niceties of life. Send little gifts on Valentine's Day and don't forget birthdays and anniversaries. Play up the romance to the hilt—with all the lovely gestures and trimmings—but tone down intensity and emotional drama (Aries and Scorpio take note). Libra needs to be surrounded by a physically tasteful atmosphere—elegant, well-designed furnishings, calm colors, good manners, and good grooming at all times.

The Scorpio Lover

Scorpios are often deceptively cool and remote on the outside, but don't be fooled. This sign always has a hidden agenda and feels very intense about most things. The disguise is necessary because Scorpio does not trust easily; but when they do, they are devoted and loyal. You can lean on this very focused sign. The secret is in first establishing that basic trust through mutual honesty and respect.

Scorpio is fascinated by power and control in all its forms. They don't like to compromise—it's all or nothing. Therefore they don't trust or respect anything that comes too easily. Be a bit of a challenge and keep them guessing. Maintain your own personal identity, in spite of Scorpio's desire to probe your innermost secrets.

Sex is especially important to those under this sign. They will demand fidelity from you though they may not plan to deliver it themselves, so communication on this level is critical. Explore Scorpio's fantasies together. Scorpio is a detective—watch your own flirtations—don't play with fire. This is a jealous and vengeful sign, so you'll live to regret it. Scorpios rarely flirt for the fun of it themselves. There is usually a strong motive behind their actions.

Scorpio has a fascination with the dark, mysterious side of life. If unhappy, they are capable of carrying on a secret affair. So try to emphasize the positive, constructive side of life with them. Don't fret if they need time alone to sort out problems. They may also prefer time alone with you to socializing with others, so plan romantic getaways together to a private beach or a secluded wilderness spot.

The Sagittarius Lover

Be a mental and spiritual traveling companion. Sagittarius is a footloose adventurer whose ideas know no boundaries. So don't try to fence them in! Sagittarius resents restrictions of any kind. For a long relationship, be sure you are in harmony with their ideals and spiritual beliefs. They like to feel that their lives are constantly being elevated and taken to a higher level. Since down-to-earth matters often get put aside by Sagittarius schemes of things, get finances under control (money matters upset more relationships with Sagittarius than any other problems), but try to avoid becoming the stern disciplinarian in this relationship (find a good accountant to do this chore).

Sagittarius is not generally a homebody (unless there are several homes). Be ready and willing to take off on the spur of the moment, or they'll go without you. Sports, outdoor activities, and physical fitness are important. Stay in shape with some of Sagittarius Jane Fonda's tapes. Dress with flair and style. It helps if you look especially good in sportswear. Sagittarius men like beautiful legs, so play up yours. And this is one of the great animal lovers, so try to get along with the dog, cat, or horse.

The Capricorn Lover

These people are ambitious, even if they are the stay-at-home partner in your relationship. They will be extremely active, have a strong sense of responsibility to their partner, and take commitments seriously. However, they might look elsewhere if the relationship becomes too dutiful. They also need romance, fun, lightness, humor, and adventure!

Generation gaps are not unusual in Capricorn romances, where the older Capricorn partner works hard all through life and seeks pleasurable rewards with a young partner, or the young Capricorn gets a taste of luxury and instant status from an older lover. This is one sign that grows more interested in romance with age! Younger Capricorns often tend to put business way ahead of pleasure.

Capricorn is impressed by those who entertain well, have class, and can advance their status in life. Keep improving yourself and cultivate important people. Stay on the conservative side. Extravagant or frivolous loves don't last. Capricorn keeps an eye on the bottom line. Even the wildest Capricorns, such as Elvis Presley, Rod Stewart, and David Bowie, show a conservative streak in their personal lives. It's also important to demonstrate a strong sense of loyalty to your family, especially to older members. This reassures Capricorn, who'll be happy to grow old along with you!

The Aquarius Lover

Aquarius is one of the most independent, least domestic signs. Finding time alone with this sign may be one of your greatest challenges. The are everybody's buddy, usually surrounded by people they collect, some of whom may be old lovers. However, it is unlikely that old passions will be rekindled if you become their best friend as well as lover, and if you get actively involved in other important aspects of their lives, such as the political or charitable causes they believe in.

Aquarius needs a supportive backup person who encourages them, but is not overpossessive when their natural charisma attracts admirers by the dozen. Take a leaf from Joanne Woodward, whose marriage to perennial Aquarius heartthrob Paul Newman has lasted more than thirty years. Encourage them to develop their original ideas. Don't rain on their parade if they decide suddenly to market their spaghetti sauce and donate the proceeds to their favorite charity, or drive racing cars. Share their goals and be their fan, or you'll never see them otherwise.

You may be called on to give them grounding where needed. Aquarius needs someone who can keep track of their projects. But always remember, it's basic friendship—with the tolerance and common ideals that implies—that will hold you together.

The Pisces Lover

To keep a Pisces hooked, don't hold the string too tight! This is a sensitive, creative sign that may appear to need someone to manage life or point the direction out of their Neptune fog; but if you fall into that role, expect your Pisces to rebel against any strong-arm tactics. Pisces is more susceptible to a play for sympathy than a play for power. They are suckers for a sob story, the most empathetic sign of the zodiac. More than one Pisces has been seduced and held by someone who plays the underdog role.

They are great fantasists and extremely creative lovers, so use your imagination to add drama and spice to your time together. You can let your fantasies run wild with this sign, and they'll go you one better! They enjoy variety in lovemaking, so try never to let it become routine.

Long-term relationships work best if you can bring Pisces down to earth and, at the same time, encourage their creative fantasies. Deter them from escapism into alcohol or substance abuse by helping them to get counseling, if needed. Pisces will stay with the lover who gives positive energy, self-confidence, and a safe harbor from the storms of life, as well as one who is a soul mate.

CHAPTER 15

Is There Prosperity in Your Future?

There are big changes in the stars ahead, so projecting astrologically a few years down the line could point your career and investments in the most profitable direction.

For long term trends, look to the outer planets, which cause major changes as they move into a different sign. Soon there will be a shift in the atmosphere as Pluto, the planet of transformation, moves into Capricorn in 2008 until 2024. (You'll notice a different kind of energy starting a few months in advance.) What's more, Jupiter, the planet of luck and expansion, also moves through Capricorn during 2008, accelerating changes and bringing luck to Capricorn, so expect many of that sign to surge into prominence. Bet on the sea goat (Capricorn's symbol) and areas associated with it. Capricorns should prepare to move into the limelight. ("It's about time," you Capricorns may well say!)

If you're headed for the fast track, set your sights on Capricorn fields, which will be going through radical changes. This will affect Capricorn-associated corporations, big business, government, institutions of all kinds, mining, land speculation, property owners and dealers, builders and building trades, contractors and engineers, civil service, providers of status products. Capricorn-influenced fields are known for function, structure, discipline, and order, so consider careers that have these qualities or can provide them to others.

Everyone Old Is New

Want to cash in on a much-neglected market? Services and care for the aging should be booming with career opportunities, thanks to our elder population explosion. Remember that the generation now entering the aging population was born with Pluto in Leo; it's the rock-and-roll generation, who will resist the idea of aging and retirement as long as possible.

This particular elder population will be highly visible and financially viable. They are big spenders who will be remaining much longer in the workforce. Those who do retire may begin second careers, so the workplace will be rethinking its relationship to grandmas and grandpas and changing to accommodate them. Since America has been a youth-oriented culture, expect a major transformation in advertising, retailing, fashion, housing, and health care.

Since the Pluto in Leo generation is one of the most image-conscious ever, anything that keeps these folks looking and feeling great is sure to succeed. Don't expect your grandma and grandpa to hang around the house. This is a curious, adventurous generation that will welcome opportunities to explore the globe that are especially tailored to their age group and interests.

Cater to Horatio Alger

Capricorn is the Horatio Alger sign of rising through one's own volition and ambition. Self-improvement courses will be booming as we search for more fulfilling careers and try to keep up with new technology.

Do you enjoy helping others fulfill their potential? Career coaching—in fact, coaching in all aspects of life—is a hot field. In the corporate area, human resources is a much-touted area of job growth. You'll need skills in training and in helping other people find jobs. Get involved with helping people adapt to the times and retrain themselves for new careers. Leos, Sagittarius, Virgos, and Aquarius make excellent trainers and teachers. Aries are the supermotivators.

Education, especially high education, will be in for a whole new approach, as gray-haired students decide to complete their educations or simply enjoy expanding their knowledge. College towns will become hot retirement destinations, which provide intellectual stimulation plus an elder-compatible atmosphere.

The demand for teachers will increase and provide a steady stream of jobs. Look into special education, private education of all kinds, and unusual approaches to teaching. The natural teaching signs—Virgo, Leo, Sagittarius, and Aquarius—are winners here.

Since the world has become a smaller place and the trend toward international involvement escalates, demand for language skills also increases. Americans may need to speak several languages including some once considered exotic for the average American, such as Chinese or Arabic. Language teachers, translators, and linguists, especially those with a Gemini emphasis in their charts, should find many opportunities.

Waste Not, Want Not

Capricorn is an intensely practical sign that dislikes waste of any kind, so consider careers in recycling and waste management, antiques, renovation, preserving old buildings, land conservation, and teaching history.

Environment-related careers are hot options, since there will be so much cleaning up of toxic wastes, rebuilding after cataclysmic natural events, and redesigning of equipment. Engineers, attorneys, designers, bankers, and researchers should slant their career search in this direction. Taurus, Scorpio, Libra, Pisces, and Aquarius could make their fortune here.

Keep Treasured Traditions Alive

It looks like a conservative time, when people will be concerned with traditional values. Hospitality businesses can capitalize on this trend by promoting the beloved holidays of all cultures, reviving the old customs and memories. Holiday vacations for the whole family to share, reunions, and celebrations could revitalize the resort and cruise business. Tourism that caters to the needs of the aging, but still adventurous, traveler should thrive.

Head for the Hills

If you're thinking about a change of scene, consider relocating to a Capricorn-influenced place, which should have growth potential now. If you're adventurous, head for Central Europe, especially mountainous regions. The Balkans, Bosnia, Bulgaria, Lithuania, Macedonia, and Albania are Capricorn places. India, Belgium, Hesse and Constance in Germany, Mexico, and New Zealand are also on the Capricorn wavelength.

Health Care for the Antiaging Population

Have you considered the health-care field? Careers in medical services are among the hottest prospects as the nation begins to reform its health-care systems. Physical therapists, nurses, physicians' assistants, and pharmacists, as well as health services administrators, will all be in demand to service the aging population. If you have strong Virgo, Scorpio, or Capricorn placements, which give you a flair for the health field and excellent organizational skills, you should consider this area. Compassionate signs such as Pisces and Cancer make excellent health caregivers.

Consider the Capricorn fields of knee surgery and therapy, bone and joint diseases, chiropractic care, dermatology. New techniques in self-enhancement, such as plastic surgery, dental work, and hair replacement, should also do well for this aging generation who'd love to look and feel forever young.

Therapists specializing in treatment of disabling conditions, optometrists, nursing home operators and managers, and home care for the aged should be thriving.

The Talent Finder

Designers and manufacturers of clothing, furniture and equipment suited to the over-sixty consumer should also do well. Look into this area if you have planets in Capricorn (ruler of old age), Pisces (creativity, compassion), Taurus and Cancer (associated with the home environment and of nurturing), and Aries (pioneering ventures).

Do you thrive on life in the fast lane? Sports and special events are high-visibility careers where salesmanship and flair count, so they're especially suited to fire signs Aries, Leo, and Sagittarius. Good communicators like Gemini and Libra do well in public relations in this market.

Capricorn-favored sports require great discipline and endurance and are luckiest when they take place in the mountains. Rock and mountain climbing, hiking, and skiing are specially favored.

There will be a continuing boom in fitness careers, with the emphasis on well-run health clubs, personal attention, and social atmosphere. As the population ages, there will be more emphasis on weight training and rehabilitation aimed at elder bodies. Virgos, Sagittarius, Leos, and Aries are specially suited to the high-energy demands of this field, while Libras, Geminis, and Pisces provide good communication, diplomacy, and compassion.

We'll be eating more consciously as America slims down (Capricorn is the sign of discipline). Diet-specific restaurants, vegetarian restaurants, diet consultants, and organic food farmers and gardeners should be expanding. We'll be especially concerned with the quality of our meat and seafood. This is a fertile area for Taurus, Virgo, Cancer, Pisces, and Leos with skills in working with agriculture, diet counseling, cooking, restaurant management, organizing farmers' markets, and managing health food stores.

High-Tech Options

Though computer fields should continue to grow, the outsourcing of high-tech service jobs is also likely to continue. The good news is that there will still be a need for software designers, trainers, salespersons, and local repair staff, as computers have become an integral part of our lives. Aquarians are natural in all areas of computer work. Sagittarius and Geminis do well in teaching and sales, while

Capricorns excel in organization, Pisces in creative software design, and Cancers in applying high tech to industry.

Video-related careers can only get bigger in 2010 as Neptune, ruler of film, moves into Pisces, its strongest position. Video stores, cameras, and viewing equipment, new uses of video for education and entertainment, technical experts in production and performing—all should be booming. Pisces, Leo, Sagittarius, and Gemini should find plenty of opportunities in performance, sales, and marketing.

Take these tips from the stars and do your career planning with the planets!

CHAPTER 16

Heath and Diet Makeovers from the Stars

Health spas, fitness resorts, gyms, yoga studios, and sports complexes are multiplying around the country. Vitamin stores and juice bars are opening up in malls. We're buying shelves of diet books. Yet we're still one of the fattest nations on the planet! This year, the stars say we'll have more discipline to make over our bad eating habits and resolve to become as healthy as possible. Astrology can clue you in to the tendencies that contribute to good or ill health (especially when it comes to controlling your appetite). Finding the right diet and health program and having the patience to stick with them over time could be your big challenge this year. So follow these sun-sign tips on how best to lose those extra pounds and make this your healthiest year ever.

Aries Tips: Avoid the Quick Fix

Thanks to your hyperactive Mars-ruled lifestyle, you're sometimes too busy to bother with healthy meals in a calm atmosphere. You're more likely to grab carbohydrate-laden, calorie-packed fast foods for instant energy on the run. You need a regimen that gives you sustained energy, rather than a quick fix or a caffeine-fueled jump start. Aim for frequent small meals and carry healthy snacks with you to recharge your batteries. Protein and fruit smoothies in the morning might provide you with a quick, healthy head start to the day.

Aries is associated with the head, your most vulnerable area, which you should be especially careful to protect by wearing the appropriate headgear during risky activities and sports. Headaches warn you to slow down and take it easy for a while. If you've been stocking up on headache remedies, it might be time to consult a nutritionist for expert dietary advice.

Superbusy, impatient Aries tends to overschedule and stress out when others don't, won't, or can't keep up to your pace. Sports to the rescue! Swatting a ball, cheering on your favorite team, training for a marathon, or just running around the block can be the best remedies for whatever ails an Aries. Sports allow you to let off steam in an atmosphere of excitement and competition where you can feel the joy of winning. Your daring moves and Mars-powered energy should earn you a stellar spot on any team. If you're older, volunteer to coach local youngsters.

Martial arts of any kind appeal to your love of action. The slower, more flowing forms, such as tai chi, can be done throughout life. You don't have to be Jackie Chan or Russell Crowe to show your Aries flair for action heroics. Try racket sports (any sport that involves hitting or working with a swordlike object), fencing, tap dancing, or aerobics if martial arts don't give you a kick. However, remember to take time to check your equipment, warm up, and wait until you're properly conditioned before you jump to expert-level challenges.

Once you've found a sport you love, try not to push yourself too hard. Listen to your body when it tells you it's time to quit (never easy for Aries). Finally, know the difference between well-exercised, fatigued muscles and the pain that signals trouble.

Taurus Tips: Downsize Portions

Taurus loves all kinds of food in large quantities—especially rich, creamy desserts and fried goodies. (Once you start eating rich food, you find it almost impossible to stop.) Deprivation in any form is not going to work for you, so find a diet that allows you healthy variations of the foods you love most. Aim for smaller portions and fill up on skinny foods like salads. First, raid your refrigerator and eliminate any foods that are not on your diet. If it's there, you'll find it and eat it. The techniques for weight loss in Cher's diet books might inspire you.

Pleasure is the key to your exercise routine. You need an attractive place to work out, not a sweaty gym. Why not plan your workout to take place in one of the scenic areas of your town? Jogging or biking along a river or through a park, exploring the woodlands and seashore in your area with long nature hikes, or horseback riding along a scenic trail can make you look forward to exercising. Or plant an extensive garden that requires lots of active maintenance. If you live in an appropriate setting, get a dog that requires lots of exercise. Working with animals can also be a joy for Taurus.

Pay special attention to the Taurus area of the body: the neck. Yoga exercises, head rolls, the proper pillow, and a good masseur can make a big difference here. Though Taurus is a hardy sign with great stamina and endurance, you can become sluggish if you're overweight or if you have a thyroid problem. So, if you can barely drag yourself off the couch, be sure to check your thyroid. If you're not getting enough sleep, it could be due to tension in your neck. Try changing your pillow to one specially designed to support your neck.

Massage is one way to soothe the raging bull in you, especially if tension is lodging in your neck. Try shiatsu massage targeted to the acupressure points in the neck area. Neck massages are a sybaritic way to release tension and promote restful sleep.

Gemini Tips: Make a Game of It

Gemini is an on-the-go sign that does not usually have a weight problem, as long as you keep moving. If life circumstances force you to be sedentary, however, you may eat out of boredom and watch the pounds pile on. Your active social life can also sabotage your weight with sumptuous party buffets and restaurant meals where you have to sample everything. Your challenge is to find a healthy eating system with enough variety so you won't get bored. Develop a strategy for eating out—at parties or restaurants—and fill up the buffet plates with salad or veggies before you sample the desserts. Sociable Geminis on a diet can benefit from group support in a system like Weight Watchers. Find a diet twin who'll support you and have fun losing weight together.

Gemini is associated with the nervous system, our body's lines of communications. If your nerves are on edge, you may be trying to do too many things at once, leaving no time for fun and laughter. When you overload your circuits, it's time to get together with friends and go out to parties. Investigate natural tension relievers, such as yoga or meditation. Doing things with your hands—playing the piano, typing, craftwork—is also helpful.

Gemini is also associated with the lungs, which are especially sensitive. If you smoke, consider quitting. Yoga, which incorporates deep breathing into physical exercise, brings oxygen into your lungs. Among its many benefits are the deep relaxation and tranquillity so needed by your sign.

Combine healthful activities with social get-togethers for fun and plenty of fringe benefits for everyone. Include friends in your exercise routines; join an exercise class or jogging club. Gemini excels at sports that require good timing and manual dexterity as well as communication with others, like tennis or golf. Those who jog may want to add hand weights or upper-body exercises, which will benefit the Gemini-ruled arms and hands. If you spend long hours at the computer, try an ergonomic keyboard for comfort and protection against carpal tunnel syndrome.

Cancer Tips: Get the Emotional Support You Need

Dieting can be difficult for Cancers, who love good cuisine, find emotional solace with goodies, and fill up with comfort foods in tough times. There are sure to be conflicts in the Cancer who wants to be fashionably thin, but also to please the family with Grandma's favorite dishes. Cancer food conflicts sometimes lead to eating disorders, as with Princess Diana. Remember that you must be nurtured emotionally as well as physically. A diet-therapy group might help you deal with issues surrounding food and give you the support you need to stick to a diet. Find nonfood ways to baby yourself, such as a visit to a spa, walks along the beach, or beauty treatments to help you feel good about yourself while you lose weight.

Get the family behind you when you diet. You'll never lose weight if they insist on eating caloric favorites in front of you. Challenge yourself to create diet-conscious variations of family recipes so the whole family can eat healthy.

Your natural water-sign element is also your best therapy. Sometimes just a walk by a pond or a brief stop by a fountain can do wonders to relieve emotional stress and tension. You will be more likely to stick to an exercise routine if it's in or near water. Pool aerobics, swimming, fishing, sailing, and all other all water sports provide ideal ways for you to stay fit.

Health-wise, Cancer is associated with the breasts. Have regular checkups, according to your age and family health history of breast-related illness, and be sure to wear the proper supportive bra. Cancer is also prone to digestive difficulties, especially gastric ulcers and eating disorders. When emotionally caused digestive problems from those stomach-knotting insecurities crop up, baby yourself with extra pampering. If you're feeling blue, a visit with loved ones, old friends, and family could provide the support you need. Plan special family activities that bring everyone close together.

Leo Tips: The Downside of the Good Life

Leo's diet downfall might be your preference for the finer things in life, like dining on gourmet food at the best restaurants. And a Leo that is not getting the love and attention you need can easily turn to food for consolation. Give yourself the royal treatment in nonfood ways and imagine how great you'll look in that sexy gold dress.

Like your lion namesake, Leos often tend to be carnivores, so a low-carbohydrate, high-protein diet might work best for you, such as the Perricone or Atkins diet. If you're having trouble getting started on your diet, give yourself a jump start with a spa vacation. Some extra pampering, plus expert advice, could see you through the first difficult week and get you on the road to healthy eating.

Leo is associated with the spine and heart, two important areas to guard throughout your life. Be sure you have a good mattress to support the vulnerable Leo spine. Learn some therapeutic exercises to strengthen and protect your back. Aerobic exercises that benefit the heart and lungs are also musts for Leo.

Ruled by the sun, you're one sign that usually loves to tan. However, considering the permanent damage sun exposure can cause, you may elect to remain porcelain pale like Madonna or to use a spray-on tanning product. Don't leave for the beach without a big hat, umbrella, and sunblock formulated for your skin type. Many makeup foundations now come with a sunblock added, a good idea for Leo ladies.

Leos are proud of your body and usually take excellent care of it. Like the archetypal Leo male, Arnold Schwarzenegger, you can summon up great discipline and determination to maintain your public image. To make your body worthy of the spotlight, consider a bodybuilding regimen in which you're supervised by a personal trainer. Be sure any exercise routine you choose emphasizes good posture. The way you carry yourself can make the most of your figure type and dramatically affect your energy level. Get that regal bearing!

Virgo Tips: Find a Diet Coach

Since Virgo is associated with the digestive system, you can make quite an issue of food quality, preparation, and diet. Many of you will select a very detailed special diet to promote health, such as a macrobiotic diet. Potassium-rich vegetables are especially important, as is your relationship to whole grains. The mind-body connection to overweight has been emphasized by Virgo diet coach, Dr. Phil MacGraw. If you become overweight, it usually comes from coping with emotional or work-related stress. To counteract this tendency, add activities to your life that promote peace of mind. Exercises that use mental as well as physical techniques could help you stay with your program.

As one of the most health-conscious signs in the zodiac, caring for the health of yourself and others is usually a high priority with Virgos. Many great doctors, nurses, and dieticians were born under Virgo, such as the noted heart surgeon Dr. Michael DeBakey.

You tend to troubleshoot your health, scheduling medical exams and appropriate diagnostic tests promptly. You have probably learned that running your life efficiently does much to eliminate health-robbing stress. It's a great comfort to know you've got a smooth health-maintenance routine in place to back you up.

Virgos benefit from exercises that stress the relationship of the mind and body, such as yoga or tai chi. Sports that require a certain technical skill to master can also challenge Virgo. The key factor in Virgo-appealing exercises is to offer self-improvement on several levels simultaneously, not just a boring or repetitive routine.

Libra Tips: Resist Sweet Temptations

One of the most famous diet doctors, Dr. Robert Atkins, was a Libra. A well-spoken gentleman with a liking for sweets, he fit your sign's profile. At first, the low-carbohydrate diet he advocated was vilified by nutritional experts. In recent years, however, he has been vindicated, and the effectiveness of the Atkins diet proven. It could be the perfect diet for Libras who often put on too much weight from indulging in sweets. Because your sign rules the kidneys, it's no surprise that this diet advocates drinking plenty of water to cleanse the system as you reduce. Since you are one of the most social signs, you may entertain or be entertained often. Plan your food choices before you go out, so you'll know exactly what to eat. Then you'll be more likely to resist sweet temptations. Dieting with your mate or a group of friends could provide the support you need and keep you on track when you go out to dinner.

Restoring and maintaining equilibrium is the Libra key to health. Balance in all things should be your mantra. If you have been working too hard or taking life too seriously, a dose of culture, art, or music or perhaps some social activity will balance your scales. Make time to entertain friends, be romantic with the one you love, and enjoy the artistic life of your city.

Since Libra is associated with the kidneys and lower back, watch these areas for misalignment or health problems. Consider yoga, spinal adjustments, or a detoxification program if your body is out of balance. Working out in a gym may be unappealing to aesthetic Libras. Since yours is the sign of relationships, you may enjoy exercising with a partner or with loved ones. Make morning walks or weekend hikes family affairs. Take a romantic bicycle tour, picnic in the autumn countryside. Libra is also the sign of grace, so any kind of dancing may appeal. Dancing combines art, music, romance, relaxation, graceful movement, social contact, and exercise.

Put more beauty in all areas of your life, and you'll be healthier and happier.

Scorpio Tips: Diet for Self-Transformation

Scorpios never do anything halfway, so they need to be fully committed to their diets. Some Scorpios will go to great lengths to transform themselves, even resorting to extreme means like stomach stapling or gastric bypass, as Roseanne Barr did. You are gifted with amazing focus and discipline and can stick with any diet, once you have made up your mind. The trick is to eliminate self-destructive food habits. Finding a diet plan you can live with for long periods, such as the South Beach Diet, which worked for Hillary Clinton, will help you avoid the yo-yo diet syndrome.

Though Scorpio usually has a strong constitution that can literally rise from the ashes of extreme illness or misfortune, resist the temptation to take this for granted or sabotage your health with self-destructive habits. Try to curb excessive tendencies in any area of your life. Know when to quit and when to seek help; don't hesitate to ask for help when you need it.

Your sign is associated with regenerative and eliminative organs. Therefore, it follows that sexual activity can be a source of good or ill health for Scorpio. It is important to examine your attitudes about sex, to follow safe-sex practices, and to seek balance in sex, as in all other areas of your life.

It's no accident that Scorpio's month coincides with football season, which reminds us that sports are a very healthy way to defuse emotions. If you enjoy winter sports, be sure to prepare ahead of time for the ski slopes or the ice rinks. Be sure to warm up your muscles before you go all out. Water sports are a terrific outlet for Scorpio, so sign up for pool aerobics or competitive swimming and be sure to treat yourself to a vacation at a spectacular tropical beach resort. Somehow, just being near a saltwater environment can restore your equilibrium.

Sagittarius Tips: Aim for Long-Range Benefits

Dieting is something Sagittarius does with great difficulty. There has to be more to it than just getting thin. Therefore, an eating plan that is part of a spiritually oriented lifestyle, such as vegetarianism, might have more appeal. Aim for long-range benefits by balancing a sane, practical eating plan with plenty of exercise. Beware of fad diets that promise instant results and come with a high-pressure sales pitch. Avoid gimmicks, pills, or anything instant; these solutions are especially tempting to impatient Sagittarius. Exercise is the greatest antidote to overeating for your sports-loving sign, so follow your guru (Jane Fonda), go for the burn, and work off those calories.

Good health for Sagittarius is often a matter of motivation. If you set a fitness goal, it will be much easier to stay motivated than if you exercise or diet haphazardly, so aim for the best you can be and then set a plan to achieve it. Once you've decided on a course of action, get going. Being on the move and physically active keeps you in the best of health, improves your circulation, and protects your arteries. Problems could come from injuries to the hip or thigh areas, as well as arterial problems, so protect yourself with the proper equipment for your sports activity and don't push yourself beyond your capacity.

Exercise is your greatest antidote to stress. Your sign loves working out in groups, so combine socializing with athletic activities and team sports. Touch football, biking, hikes, and long walks with your dog are fun as well as healthy. Let others know that you'd like a health-promoting birthday gift, such as sports equipment, a gym membership, or an exercise video. In your workouts, concentrate on Sagittarius-ruled areas—the hips, legs, and thighs.

If you're already in shape, try out Sagittarius sports such as downhill or cross-country skiing, Rollerblading, and basketball. Since you like to travel, plan an exercise routine that can be done anywhere. Isometric exercises, which use muscle resistance and can be done in a car or plane seat, are a good travel option. If you are always on the road, investigate equipment that fits easily in your suitcase, such as water-filled weights, home gym devices, elastic exercise bands. Locate hotels with well-equipped gyms or parks nearby where you can jog.

Capricorn Tips: Disciplined Dieting

It was a Capricorn hostess and decorator, Lady Elsie de Wolfe Mendl, who introduced dieting to America, via the 1920s health guru Gayelord Hauser. Lady Mendl served very small portions of exquisitely prepared health food at her elegant dinner parties, a good tip for you who may need to downsize portions. One of the skinny signs, Capricorn has amazing self-discipline, a big help in maintaining weight loss. Exercise or active sports should help you keep the pounds off without strenuous dieting. Food and mood are linked with Capricorn, so avoid eating to console or comfort yourself; instead, choose upbeat relaxed companions. Since you are likely to mix business with pleasure, plan your work-related lunches and dinners in advance so you won't be led astray by the dessert tray.

As a Capricorn, you naturally take good care of yourself, getting regular medical checkups and tending toward moderation in your lifestyle. You're one of the signs that ages well and remains physically active in your senior years. But Capricorn's fast-paced, action-packed life can be stressful, so here are some ways to unwind and put the spring back into your step.

Since Capricorn is associated with the bone structure, you need to watch for signs of osteoporosis and take preventive measures. Good posture and stretching exercises such as yoga are essential to remain flexible. You might practice yoga, as Christy Turlington does. Another way to counteract osteoporosis is by adding weight-bearing exercise to your routine. If your knees or joints are showing signs of arthritis, calcium supplements may be helpful. For those who enjoy strenuous sports, remember to protect your knees by doing special exercises to strengthen this area, and always warm up beforehand.

Capricorn's natural self-discipline is a big help in maintaining good health. Keep a steady, even pace for lasting results. Remember to balance workouts with pleasurable activities in your self-care program. Grim determination can be counterproductive, especially if one of your exercise goals is to relieve tension. Take up a sport for pure enjoyment, not necessarily to become a champion.

Since you probably spend much of your life in an office, check your working environment for hidden health saboteurs like poor air quality, bad lighting, and uncomfortable seating. Get an ergonomically designed chair to protect your back, or buy a specially designed back-support cushion if your chair is uncomfortable. If you work at a computer, adjust your keyboard and the height of the computer screen for ergonomic comfort.

Capricorn, the sign of Father Time, brings up the subject of aging. If sags and wrinkles are keeping you from looking as young as you feel, investigate plastic surgery to give you a younger look and psychological lift. Teeth are also associated with your sign, a reminder to have regular dental cleanings and checkups.

Aquarius Tips: The Diet Trendsetter

Aquarius is a sign of reaching out to others, a cue to make your diet program a social one. Sharing your diet with friends might keep you interested and prevent boredom. It worked for Oprah Winfrey, an Aquarius whose yo-yo weight gains and losses became media events. If you know you'll be going public for a party or wedding, you'll be motivated to look your best. The trick is to segue from dieting to an ongoing healthy lifestyle. Otherwise you'll be back up the scale again. Try to find a flexible plan that adapts to individual personalities rather than one that imposes a rigid diet structure. Keep a diet diary or online blog to help monitor yourself, a tip from Oprah.

Clean air is top priority for a health-wise air sign especially vulnerable to airborne allergies and viruses. The effects of air pollution might influence where you choose to live. If you life in a polluted environment, get an air purifier, ionizer, or humidifier. Aquarius tends to travel a lot (or may fly your own plane, as John Travolta and Lorenzo Lamas do). Protect yourself from infections that flourish in the enclosed environments of trains, buses, and planes.

Since Aquarius is associated with the circulatory system, you especially benefit from a therapeutic massage. Find your local day spa and schedule one of their relaxing hands-on treatments. New Age treatments are favored by experimental Aquarius, so consider alternative approaches to health and fitness. Perhaps the Ayurvedic approach from India or Chinese massage therapies might work for you. Calves and ankles are also Aquarius territory, which should be emphasized in your exercise program. Be sure your ankles are well supported. Be careful of sprains and strains, especially if you're a jogger.

You'll follow a fitness routine only if you can make your own rules and exercise at a convenient time, which could mean odd moments. If your schedule makes it difficult to get to the gym or if you dislike the routine of regular exercise classes, videos might solve your problem. There is a vast selection of exercise videos to choose from. Exercising with friends could make staying fit more fun. Try several different kinds of exercise so you can vary your routine from yoga to kick-boxing when you get bored. Or set up a gym at home with portable home exercise equipment. (You're the type who will combine your treadmill sessions with a telephone conversation or TV news show.)

Pisces Tips: The Addictive Eater

Pisces is a sign of no boundaries, one of the most difficult to discipline diet-wise. You can get hooked on a fattening food like French fries (or alcohol), a habit like coffee with lots of sugar and a roll, and easily gain weight. Your water-sign body may have a tendency to bloat, holding water weight at certain times, especially around the full moon. The key for you, as with so many others, is commitment and support. Don't try to go it alone. Get a partner, a doctor, a group, or one of the online diet-related sites to help. Since you're influenced by the atmosphere around you, choose to be with slim healthy friends and those who will support your efforts. Avoid those seemingly well-meaning diet saboteurs who say just one cookie won't do any harm. A seafood-based diet, like the Perricone diet, could be the right one for you. Your Pisces sisters—Queen Latifah, Liza Minnelli, Camryn Manheim, and Elizabeth Taylor—have slimmed down, and so can you!

Health-wise, supersensitive Pisces, associated with the lymphatic system, reacts strongly to environmental toxins and emotional stress. It's no accident that we often do spring cleaning during the Pisces months. Start your birth day off right by detoxing your system with a liquid diet or supervised fast. This may also help with water retention, a common Pisces problem. Lympathic drainage massage is especially relaxing and beneficial to Pisces.

The feet are Pisces territory. Consider how often you take your feet for granted and how miserable life can be when your feet hurt. Since our feet reflect and affect the health of the entire body, devote some time to pampering them. Check your walking shoes or buy ones designed for your kind of exercise. Investigate custom-molded orthotic inserts if your arches are high. They could make a big difference in your comfort and performance.

Just as the sign of Pisces contains traces of all the previous signs, the soles of our feet contain nerve endings that connect with all other parts of our body. This is the theory behind reflexology, a therapeutic foot massage that treats all areas of the body by massaging the soles of the feet. For the sake of your feet, as well as your entire body, consider treating yourself to a session with a local practitioner of this technique.

Exercise is not a favorite Pisces activity, unless it is a creative activity like dance or ice-skating, or is related to your water element, such as water aerobics or swimming. A caring exercise instructor who gives you personal attention can also make a difference in your motivation. Walking regularly releases tension, gets you outdoors, and can be a way to socialize with friends away from the temptation of food and drink. Try doing local errands on foot, if you live in a city, or find a local park where you can take a daily hike. Invite someone you love or would like to get to know better to share this time with you, or get an adorable dog to accompany you.

CHAPTER 17

Discover Your Gemini Personality

Did you know that your Gemini sun sign colors all areas of your life? What and whom you like, how you behave as a parent, your attitude toward your career—all have a strong Gemini influence. The more you know about the Gemini in you, the better you can use your personal solar power to help you make good decisions, from something as basic as what to wear today to deeper psychological issues, such as what compromises you might need to make in order to get along with a different boss or new lover. Your sun sign provides a time-honored guide to what's right for you, so why not turn to it when you're at a crossroads in your career, choosing a new hue for your walls, or deciding whether or not to pursue a romantic relationship? Let the following chapters empower you with the confidence that you're moving in harmony with your natural inclinations.

The basic characteristics of a Gemini are determined by blending several ingredients. First there's your Gemini element: air. Air signs are distinguished by their mental orientation. Gemini functions like a mutable sign, constantly changing. Then there's your sign's polarity, which adds a positive, masculine, yang dimension. Let's not forget your planetary ruler: Mercury, the planet of communications and mental functioning. Add your sign's location in the zodiac: third, in the house of communication. Finally, stir in your symbol, the twins, which indicates the dual nature of your sign.

This recipe influences everything we say about Gemini.

For example, you could easily deduce that an air sign with a Mercury ruling planet should have a quick mind and a facility with words. Is a Gemini likely to sit around the house? Only if there's a dual-line phone or a party going on. Gemini can multitask, easily able to do two things at once. If you're a typical Gemini, a desert island is unlikely to be your favorite vacation spot. But your total astrological personality contains a blend of many other planets, colored by the signs they occupy, plus factors such as the sign coming over the horizon at the exact moment of your birth. However, the more Gemini planets in your horoscope, the more likely you'll follow your sun sign's prototype. On the other hand, if many planets are grouped together in a different sign, they will color your horoscope accordingly, sometimes making a communicative sign like yours appear more withdrawn. So if the Gemini traits mentioned here don't describe you, there could be other factors flavoring your cosmic stew. (Look up your other planets in the tables in this book to find out what they might be!)

The Gemini Man: The Quick-Change Artist

The Gemini man is on a perpetual journey in search of the new. You seem to be forever in motion. Even when you're sitting still, your mind is racing. You are a lover of games on every level who can make a game of the most complicated situations. On the negative side, it is difficult for you to take anything or anyone too seriously. Weighty matters tend to drag you down, unless your mind is challenged by a crisis situation. You'd rather dabble in lots of different projects than fly off when things get sticky.

In childhood, Gemini is the bright, funny little boy who gets bored in school and could devise some jolly pranks to amuse yourself. You'll have many interests, which keep changing constantly. In your early years you should learn self-discipline as well as the satisfaction of setting goals and reaching them. Otherwise, you'll have a tendency to skim the surface of life, with much activity but few real accomplishments.

Young adulthood is an experimental time, and you're not about to deny yourself any adventures. Like the characters portrayed by Gemini idol Johnny Depp, you're the elusive and scintillating lover who dazzles, then disappears. A born flirt and charming chameleon who can't resist an exciting affair of the heart, you usually opt for several romantic experiences at once. This could result in your becoming a perennial playboy, even to leading a double life, both hazards of the ever-curious and charming Gemini man.

In a Relationship

The woman who succeeds in tying Gemini down would be well advised to give him lots of rope and keep an open mind. This is likely to be a nontraditional marriage—exciting but not particularly stable. Though Gemini is not naturally inclined to be monogamous, he will stick with a woman who is bright, entertaining, sociable, interesting, and companionable. It would help if she is involved in his professional life, too, as well as having strong interests of her own. His hot-cold temperament and roving eye could cause his mate a great deal of insecurity, unless she is an independent person as well. This mercurial man makes the perfect husband for an intelligent woman who longs for a witty conversationalist, a flirtatious and inventive lover, and an ever-youthful companion throughout life. With Gemini, she'll never be bored.

The Gemini Woman: The Great Communicator

It's no surprise that the comedienne whose signature line is "Can we talk?" is a Gemini—Joan Rivers. Your verbal skills are legendary, giving you the ability to talk yourself into or out of any situation. The written and spoken word is your means of seduction, sales, and self-defense. You'll talk with your expressive hands (the Gemini part of the body), and use body language to add extra emphasis.

You're highly charged with nervous energy, seeming to be everywhere at once. And you have enough sides to your personality to dazzle even those close to you. One moment you are a capable executive, the next a little girl filled with wonder, the next an earthy sensualist, the next an expert in verbal karate, the next a comedienne. It's no wonder there are so many actresses under this sign. And, best of all, you do everything with a light, quicksilver touch, so the effort never shows.

While your brain is busily skipping about, juggling many people and projects at once, you manage to skip away from heavy emotional involvements. You're not one to be tied down in any way. However, though variety may be the spice of your life, it can also be hard to digest. You need a substantial anchor and truly caring relationships to get you through the tough times. If you learn to live with a few normal human flaws and foibles (you can't laugh everything off!) instead of constantly changing your mind, you'll find your twin sides working together more smoothly. Then you will have a much better idea of what you're really looking for.

The little Gemini girl is the bright, precocious one who learns to read and write ahead of everyone. She is very well-coordinated, moves quickly, and talks even more rapidly. She bores easily with her toys, and may even invent new games to play with them.

Gemini's problem is making up her mind. There is always something more interesting to do, a more exciting place to go, people who might be more fun. You must learn early to stick to one thing until you have mastered it—or you'll end up being the proverbial "jill-of-all-trades."

Propelled by a great reservoir of nervous energy, the young Gemini is likely to have more than one job, more than one boyfriend, and a full schedule of social activities. Juggling is second nature to you. The more balls in the air, the less likely you are to get bored. One challenge is to find situations that give you a chance to grow. Otherwise, you'll skip from job to job, love affair to love affair, at a great strain on your nerves.

When you find a man who stimulates you mentally as well as emotionally and physically, you may be tempted to take a chance on love. It is important that you separate dream from reality here—and not confuse surface attraction with true communication. Otherwise, you may marry on impulse, quickly tire of the situation, and search for excitement elsewhere. Since you often retain your looks and youthful outlook, it is not unusual for you to finally settle with a much younger man.

In a Relationship

Keeping your foothold in the working world after marriage provides you with the outside stimulation you need and also the financial means to delegate the more boring routine tasks of housekeeping to someone else. If you apply your creativity to making the marriage special, you can keep the union lively, with no need to look for greener pastures. You're sure to promote a social life, entertain frequently, and decorate with flair and originality. Your relationship may also benefit if you take an active part in your husband's business. But too much togetherness can seem confining for your restless sign. If your husband is too progressive and demanding, you may be tempted to take flight. However, if you can negotiate enough room for personal freedom, you'll provide a life of sparkle and variety.

Gemini in the Family

The Gemini Parent

Geminis take a great interest in their child's different stages, watching the young personality unfold. You may find the early babyhood years most difficult, when the child is dependent and needs steady, routine care. After the child learns to communicate, you'll take on the role of teacher, introducing the child to the world of ideas and mental pursuits, helping with homework, and making difficult subjects easier to understand. One of your greatest assets as a parent is your own insatiable curiosity about the world, which you can communicate to the children by introducing them early to the world of ideas and books. You are also an excellent coach, teaching your child social abilities and the art of handling others at an early age. As your child matures, your youthful, ever fresh outlook makes you a wonderful friend and companion through the years.

The Gemini Stepparent

Your verbal skills and sense of humor will often come to the rescue in the initial stages of starting up a new family. You're a communicator who can quickly get shy youngsters to open up and difficult personalities to communicate. Your natural sociability and flair for entertainment encourages everyone to have fun, making family get-togethers seem like parties. Since you have many outside activities and interests, the children will be able to have as much time as they need alone with their parent. Soon your new family will find that you are a fun-loving addition to their lives, a wise adviser, and an excellent noncompetitive companion.

The Gemini Grandparent

You're an upbeat grandparent who still finds life an interesting adventure. You're always the life of the party, up on all the latest family gossip, as well as what's happening with the rest of the world. Visits with you are full of laughter and good stories! You'll take a special interest in your grandchildren's education and support them in whatever career path they choose. Like Barbara Bush, you may have a large extended family that reaches out to the children of your community. You'll give your own children plenty of space to rear the grandchildren as they please, never interfering with Mother's rules or taking over the grandchildren's upbringing.

"Never complain" was the motto of the Duchess of Windsor (a Gemini), and it could be yours, too. You accentuate the positive and keep a cheerful attitude. Your mentor should be the famous Gemini pastor Norman Vincent Peale, author of *The Power of Positive Thinking,* one of the most influential self-help books of all time. Dr. Peale lived a productive life well into his nineties, still writing and preaching. You, too, realize how the right mental attitude can influence any situation for the better, and you'll be sure to pass on your wisdom to your grandchildren.

CHAPTER 18

Gemini Stellar Style: The Fashion Trends, Home Decor, Colors, and Getaways That Suit Gemini Best

Whether you're ready for an extreme makeover or simply want to update your wardrobe, look to your sun sign for the trends and colors that will harmonize with your Gemini personality.

Gemini Chic

Gemini always likes to do something interesting with your clothes, have fun with fashion, and never takes your fashion image too seriously. Nicole Kidman dresses with great Gemini flair, in clothes that get people talking. Annette Bening opts for simple, elegant clothes that set off her delicate beauty. Other Gemini beauties, like Liz Hurley, who once attended the Academy Awards in a gown held together with safety pins, and Angelina Jolie, enjoy being downright outrageous to keep their fans guessing! Some Geminis, like the late Marilyn Monroe, love to flaunt their sex appeal. And then there is Joan Rivers, mistress of the red carpet, whose fashion flair and crusade for more elegance has literally transformed the way celebrities dress!

Since you have such a changeable personality, you'll probably experiment before you find the style that suits you. Double-duty clothes that change personality with a scene-stealing accessory or two are ideal for your gadabout life, when you're just too busy to fuss. A hairstyle that can be combed several different ways would satisfy your need for constant change. Add a witty, scene-stealing jewel or two, a dramatic scarf or trendy shoes and handbag to quick-change your outfit's personality and you're ready to go!

Geminis often talk with their hands, so make your gestures count. Stay well-manicured and accent your expressive hands with hot-colored nail polish and fabulous rings.

The Gemini palette—soft silvery gray, pale yellow, and airy Wallis Windsor blue—consists of great background colors, elegant ones you can live with over a period of time. They adapt to different seasons and climates, and they won't compete with your personality or distract from your total image. You can change the look of these colors at will, accenting them with bright touches or blending with other pastels. And they can tolerate a frequent change of accessories, according to your mood of the moment.

Some legendary fashion icons, like the late Duchess of Windsor, were born under your sign, and you couldn't find better inspiration than that scandalous siren who made fashion history as well. We remember Wallis Simpson for her witty way with accessories, like those fabulous jewels she wore with casual aplomb (some engraved with secret messages from the duke.) Yet she never varied her signature swept-back hairdo or her elegantly simple style of dressing.

The fashion duo Dolce and Grabbana, the with-it looks of Anna Sui, or the newest androgynous menswear styles would be fun for you to try on for size. Gemini models who express your flair, like Naomi Campbell, Liz Hurley, and Brooke Shields, have the ability to change their image with their hairstyle, acting like a vamp one moment and the innocent girl next door the next.

Time for a Home Makeover? Bring Gemini into Every Room!

Your home should be multipurpose to accommodate your many interests and ongoing projects, yet it should also be a place where you can conduct your active social life, and finally, a relaxing haven. Keep your atmosphere and colors light and airy. Give heavy drapes, intense colors, and dark furniture a pass.

Let the colors of your room be a background for all the interesting things that will happen there. Pale neutrals and pastels on the walls are versatile and easy to live with over a period of time. (You might get quickly bored with more vibrant shades.) Then shift into color with bright slipcovers and accessories to give your room a quick change of personality.

Since you may have several activities going on at once, your decor strategy should help you avoid confusion and stay on top of your schedule. Choose furniture that can be rearranged in different combinations and settings. Clever cabinets and storage containers allow you to sweep your projects out of sight when friends drop in. Line a room with bookcases if you're one of the Gemini readers who collect the latest magazines, books, and newspapers.

Set up your communications center carefully. (You're the sign with a telephone on both sides of the bed and alongside the bathtub.) Have a separate room or corner with a desk where you can organize lists, equipment, and books so you won't waste time looking for them. Many Geminis have houses in more than one place (you're often bicoastal), so you can switch environments. At each place, there should be a space to stash whatever you need to stay connected to your network. With a laptop computer, you can work wherever you go.

Geminis love to entertain casually and frequently, so your kitchen should be set up for impromptu parties, with plenty of glassware and buffet plates handy. Have multipurpose tables that can be set up anywhere and folding chairs for instant group seating. Then get ready to party!

The Gemini Sound Track

Gemini has sophisticated, eclectic musical tastes, and perhaps has accumulated a varied collection of sounds. You may enjoy instrumentals that require manual dexterity, such as piano concertos. In popular music, you pay attention to the words as well as the melody, so the witty lyrics of Cole Porter and the poetry of Bob Dylan appeal, as do the hottest rap artist and the latest experiment of Sir Paul McCartney. You like abstract classical music, but nothing too heavy or loud that might distract from conversation or bring on the blues. You're a natural disk jockey, so customize your own mix of musical moods on tapes or CDs. Paula Abdul, Miles Davis, Alanis Morrisette, rap music, Kylie Minogue, Cole Porter, Prince, Judy Garland, and continental tunes from Charles Aznavour would give you the full range of Gemini sounds.

Gemini Away from Home

Sometimes you just have to get away from it all! But Gemini never likes to get too far away from civilization. Stay away from desert islands, unless you need some peace and quiet to write your novel. Stick to places where there's a lively social scene, some interesting scenery, local characters who provide good conversation, and an Internet café to keep up with your e-mail.

Improve your language skills by visiting a foreign country; you'll have no trouble communicating in sign language, if necessary. Consider a language school in the south of France or in Switzerland, where you'll mix with fellow students of many nationalities while you perfect your accent. In the USA, visit some of the Gemini states: Wisconsin, Tennessee, Kentucky, Rhode Island, South Carolina, and Arkansas.

Lightness is the key to Gemini travel. Don't weigh yourself down with luggage. Dare to travel with an empty suitcase, then acquire clothes and supplies at your destination. Imagine how fast you'll speed through the airport! Invest in a fabulous carry-on that you can throw your life in and go.

Keep a separate tiny address book for each city, so the right numbers are always handy. Invest in beautifully designed travel cases and briefcases, since you're on the go so much. Spend some time looking for the perfect luggage, portable notebook computer (with a modem and wifi), and a worldwide cell phone to keep you in touch at all times.

CHAPTER 19

Your Gemini Career Finder

What Does Gemini Bring to the Table?

What makes some Geminis more successful than others? Gemini has a special combination of talents and abilities that makes you stand out. By discovering and developing your special sun-sign strengths, you'll not only be likely to find a career you truly enjoy, but you'll be able to channel your efforts to areas where you'll be most successful.

Follow your natural Gemini tendencies. Gemini has many winning cards to play in the career game. Your quick mind works best in a career where there is enough mental stimulation to keep you from getting bored. High-pressure situations that would be stressful to others are stimulating to you. Many things happening simultaneously—phones ringing off the hook, daily client meetings, constant changes—create a situation in which you thrive, getting to use all your communication skills. Consider the way the Gemini mayor of New York City, Rudolph Giuliani, masterfully handled the World Trade Center crisis, for the prime example of Gemini grace under pressure.

Where to Find Opportunity

Your ability to communicate with a variety of people works well in sales, journalism, public relations, politics, agent or broker work, personnel or consulting—literally any job that requires verbal or writing skills. You learn languages easily, so you could be a language teacher or an interpreter. Manual dexterity is another Gemini gift that can find craft, musical, or medical expression (especially surgery or chiropractic work).

What to avoid: a job that is too isolated, routine, detail-oriented, or confining. Stay away from companies with too many rigid rules. Look for a place that gives you strong backup as well as free rein. Gemini often succeeds in a freelance position, provided you have a solid support system to help with the details and routine chores.

The Gemini Leader

Gemini's natural analytical mind and way with words can be used to wheel and deal your way to the top. The works of real estate tycoon Donald Trump, who has written several books on his techniques, should make fascinating reading for ambitious Geminis. Be inspired and entertained by this colorful tycoon, who changed the skyline of New York and became a TV star as well.

As a leader, Gemini is fun to work for—sociable, witty, and clever. Your office will be a beehive of activity, with telephone lines buzzing and clients coming and going. What is lacking in job security you make up in opportunities for others to experiment and to develop flexibility and a sense of gamesmanship.

You operate best as an entrepreneur rather than a designer or producer. You often change your mind, so you should hire assistants who are adaptable enough to keep up with you, yet who can provide organization, follow-up, and structure. You rule by multitasking, and sometimes have so many projects going on at once that others are dizzy, yet you are known for innovative ideas and cool analysis of problems. You are especially gifted in making a deal, coordinating the diverse aspects of a project.

The Gemini Team Player

You work beautifully on a team, where your light sense of humor, friendliness, and ability to express yourself clearly are appreciated. Your work should be dealing with the public in a sales or communications position. You are also skilled at office politics. It's all part of the game to you; you rarely get emotionally involved. Let someone else do the record keeping, financial management, or accounting. As a Gemini you can handle a position where you report to several different people or juggle several different assignments, though you may do less well if the job requires intense concentration, patience, and perseverance.

Promote Yourself!

You're behind the steering wheel of your life. Use your special Gemini talents and abilities to bring you the highest return on your investment of time and energy. To get ahead fast, pick a job with variety and mental stimulation. Play up your best attributes, especially the following:

- Verbal and written communication skills
- Ability to handle several tasks at once
- Charm and sociability
- Manual dexterity
- Ability to learn quickly
- Analytical ability

CHAPTER 20

Let Gemini Celebrities Teach You About Your Sun Sign

It's fun to find out who else was born under Gemini, especially if it's one of your favorite celebrities. Someone in the public eye who was born on or near your birthday is sure to have many of the traits you do. You may even have a Gemini twin born the same day and year. Notice how your famous mates used their Gemini qualities for better or for worse, how they rose from obscurity to fame (and vice versa), what helped or hindered their success, even how they dress to play up their Gemini star quality. Could this work for you as well?

You have a host of fabulous Geminis to inspire you. Sir Paul McCartney, Rudy Giuliani, and Joan Rivers display the Gemini brilliance and verbal skill. Fascinating Gemini beauties include Angelina Jolie, Nicole Kidman, Annette Bening, and the Olsen twins, Ashley and Mary Kate. Interesting Gemini male types include Johnny Depp, Morgan Freeman, Christo, and Bill Moyers. If you're a tabloid fan, how do your sun-sign mates like Elizabeth Hurley and Brooke Shields show their Gemini traits as they cope with difficulties and reinvent themselves?

If there's someone who intrigues you, go deeper into his life by finding his other planets in the tables in this book. You'll learn more about him as you apply the effects of Venus, Mars, Saturn, and Jupiter to his sun-sign traits. You'll be amazed at how the total planetary picture lights up when you have a living example to refer to.

If you've caught the astrology bug, you can move on to

analyze the charts of current newsmakers and match your astrology skills with the experts. Of the many celebrity sites on the Internet, the most accurate source of famous birthdays is www.astrodatabank.com, which has charts of world events and headline makers, plus the observations of amateur and professional astrologers. Try it!

Gemini Celebrities

Raymond Burr (5/21/17)
Laurence Olivier (5/22/1907)
Naomi Campbell (5/22/70)
Douglas Fairbanks (5/23/1883)
Drew Carey (5/23/58)
Bob Dylan (5/24/41)
Priscilla Presley (5/24/45)
Roseanne Cash (5/24/50)
Kristin Scott-Thomas (5/24/60)
Miles Davis (5/25/26)
Dixie Carter (5/25/39)
Sir Ian McKellen (5/25/39)
Connie Selleca (5/25/55)
Mike Myers (5/25/63)
Anne Heche (5/25/69)
John Wayne (5/26/1907)
Peggy Lee (5/26/20)
Stevie Nicks (5/26/48)
Lenny Kravitz (5/26/64)
Helena Bonham-Carter (5/26/66)
Vincent Price (5/27/11)
Henry Kissinger (5/27/23)
Tony Hillerman (5/27/25)
Louis Gossett, Jr. (5/27/36)
Siouxie Sioux (5/27/57)
Joseph Fiennes (5/27/70)
Paul Bethany (5/27/71)
Gladys Knight (5/28/44)
Rudolph Giuliani (5/28/44)
Kylie Minogue (5/28/68)

Bob Hope (5/29/1903)
John F. Kennedy (5/29/17)
Kevin Conway (5/29/42)
Anthony Geary (5/29/47)
Annette Bening (5/29/58)
Rupert Everett (5/29/59)
Benny Goodman (5/30/1909)
Prince Ranier (5/31/23)
Clint Eastwood (5/31/30)
Peter Yarrow (5/31/38)
Sharon Gless (5/31/43)
Tom Berenger (5/31/50)
Joe Namath (5/31/50)
Lea Thompson (5/31/61)
Brooke Shields (5/31/65)
Andy Griffith (6/1/26)
Marilyn Monroe (6/1/26)
Edward Woodward (6/1/30)
Pat Boone (6/1/34)
Morgan Freeman (6/1/37)
Rene Auberjonois (6/1/40)
Jonathan Pryce (6/1/47)
Ron Wood (6/1/47)
Heidi Klum (6/1/73)
Alanis Morrisette (6/1/74)
Hedda Hopper (6/2/1890)
Sally Kellerman (6/2/37)
Stacey Keach (6/2/41)
Marvin Hamlisch (6/2/44)
Tony Curtis (6/3/25)
Curtis Mayfield (6/3/42)
Denicce Williams (6/3/51)
Dr. Ruth Westheimer (6/4/28)
Bruce Dern (6/4/36)
Michelle Phillips (6/4/44)
Parker Stevenson (6/4/52)
Angelina Jolie (6/4/75)
Bill Moyers (6/5/34)
Mark Wahlberg (6/5/71)
Sandra Bernhard (6/6/55)
Jessica Tandy (6/7/1909)
James Ivory (6/7/28)

Tom Jones (6/7/40)
Liam Neeson (6/7/52)
Prince (6/7/58)
Anna Kournikova (6/7/81)
Barbara Bush (6/8/25)
Joan Rivers (6/8/33)
Kathy Baker (6/8/50)
Juliana Margulies (6/8/66)
Cole Porter (6/9/1892)
Helena Rubenstein (6/9/1892)
Charles Saatchi (6/9/43)
Michael J. Fox (6/9/61)
Johnny Depp (6/9/63)
Natalie Portman (6/9/81)
Prince Philip (6/10/21)
Lionel Jeffries (6/10/26)
Grace Mirabella (6/10/30)
Elizabeth Hurley (6/10/65)
Tara Lipinski (6/10/82)
Gene Wilder (6/11/35)
Chad Everett (6/11/37)
Adrienne Barbeau (6/11/45)
George Bush (6/12/24)
Timothy Busfield (6/12/57)
Basil Rathbone (6/13/1892)
Christo (6/13/35)
Tim Allen (6/13/53)
Ashley and Mary Kate Olsen (6/13/86)
Donald Trump (6/14/46)
Boy George (6/14/61)
Steffi Graf (6/14/69)
Mario Cuomo (6/15/32)
Waylon Jennings (6/15/37)
Helen Hunt (6/15/63)
Courteney Cox Arquette (6/15/64)
Corin Redgrave (6/16/39)
Sonia Braga (6/16/50)
Yasmine Bleeth (6/16/68)
Dean Martin (6/17/17)
Joe Piscopo (6/17/51)
Jason Patric (6/17/66)
E. G. Marshall (6/18/10)

Roger Ebert (6/18/42)
Paul McCartney (6/18/42)
Isabella Rossellini (6/18/52)
Gena Rowlands (6/19/34)
Phylicia Rashad (6/19/48)
Kathleen Turner (6/19/54)
Paula Abdul (6/19/63)
Danny Aiello (6/20/33)
Lionel Richie (6/20/40)
John Goodman (6/20/52)
Cyndi Lauper (6/20/53)
Nicole Kidman (6/20/67)

CHAPTER 21

The Gemini Power of Attraction: Your Chemistry with Every Other Sign

Understanding how your sun sign works as part of a couple can help you make wise decisions about your most important relationships: romantic, business, or friendship.

Traditional astrological wisdom holds that signs of the same element (for Gemini, that means other air signs: Libra and Aquarius) are naturally compatible. So are signs that are in complementary elements, such as air signs with fire signs. In these relationships communication flows easily and you'll feel most comfortable with each other.

But do you want comfort at certain times of your life? What happens when you meet someone, sparks fly, and an irresistible magnetic pull draws you together or when disagreements and challenges fuel intrigue, mystery, and passion? (Think of the sexy verbal sparring in Jane Austen's novel *Pride and Prejudice*.) Even though it may end sadly, you'll never forget or regret that passionate encounter. Indeed, many lasting marriages happen between incompatible sun signs, while some ideally matched couples fizzle after a few years.

Once you understand how your partner's sun sign is likely to view yours and what each of you wants from a relationship, you'll be in a much better position to judge whether this combination has happiness potential. Will there be chemistry or challenges where you'll both need to compromise . . . and are you willing to make them?

The celebrity couples can help you visualize each Gemini combination. Notice that some are legendary couples, others showed promise but broke up after a few years, and still others existed only in the fantasy world of film or television (but still captured our imagination).

Gemini/Aries

GOOD CHEMISTRY:

There is fast-paced action here. Gemini gets a charge of excitement. Aries gets constant changes to keep up with. Both are spontaneous, optimistic, and energetic. Differences of opinion only keep the atmosphere stimulating.

COMPROMISES:

Juggling life with you could have Aries seeing double. Aries is direct and to the point, but Gemini can't or won't be pinned down. This hyperactive combination could get on both your nerves unless you give each other plenty of space. Gemini, tone down the flirting. Aries must be number one!

SIGN MATES:

Gemini Annette Bening and Aries Warren Beatty

Gemini/Taurus

GOOD CHEMISTRY:

The sign next door can be your best friend as well as lover. In this case, you drag Taurus out of the house and into social life, adding laughter to love. Taurus has a soothing, stabilizing quality that supports your restlessness and allows you to be more creative than ever.

COMPROMISES:

Homebody Taurus usually wants one-on-one relations, while social Gemini loves to flirt with a crowd. You will have to curb roving eyes and bodies and plan to spend more time at home, which might cramp your style and leave you gasping for air. Infidelity can be serious business with Taurus, but taken lightly by Gemini. The line between freedom and license swings and sways here. You could feel Taurus is holding you back.

SIGN MATES:

Gemini Liam Neeson and Taurus Natasha Richardson
Gemini Steffi Graf and Taurus Andre Agassi
Gemini Anna Kournikova and Taurus Enrique Iglesias

Gemini/Gemini

GOOD CHEMISTRY:

When Gemini twins find each other, you know you'll never be bored. There is enough multifaceted mental activity, games, and delightful social life to double your pleasure. Your partner will understand the complexities of your sign as only a fellow Gemini can

COMPROMISES:

When the realities of life hit, you may go off in four directions at once. This combination lacks focus. It functions best in a light, creative atmosphere where there are no financial concerns. Serious practical problems could split your personalities and send you running elsewhere for protection and guidance.

Twins Mary Kate and Ashley Olsen

Gemini/Cancer

GOOD CHEMISTRY:

This is a very public pair with charisma to spare. Your sparkling wit sets off Cancer poise with the perfect light touch. Cancer adds warmth and caring to Gemini. This sign's shrewd insight can make your ideas happen. You can go places together!

COMPROMISES:

It's not easy for Gemini to deliver the kind of devotion Cancer needs. There are too many other exciting options. Nor do you react well to the Cancer need to mother you or to Cancer pleas for sympathy. Their up-and-down moods get on your nerves. Why can't they learn to laugh away their troubles or to find new interests? When Cancer clings, Gemini does a vanishing act. You need to have strong mutual interests or projects to hold this combo together. But it has been done!

SIGN MATES:

Gemini Michael J. Fox and Cancer Tracy Pollan
Gemini Nicole Kidman and Cancer Tom Cruise

Gemini/Leo

GOOD CHEMISTRY:

Gemini good humor, ready wit, and social skills delight and complement Leo. Here is someone who can share the spotlight without trying to steal the show from the regal lion. This is one of the most entertaining combinations. Steady Leo provides the focus Gemini often lacks, and directs the twins toward achieving goals and status.

COMPROMISES:

Gemini loves to flirt and flit among many interests, romantic and otherwise. This is sure to irritate the lion, who does one thing at a time and does it well. Gemini might be a bit bored with Leo self-promotion, and might poke fun at this sign's notorious vanity. The resulting feline roar will be no laughing matter!

SIGN MATES:

Gemini Angelina Jolie and Leo Billy Bob Thornton

Gemini/Virgo

GOOD CHEMISTRY:

You are both Mercury-ruled, and your deepest bond will be mental communication and appreciation of each other's intelligence. The Virgo Mercury is earthbound and analytical, while the Gemini Mercury is a jack-of-all-trades. Gemini shows Virgo the big picture; Virgo takes care of the details. Your combined talents make a stimulating partnership. Virgo becomes the administrator here, Gemini the idea person.

COMPROMISES:

Your different priorities can be irritating to each other. Virgo needs a sense of order. Gemini needs to experiment and is forever the gadabout. An older Gemini who has slowed down somewhat makes the best partner here.

SIGN MATES:

Gemini Liz Hurley and Virgo Hugh Grant
Gemini Courteney Cox and Virgo David Arquette

Gemini/Libra

GOOD CHEMISTRY:

Air signs Gemini and Libra have both mental and physical rapport. This is an outgoing combination, full of good talk. You'll never be bored. Libra's good looks and charm, as well as fine mind, could keep restless Gemini close to home.

COMPROMISES:

Both of you have a low tolerance for boredom and practical chores. The question of who will provide, do the dirty work, and clean up can be the subject of many a debate. There could be more talk than action here, leaving you turning elsewhere for substance.

SIGN MATES:

Tiger tamers Gemini Siegfried Fischbacher and Libra Roy Horn

Gemini/Scorpio

GOOD CHEMISTRY:

You're a fascinating mystery to each other. Gemini is immune from Scorpio paranoia, laughs away dark moods, and matches wits in power games. Scorpio intensity, focus, and sexual magnetism draw Gemini like a moth to a flame. You're intrigued by Scorpio secrets. Here's a puzzle that would be fun to solve! And steamy Scorpio brings intensity and a new level of thrills to your sex life.

COMPROMISES:

Scorpio gets heavy, possessive, and jealous, which Gemini doesn't take seriously. To make this one last, Gemini needs to treat Scorpio like the one and only, while Scorpio must use a light touch, and learn not to take Gemini flirtations to heart.

SIGN MATES:

Gemini Prince Ranier and Scorpio Grace Kelly

Gemini/Sagittarius

GOOD CHEMISTRY:

These polar opposites shake each other up happily. Sagittarius helps Gemini see higher truths, to look beyond the life of the party and the art of the deal. Gemini adds mental challenge and flexibility to Sagittarius.

COMPROMISES:

Gemini pokes holes in Sagittarius theories. Sagittarius can brand Gemini as a superficial party animal. Work toward developing nonthreatening, nonjudgmental communication. However, you can't talk away practical financial realities. You need a carefully thought-out program to make things happen.

SIGN MATES:

Gemini Marilyn Monroe and Sagittarius Joe DiMaggio
Gemini Angelina Jolie and Sagittarius Brad Pitt

Gemini/Capricorn

GOOD CHEMISTRY:

Capricorn benefits from the Gemini abstract point of view and lighthearted sense of fun. Gemini shows Capricorn how to enjoy the rewards of hard work. Support and structure are Capricorn gifts to Gemini. (Taking that literally, Capricorn Howard Hughes designed the famous bra that supported Gemini sexpot Jane Russell's physical assets!)

COMPROMISES:

Capricorn can be ultraconservative and tightfisted with money, which Gemini will not appreciate. The Gemini free-spirited, fun-loving attitude could grate against the Capricorn driving ambition. Gemini will have to learn to take responsibility and to produce solid results.

SIGN MATES:

Gemini Kylie Minogue and Capricorn Olivier Martinez

Gemini/Aquarius

GOOD CHEMISTRY:

In this open and spontaneous relationship, the pressure's off. You two air signs have room to breathe freely. At the same time, you can count on each other for friendship, understanding, and mental stimulation plus highly original romantic ideas. You'll keep each other entertained, and your love life will be fresh and stimulating.

COMPROMISES:

Be sure to leave time in your busy schedule for each other. If there is no commitment, you could both fly off. A sharing of causes, projects, or careers could hold you together.

SIGN MATES:

Costars Gemini Marilyn Monroe and Aquarius Clark Gable

Gemini/Pisces

GOOD CHEMISTRY:

You are both dual personalities in mutable, freedom-loving signs. You fascinate each other with ever-changing facets. You keep each other from straying by providing constant variety and new experiments to try together.

COMPROMISES:

At some point, you'll need a frame of reference for this relationship to hold together. Since neither likes structure, this could be a problem. Overstimulation is another monster that can rise to the surface. Pisces sensitive feelings and Gemini hyperactive nerves could send each other searching for more soothing, stabilizing alternatives.

SIGN MATES:

Gemini Donald Trump and Pisces Ivana Trump

CHAPTER 22

Astrological Overview for Gemini in 2007

Welcome to 2007, Gemini!

The year begins with Mercury, Venus, and Neptune in Aquarius, forming harmonious angles to your sun. Mercury, your ruler, takes your conscious thoughts to exotic locales. Which one falls within your budget? Venus whispers that you can afford it and tantalizes you with the possibility of romance abroad. Then Neptune adds his voice to the chorus, urging you to scrutinize your spiritual and creative beliefs.

If you plan an overseas trip, be sure that it falls outside of the Mercury retrograde periods listed at the end of the chapter.

The partnership area of your chart is lit up this year while expansive Jupiter continues its journey through your solar seventh house. Pluto in Sagittarius is also there, transforming both your personal and business partnerships. Sometimes these transformative events don't feel comfortable, but be assured that when the dust has settled, you will be in a much better place, particularly with Jupiter helping things along.

For romance, the best times fall between April 11 and May 7, when Venus is in your sign. Other excellent dates are November 8 to December 4, when Venus is in your fifth house of romance and pleasure, and August 7 to September 27, when Mars—your sexual and physical energy—is in your sign.

For those of you born in the first week of June, Uranus

will be forming a challenging aspect to your sun for much of the year. This aspect—a square—will affect your house of career and profession. You could experience sudden, unexpected changes in your career, but these changes should be exciting and shake you out of your usual routine. You may be able to interject your spiritual beliefs more readily into your work.

On September 2, Saturn moves from Leo and into Virgo and your solar fourth house. If you've hoped to establish a home-based business, this could be the year it happens. Any move from one house to another, however, could be delayed. One of your parents may need emotional support this year.

Very late in the year, on December 18, Jupiter moves into Capricorn and your eighth house. This transit, which lasts for about a year, should expand any resources you share with others. It will be easy to obtain mortgages and loans. It's possible that your partner or spouse will get a raise. If you have a moon or rising in Capricorn, this transit should bring some beautiful surprises!

For daily work issues, look to the Saturn transit that begins on September 2 to increase your responsibility and to make you accountable. This would be a great time to join a gym or set up some kind of regular exercise routine.

Here are some dates to watch for this year:

April 12: Mercury and Venus are moving at favorable angles to each other, stimulating activities in your friendships and in the way other people perceive you.

June 1–21: The sun and Mars travel very close together during this time, galvanizing your friendships, your dreams, and how others perceive you. You can accomplish a great deal during these three weeks.

October 13–19: During this time, Venus and Saturn travel close together through your solar fourth house. This combination can bring delays or restrictions in terms of moving, but certainly heats up your love life. It could be a good time to establish a home office or business.

December 22: Today could be one of the best for you this year. The sun, Mercury, and Jupiter are traveling together through your solar eighth house—excellent for obtaining mortgages and loans and for delving into metaphysics.

There are four eclipses this year. Two of them involve Virgo, two involve Pisces. Lunar eclipses tend to bring up emotional issues related to the sign and house in which they fall and solar eclipses tend to reveal something that has been hidden. On March 3, the lunar eclipse in Virgo could bring up an emotional issue related to your home or family. Two weeks later, on March 18, the solar eclipse in Pisces brings to light something that has been hidden from you in your profession.

On August 28, there's a lunar eclipse in Pisces. This eclipse hits your tenth house, indicating that an emotional issue concerning your career may surface. On September 11, the solar eclipse is in Virgo, so something about home and family that has been hidden from you will be revealed.

Every year, your ruler, Mercury, turns retrograde three times; during these periods, it's easy to be misunderstood, travel plans often go awry, and computers and other appliances act up. It's a good idea not to negotiate or sign contracts. The times to watch for are:

February 13–March 7—Mercury retrograde in Pisces (your tenth house). This hits your career. It's a good time to review, rewrite, reevaluate.

June 15–July 9—Mercury retrograde in Cancer (your second house). Checks and other money you're expecting could be delayed.

October 11–November 1—Mercury retrograde in Scorpio (your sixth house). Be clear and concise in your communications at work!

CHAPTER 23

Eighteen Months of Day-by-Day Predictions—July 2006 to December 2007

Moon sign times are calculated for Eastern Standard Time and Eastern Daylight Time. Please adjust for your local time zone.

JULY 2006

Saturday, July 1 (Moon in Virgo)   Visitors arrive for the Fourth of July weekend. You actually enjoy being surrounded by family and friends and accept the fact that your schedule will be disrupted for a few days.

Sunday, July 2 (Moon in Virgo to Libra 1:07 p.m.)   You and a friend or family member take a long walk this morning or perhaps go horseback riding or even swimming. Whatever the activity, there's an element of beauty about it, an aesthetic satisfaction.

Monday, July 3 (Moon in Libra)   Your mediation skills are called into play today. You're able to help, and you feel good about it. The others are grateful the dispute is resolved.

Tuesday, July 4 (Moon in Libra)   Today marks the second Mercury retrograde of the year. It impacts your fourth house. Be clear and concise about what you say, to minimize possibilities of miscommunication, and try to postpone travel plans until after July 28.

Wednesday, July 5 (Moon in Libra to Scorpio 1:14 a.m.) Back at work today, you are immediately confronted with a mystery or puzzle that begs to be solved. In typical Gemini fashion, you tackle the challenge, digging for information.

Thursday, July 6 (Moon in Scorpio)   Jupiter turns direct today in Scorpio, in your sixth house. Energy is now freed up in your daily work routine that allows expansion and success to unfold. You feel emotionally expansive toward coworkers.

Friday, July 7 (Moon in Scorpio to Sagittarius 10:14 a.m.)   As the moon moves into your seventh house, you and your partner decide to leave for a long weekend together. You both love to travel and this trip proves particularly enlightening.

Saturday, July 8 (Moon in Sagittarius)   Your perception opens wider now, allowing you to see the world through your partner's eyes and values. When you walk in someone else's shoes like this, your understanding is immediate and profound.

Sunday, July 9 (Moon in Sagittarius to Capricorn 3:25 p.m.)   You're interested in a piece of property for possible investment purposes. You and your spouse should look at the property and gather your facts, but don't make an offer yet.

Monday, July 10 (Moon in Capricorn)   Look for long-term investments that are safe, even if the immediate profit isn't as much as you would like. Your spouse's income is fluctuating a lot this month.

Tuesday, July 11 (Moon in Capricorn to Aquarius 5:46 p.m.)   When the moon transits visionary Aquarius, you feel nearly as good as when it's in your own sign. Anything you do today related to your continuing education pays off down the line.

Wednesday, July 12 (Moon in Aquarius)   With both the moon and Neptune in your ninth house, there may be some confusion about in-laws. One of your in-laws needs help and support right now. In your usual direct fashion, you get the problem straightened out by the end of the day.

Thursday, July 13 (Moon in Aquarius to Pisces 7:00 p.m.)   Anything you do today related to your career furthers your standing with your company or boss or both. The higher-ups notice your initiative.

Friday, July 14 (Moon in Pisces)   Your imagination and intuition are powerful forces. Use them today to make a career decision. A Pisces is helpful in this regard.

Saturday, July 15 (Moon in Pisces to Aries 8:39 p.m.)   Publicity and promotion are highlighted today. But have a plan and a strategy ready—don't just rush into it.

Sunday, July 16 (Moon in Aries)   The moon now forms a harmonious angle to your sun, which facilitates communication and increases your passion and sex appeal. Romance is possible with someone you meet through friends.

Monday, July 17 (Moon in Aries to Taurus 11:45 p.m.)   As the moon moves into your twelfth house, you may feel the need to withdraw from your usually busy social calendar. Nurture your own creativity now.

Tuesday, July 18 (Moon in Taurus)   Venus moves into Cancer and your second house. This transit favors financial matters. It could mean a raise or a promotion. Romance is possible with someone you meet serendipitously.

Wednesday, July 19 (Moon in Taurus)   A long walk this morning stimulates your creativity and offers an insight into a particularly challenging pattern in your life. You and a close friend have dinner and take in a movie later this evening.

Thursday, July 20 (Moon in Taurus to Gemini 4:39 a.m.)   The good times are here again! As the moon moves into your sign early this morning, you awaken refreshed, ready to tackle whatever comes your way.

Friday, July 21 (Moon in Gemini)   Books, writing, and self-expression come into play today. Something you've written is accepted for publication.

Saturday, July 22 (Moon in Gemini to Cancer 11:29 a.m.) Mars moves into Virgo and your fourth house. This transit can increase tensions or activities in your home. Your temper may be somewhat short; nurture patience.

Sunday, July 23 (Moon in Cancer)   As the moon joins Venus in your second house, your artistic sensibilities increase. A woman in the arts (or your mother) proves helpful.

Monday, July 24 (Moon in Cancer to Leo 8:25 p.m.)   By this evening, you're in a party mood. You and friends or neighbors get together for a festivity that goes on late into the night.

Tuesday, July 25 (Moon in Leo)   Your kids have put together a neighborhood theater group. Today is their first production. Their creativity astounds you.

Wednesday, July 26 (Moon in Leo)   You're in a flamboyant mood and dress the part. You attract the attention of a neighbor who has watched you from a distance for a long time now. The chemistry clicks.

Thursday, July 27 (Moon in Leo to Virgo 7:37 a.m.)   As the moon joins Mars in your fourth house, your sex life and your love life pick up considerably. A lot of people are coming and going in your personal environment now, and you may consider doing your creative work at night when it's quieter.

Friday, July 28 (Moon in Virgo)   Mercury, your ruler, turns direct today in Leo. Celebrate, Gemini! It's always good news for you when Mercury retrograde periods are over. Any electrical or computer problems you've been having should straighten out now.

Saturday, July 29 (Moon in Virgo to Libra 8:28 p.m.)   The Libra moon is comfortable for you because it forms a harmonious angle to your sun. You're in a much more social mood now and may toss a party for your coworkers.

Sunday, July 30 (Moon in Libra)   You're networking now and it's stimulating the creative side of your life. Any romance that begins in the next two days may be a passing fling for you, Gemini. But that's okay. Have fun while it lasts.

Monday, July 31 (Moon in Libra)   Creativity is the name of the game you play today with your children. It's hard to say, though, whose ideas have more of an impact. Your creativity is always stimulated by watching and interacting with your children.

Tuesday, August 1 (Moon in Libra to Scorpio 9:08 a.m.)
Some adjustment that is related to work or to your health is required in your thinking today. A few minutes of meditation on the problem will help you solve it.

Wednesday, August 2 (Moon in Scorpio)   You usually avoid emotional confrontations. But a coworker does or says something insensitive to you and you take umbrage and speak your mind.

Thursday, August 3 (Moon in Scorpio to Sagittarius 7:14 p.m.)   Even though this moon is opposite your sun, you enjoy the Sagittarius fire. It stimulates both your passion and your independence and helps you to see the larger picture of a partnership.

Friday, August 4 (Moon in Sagittarius)   If there's a way through a bumpy time in a relationship, you find it today. Take steps now to remedy the problem. An Aries or a Leo helps you clarify your own intentions.

Saturday, August 5 (Moon in Sagittarius)   Your independence bothers someone who is close to you. Be gentle but firm about what you expect in a partnership. State your rules up front to avoid problems later on.

Sunday, August 6 (Moon in Sagittarius to Capricorn 1:20 a.m.)   A visit with your tax attorney or accountant provides insight into your joint financial affairs. A Libra offers another viewpoint. Back off for the time being on a joint venture.

Monday, August 7 (Moon in Capricorn)   You and a friend attend an estate sale. It triggers certain thoughts you have about your own mortality. Perhaps now is the time to begin investigating metaphysical topics that interest you.

Tuesday, August 8 (Moon in Capricorn to Aquarius 3:48 a.m.)   Here it comes again, the lure of foreign lands. You've got the travel bug, Gemini; maybe it's time to indulge it. Pick a place and then decide if you can afford it.

Wednesday, August 9 (Moon in Aquarius)   You may sign up for an adult-education class in Web design or in some other area that involves computers. You convince a Gemini friend to take the class with you.

Thursday, August 10 (Moon in Aquarius to Pisces 4:11 a.m.)   Your dream recall now is extraordinary. You may even join a group that discusses dreams so that you can better understand the symbolism of your own dreams.

Friday, August 11 (Moon in Pisces)   You experience something filled with symbolism that seems rather dreamlike. The work you've been doing with your dream group helps you to understand the meaning behind the experience.

Saturday, August 12 (Moon in Pisces to Aries 4:23 a.m.) Venus moves into Leo and your third house. This lucky transit brings romance with someone who lives in your neighborhood or nearby. You could also get a break related to something you've written.

Sunday, August 13 (Moon in Aries)   A radio show or other type of public appearance is possible today. It may come out of the blue; if so, take advantage of it. It benefits you in the long run.

Monday, August 14 (Moon in Aries to Taurus 6:01 a.m.)   A Capricorn convinces you to help out behind the scenes. It could be in an institutional setting. You discover something insightful about yourself.

Tuesday, August 15 (Moon in Taurus)   You spend time at home today, adding touches of color to your workspace. You may add fresh flowers and scents too. Aromatherapy may be just the ticket to improve your mood.

Wednesday, August 16 (Moon in Taurus to Gemini 10:08 a.m.)   The moon is finally in your sign again, and you can actually feel the shift in your mood. You're suddenly more sociable, more optimistic, and more, well, Gemini!

Thursday, August 17 (Moon in Gemini)   You're feeling lucky, so you gamble today on buying a rare book. Hold on to it for your kids. Thirty years down the road, they'll be reading it to their kids.

Friday, August 18 (Moon in Gemini to Cancer 5:04 p.m.)   You're feeling restless to move. You and your spouse or partner may look at homes or property in another neighborhood. Just remember that the grass isn't always greener elsewhere.

Saturday, August 19 (Moon in Cancer)   Your mother or a female relative visits you, and the two of you head to antique stores in a nearby town. You're not too interested in antiques, so you slip away and find the perfect bookstore.

Sunday, August 20 (Moon in Cancer)   There's a certain element of nostalgia with this moon. Even though you don't usually cling to the past, you find your mind moving backward through time, seeking an answer.

Monday, August 21 (Moon in Cancer to Leo 2:34 a.m.)   Now you're moving forward again. The past is where it belongs, and the future waits ahead of you. An Aries or a Leo invites you out for the evening.

Tuesday, August 22 (Moon in Leo)   Your writing is going extremely well. You've gotten good feedback from an agent or an editor; you are inspired to keep moving forward. Success comes to those who never give up!

Wednesday, August 23 (Moon in Leo to Virgo 2:08 p.m.)   With the moon in Virgo in your fourth house, you may be something of a perfectionist today. Nothing wrong with that. But don't criticize others.

Thursday, August 24 (Moon in Virgo)   Your quest for perfection gets on everyone else's nerves. Chill out, Gemini. Life is rarely perfect.

Friday, August 25 (Moon in Virgo)   You're concerned about details today. Apply it to your creative endeavors, and everyone around you will breathe more easily.

Saturday, August 26 (Moon in Virgo to Libra 3:01 a.m.)   One of your children brings home a stray kitten. Your heart melts. You all decide to keep the kitten.

Sunday, August 27 (Moon in Libra)   Mercury moves into Virgo, one of the signs that it rules. Your mind is finely tuned now, discriminating, able to pick out what is important and what isn't.

Monday, August 28 (Moon in Libra to Scorpio 3:56 p.m.)   You and coworkers get together on a joint project. Your ability to cull information and get to the bottom line helps the project go more quickly.

Tuesday, August 29 (Moon in Scorpio)   Yesterday's project becomes today's bonus! Your boss loves what you've done. A bonus may be in the offing.

Wednesday, August 30 (Moon in Scorpio)   Keep on the path you're following, Gemini. Even on days when you feel discouraged, things are rarely as bad as they seem.

Thursday, August 31 (Moon in Scorpio to Sagittarius 3:00 a.m.) You and your partner take advantage of a long weekend. You get away alone and renew your commitment to each other.

SEPTEMBER 2006

Friday, September 1 (Moon in Sagittarius) You're able to see the broader picture of your marriage or primary love relationship. If you like what you see, take steps to continue whatever you're doing that makes the relationship work.

Saturday, September 2 (Moon in Sagittarius to Capricorn 10:35 a.m.) You're laying a metaphysical foundation for your life. This could involve taking courses, reading books, or talking with people in the field. You've got many questions begging for answers.

Sunday, September 3 (Moon in Capricorn) Your mother or father or an elderly relative asks for your help. If you can't do everything that's required, find the experts who can.

Monday, September 4 (Moon in Capricorn to Aquarius 2:15 p.m.) Pluto turns direct in Sagittarius today, in your seventh house. The effects of this movement are likely to be subtle. Energy is now released that allows your partnerships to move forward.

Tuesday, September 5 (Moon in Aquarius) Expect news from overseas or related to publishing and education. You get a break on a book you've been writing.

Wednesday, September 6 (Moon in Aquarius to Pisces 2:57 p.m.) Venus moves into Virgo today. This transit indicates that your love life picks up at home. Any relationship that begins under this transit, which lasts until September 30, will be founded on excellent communication.

Thursday, September 7 (Moon in Pisces)   Mars moves into Libra and your fifth house. This transit triggers your creative adrenaline and your sexual appetite.

Friday, September 8 (Moon in Pisces to Aries 2:24 p.m.)   The Aries moon stimulates your interest and involvement in group projects. You may join a theater group or some other group that shares your creative interests.

Saturday, September 9 (Moon in Aries)   Your idealism today is strong and powerful. It infects other people you're around and brings out your pioneering spirit.

Sunday, September 10 (Moon in Aries to Taurus 2:31 p.m.)   You and a Virgo friend work behind the scenes for a political campaign or some other endeavor where your work is needed but perhaps not acknowledged. You may visit a sick friend who is in the hospital.

Monday, September 11 (Moon in Taurus)   You're physically strong today, and the spirit moves you to display it. The gym or a long run is in order.

Tuesday, September 12 (Moon in Taurus to Gemini 5:00 p.m.)   Mercury moves into Libra and your fifth house. Your mind is judicious and balanced now. You're able to see your way clear to the end of the book you're working on.

Wednesday, September 13 (Moon in Gemini)   With the moon in your sign, you're pretty much on top of the world. Things come your way without any apparent effort on your part.

233

Thursday, September 14 (Moon in Gemini to Cancer 10:54 p.m.)   How far are you willing to go with your money? Is risk what you're about? These are some of the questions you're asking yourself today about your financial affairs.

Friday, September 15 (Moon in Cancer)   You may feel emotionally vulnerable where money is concerned. Resist splurging on anything for the next couple of days. Gain some perspective.

Saturday, September 16 (Moon in Cancer)   Your mother or a close female friend offers financial advice. Test it against your own intuition before you follow it.

Sunday, September 17 (Moon in Cancer to Leo 8:15 a.m.) Flamboyance and flair are part of who you are today. You're developing your own style in the communication business.

Monday, September 18 (Moon in Leo)   You're doing a lot of running around today related to children: carpooling, soccer games, the usual school-year chaos. Sit back and enjoy it, Gemini.

Tuesday, September 19 (Moon in Leo to Virgo 8:07 p.m.)   Your mother criticizes you or your home. She doesn't intend to be mean about it, but that's how you take it. Get over it, Gemini.

Wednesday, September 20 (Moon in Virgo)   One of your kids or your spouse needs your attention today. It's nothing serious. It's just that you've been distracted lately, and your family feels that.

Thursday, September 21 (Moon in Virgo)   Pay attention to the small details today. If paint is chipped, repaint. If the icemaker doesn't work, get it fixed. You get the idea here.

Friday, September 22 (Moon in Virgo to Libra 9:07 a.m.)   You're going great guns today on your creative projects. One of your children may provide clues about how to do something a bit differently.

Saturday, September 23 (Moon in Libra)   Romance is in the air again. Look as good as you feel today. Get your hair cut, buy a new outfit, or do something that makes you feel as beautiful as you are.

Sunday, September 24 (Moon in Libra to Scorpio 9:55 p.m.)   This evening, you may not be in the best of moods. Your emotions run through you like a powerful river, sweeping away everything that gets in your way.

Monday, September 25 (Moon in Scorpio)   You've calmed down now. At work, you do what you have to do to get through the day. Is it time to start looking for another job, Gemini?

Tuesday, September 26 (Moon in Scorpio)   Figure out what you love to do most of all; then try to figure out how to earn money doing it. You're multitalented. You can pick and choose. You just have to believe in yourself.

Wednesday, September 27 (Moon in Scorpio to Sagittarius 9:17 a.m.)   It's time to negotiate a fair contract for yourself. Hold out for what you want. Do it nicely, but do it.

Thursday, September 28 (Moon in Sagittarius)   An overseas visitor arrives. You feel somewhat put out that the person comes unannounced, but you enjoy this person's company nonetheless.

Friday, September 29 (Moon in Sagittarius to Capricorn 6:02 p.m.)   You and your spouse draw up your wills. It may not be pleasant work, but it's necessary.

Saturday, September 30 (Moon in Capricorn) Venus moves into Libra today. This beautiful transit indicates good fortune related to creative endeavors. Love and romance may come your way too and will be founded on mutual aesthetic and artistic passions.

OCTOBER 2006

Sunday, October 1 (Moon in Capricorn to Aquarius 11:25 p.m.) Mercury moves into Scorpio today. For the next two weeks, you're deeply intuitive and have terrific insights into yourself and others. Expect news related to work or your health.

Monday, October 2 (Moon in Aquarius) Your spiritual interests and studies could take you overseas, to some faraway corner of the world. Or you may find a book or Internet site that satisfies your curiosity.

Tuesday, October 3 (Moon in Aquarius) Your political views may not be to the liking of the people around you. But hey, guess what? You're not here to please everyone. You're here, Gemini, to sample everything.

Wednesday, October 4 (Moon in Aquarius to Pisces 1:34 a.m.) As the transiting moon joins Uranus in your tenth house, you're suddenly in the right place at the right time. A TV or radio appearance is a possibility.

Thursday, October 5 (Moon in Pisces) There could be some tension or friction today with a boss, your father, or some other authority figure in your life. Don't lose your cool, Gemini. Just let it all roll away from you.

Friday, October 6 (Moon in Pisces to Aries 1:33 a.m.) You're short on patience today and your friends notice it. It seems that your life is jammed in fast-forward right now. Perhaps you need to start delegating responsibility to others.

Saturday, October 7 (Moon in Aries)   You're redefining your goals and dreams. This isn't necessarily a conscious process, but on some level, your priorities are shifting.

Sunday, October 8 (Moon in Aries to Taurus 1:05 a.m.)   Any relationship that begins in the next two days could be quite physical and sexual and may take place in secret. The secrecy part of it won't last long for you.

Monday, October 9 (Moon in Taurus)   You're not very good at keeping secrets. And today, you're entrusted with more than your share. Instead of divulging them, you may use them as fodder for your next book.

Tuesday, October 10 (Moon in Taurus to Gemini 2:06 a.m.)   With the moon in your sign, life suddenly looks brighter. You get a fortunate break with a publishing project you've been working on. It could be that you're going to see your novel or nonfiction book in print!

Wednesday, October 11 (Moon in Gemini)   You throw a party for friends, who end up bringing other friends. Pretty soon, your home is filled with people and music. Romance could be on the horizon with someone you meet at this party.

Thursday, October 12 (Moon in Gemini to Cancer 6:21 a.m.)   Keep your options open. You may be tempted to get involved in a get-rich-quick scheme. Resist. There're no free rides.

Friday, October 13 (Moon in Cancer)   You're feeling vulnerable now about your finances. Stash some money away. And keep stashing.

Saturday, October 14 (Moon in Cancer to Leo 2:38 p.m.) Your mood improves a hundred percent by this afternoon. You and friends hit the mall, a bookstore, or even a café. You find a special gift for your sister or brother.

Sunday, October 15 (Moon in Leo) You're quite the actor today. Even though a neighbor has angered you, you're able to act as if nothing has happened. You should probably express your anger and be done with it!

Monday, October 16 (Moon in Leo) A proposal you've written catches the attention of the right editor or agent or your boss loves it. Your ideas are clear and succinct.

Tuesday, October 17 (Moon in Leo to Virgo 2:16 a.m.) A love affair is deepening to the next level. Are you ready to commit, Gemini? Be sure before you do. You're known for your fickle heart.

Wednesday, October 18 (Moon in Virgo) Follow the three rules for this moon: attend to details, don't criticize yourself or others, and take care of your physical body. And while you're at it, finish your novel!

Thursday, October 19 (Moon in Virgo to Libra 3:20 p.m.) Your emotions seesaw today. You're like a teenager pulling petals off a daisy: loves me; loves me not. Make up your mind!

Friday, October 20 (Moon in Libra) Okay, it's official. It's a romance. Your new lover has brought you flowers and your favorite book, and asked you out to see a movie with some of your favorite actors in it.

Saturday, October 21 (Moon in Libra) The moon feels very comfortable for you. You're able to focus on your artistic projects, whatever they are, and have a barrel of fun while doing them. Remember, what makes you feel like this, Gemini, so you can conjure it later.

Sunday, October 22 (Moon in Libra to Scorpio 3:55 a.m.) High emotions and profound insights mark your day. Fortunately, you're not at work, but the event that precipitates your mood is work-related.

Monday, October 23 (Moon in Scorpio) As Mars moves into Scorpio, a sign that it corules, an affair with a coworker proves to be more than you bargained for. Your sexuality, however, is taken to new heights.

Tuesday, October 24 (Moon in Scorpio to Sagittarius 2.54 p.m.) When Venus goes into emotionally intense Scorpio, your romance isn't just a passing fling with a coworker. It's sexually charged, secretive, and probably has past-life connections.

Wednesday, October 25 (Moon in Sagittarius) You've got the bigger picture today on your personal relationships. If your partner is also your business associate, so much the better. Now you can brainstorm together for where you would like your company to be five years from now.

Thursday, October 26 (Moon in Sagittarius to Capricorn 11:48 p.m.) You visit a psychic. You may have reservations or skepticism about these people, but the person you see blows your socks off.

Friday, October 27 (Moon in Capricorn) Your metaphysical journey has begun now. You're buying books on the topics that interest, attending seminars. In typical Gemini fashion, you're on a quest to get as much information as you can find.

Saturday, October 28 (Moon in Capricorn)   Today marks the beginning of the last Mercury retrograde this year. It falls in Scorpio, your house of daily work. Be very clear now in your communications with coworkers so that you aren't misunderstood. This retrograde period lasts until November 17.

Sunday, October 29—Daylight Saving Time Ends (Moon in Capricorn to Aquarius 5:17 a.m.)   You've bought your tickets. You're headed for someplace you've always wanted to visit. Now there are a few more landmarks to include in your itinerary.

Monday, October 30 (Moon in Aquarius)   With the moon in visionary Aquarius, you're all intellect today. Even your heart is moved by ideas, speculations. Record the ideas. You can use them later in your novel.

Tuesday, October 31 (Moon in Aquarius to Pisces 9:11 a.m.)   Happy Halloween! Put on a costume and go trick or treating with your kids. Or get together with your group of pagan friends and celebrate the most powerful day among Wiccans.

NOVEMBER 2006

Wednesday, November 1 (Moon in Pisces)   The energy of this moon sometimes feels strange to you, rather dreamy. It's because your imagination and intuition are working overtime. Use these qualities to your advantage.

Thursday, November 2 (Moon in Pisces to Aries 10:47 a.m.)   A friend introduces you to someone. The chemistry is right. Even if the relationship is short-lived, you enjoy it.

Friday, November 3 (Moon in Aries)   You take a risk today and arrange a promotion for your company's product. Your gall works!

Saturday, November 4 (Moon in Aries to Taurus 11:05 a.m.)   It's not empty talk. Regular physical exercise prolongs your life. Go get some, Gemini.

Sunday, November 5 (Moon in Taurus)   A Capricorn talks you into taking a yoga class. You find that it really does make you more flexible. Now you're an advocate.

Monday, November 6 (Moon in Taurus to Gemini 11:47 a.m.)   The moon is finally in your sign again and we know what that means, right? Get yourself in shape. Romance is just around the corner, and the likely candidate is a Libra or an Aquarius who has been interested in you for some time.

Tuesday, November 7 (Moon in Gemini)   Your focus is on books, writing, and other forms of communication. Your skills are especially strong now. Take advantage of it.

Wednesday, November 8 (Moon in Gemini to Cancer 2:46 p.m.)   Okay, it's time for some moneymaking ideas to roll in. But they can originate within you. Use your intuition.

Thursday, November 9 (Moon in Cancer)   Your mother or another female has advice for you about money. You may not like the advice, but be polite. Listen.

Friday, November 10 (Moon in Cancer to Leo 9:35 p.m.)   As the moon joins Saturn in your fourth house, you may feel emotionally burdened and restricted in some way. Just take it easy.

Saturday, November 11 (Moon in Leo)   Feeling flashy and flamboyant today? Good. Go dress the part. Play the part. Become the part.

Sunday, November 12 (Moon in Leo)   Your children are filled with energy today. Take them out to someplace fun. You won't regret it!

Monday, November 13 (Moon in Leo to Virgo 8:20 a.m.) Picky, picky, picky. Just back off from this perfectionist streak you're on. Things will get done without you picking at everyone.

Tuesday, November 14 (Moon in Virgo)   Turn your perfectionism toward your creative projects. You'll spot details now that don't fit or that should be changed.

Wednesday, November 15 (Moon in Virgo to Libra 9:15 p.m.)   By tonight, you're in rare form. You feel better when the moon is in Libra, forming a harmonious angle to your sun. You're also easier for others to be around!

Thursday, November 16 (Moon in Libra)   It's a beauty day. Get your hair cut, do your nails, clean out your closet, and make way for the new.

Friday, November 17 (Moon in Libra)   Venus moves into Sagittarius today, and your love life heats up! Perhaps a business partner now becomes a lover. Perhaps you and your partner finally tie the knot. However this transit unfolds for you, it happens between now and December 11. Mercury also turns direct today—always good news for you, Gemini!

Saturday, November 18 (Moon in Libra to Scorpio 9:48 a.m.)   Here you are again, back with the most intense moon in the zodiac. Just remember to make space in your life for fun when the transiting moon is in Scorpio and to remember that it's not really the end of the world.

Sunday, November 19 (Moon in Scorpio)   Uranus moves direct in Pisces. The effects of this transit are subtle and release energy so that you can move forward in your career. But how can you integrate your spiritual beliefs into your profession?

Monday, November 20 (Moon in Scorpio to Sagittarius 8:16 p.m.)   You and your honey see eye to eye on many things, but today that agreement could fall briefly into disarray. It's a phase, nothing more.

Tuesday, November 21 (Moon in Sagittarius)   You and your spouse rent a home in a foreign country for the Christmas holidays. Your brochures on the place arrive. Everyone is filled with anticipation.

Wednesday, November 22 (Moon in Sagittarius)   You sell a piece of property and split the proceeds with your ex. It galls you, but you're free now of further obligations.

Thursday, November 23 (Moon in Sagittarius to Capricorn 4:26 a.m.)   Jupiter moves into Sagittarius for the first time in twelve years and remains there for about a year. This transit expands your professional and personal partnerships in ways that you can't even imagine now.

Friday, November 24 (Moon in Capricorn)   A Virgo offers advice that you need about a nursing home for an aging relative. It's sad business, yes, but it's up to you to make sure that the care the person receives is top-notch.

Saturday, November 25 (Moon in Capricorn to Aquarius 10:41 a.m.)   Just how far into the future can you see?

243

Try it today through meditating or some kind of divination technique.

Sunday, November 26 (Moon in Aquarius)   You may decide to take a course in astrology or you could start buying books that will help in your studies. While you're at it, buy a good astrology software program.

Monday, November 27 (Moon in Aquarius to Pisces 3:21 p.m.)   You make significant professional strides today. And it's surprisingly easy to do. All you have to do is listen.

Tuesday, November 28 (Moon in Pisces)   A colleague is impressed with your intuitive awareness. The chemistry between you is electric. This one may go somewhere, Gemini. Pay attention.

Wednesday, November 29 (Moon in Pisces to Aries 6:30 p.m.)   As the holidays approach, you've already got your shopping list ready. Get an early jump on things.

Thursday, November 30 (Moon in Aries)   You're rethinking your goals and ambitions for the new year. Yes, you're a month ahead of everyone else. But that's how it usually is with you.

DECEMBER 2006

Friday, December 1 (Moon in Aries to Taurus 8:27 p.m.)   You don't mind shopping by yourself. Sometimes you actually prefer it that way. You can move at your own pace today at the mall. You find precisely the right gifts.

Saturday, December 2 (Moon in Taurus)   You buy some green plants for the house. It satisfies the Taurus moon need for beauty.

Sunday, December 3 (Moon in Taurus to Gemini 10:06 p.m.)   The moon moves into your sign. You've changed your mind a dozen times today about someone or about a particular situation. Make your decision; then stick to it.

Monday, December 4 (Moon in Gemini)   They say you're fickle, but it's not really that, is it? It's just that life is filled with so many things and people to sample and taste. You need an entire lifetime just to read all the books sitting on your shelves!

Tuesday, December 5 (Moon in Gemini)   Mars moves into Sagittarius today and Saturn turns direct to Leo. The Mars transit stimulates your sex life. The Saturn movement releases energy that helps tensions ease up at home.

Wednesday, December 6 (Moon in Gemini to Cancer 1:02 a.m.)   A real estate investment looks awfully good. Before you make a decision, do your left-brain Gemini thing and gather all the facts.

Thursday, December 7 (Moon in Cancer)   You've uncovered some things about the property you saw yesterday that you don't like. Some other opportunity will come your way before the end of the month.

Friday, December 8 (Moon in Cancer to Leo 6:53 a.m.) Mercury joins Mars in Sagittarius in your seventh house. You and your partner are not only enjoying a great sex life now, but your minds are completely in sync.

Saturday, December 9 (Moon in Leo)   You and a neighbor feel a certain chemistry. Who will act on it first? Is this the direction in which you want to move?

Sunday, December 10 (Moon in Leo to Virgo 4:32 p.m.)   Once the moon moves into Virgo, you have a

245

clearer idea about yesterday's chemistry. If there are sparks, then you're interested.

Monday, December 11 (Moon in Virgo)   Venus moves into Capricorn today. This transit not only increases your opportunities for romance, but brings a change to your spouse or to someone with whom you share bank accounts and resources. A raise perhaps? Even an inheritance is possible.

Tuesday, December 12 (Moon in Virgo)   Any relationship starting under the Venus transit that began yesterday is sure to be emotionally intense yet practical, loving yet ambitious. A strange dichotomy, but you're accustomed to living with dichotomies and paradoxes.

Wednesday, December 13 (Moon in Virgo to Libra 5:01 a.m.)   Here's the beautiful Libra moon again. Romance is in the air, in your heart, and in everything you look at. You're in love with love, but that's okay too. Just enjoy it.

Thursday, December 14 (Moon in Libra)   Your love story is the one you may write. Be sure it's as interesting to other people as it is to you.

Friday, December 15 (Moon in Libra to Scorpio 5:43 p.m.)   You and a coworker head out of town for the weekend. You're off to see a psychic. You've got big questions to which you need answers.

Saturday, December 16 (Moon in Scorpio)   Your emotional intensity needs an outlet today. Find one—and fast!

Sunday, December 17 (Moon in Scorpio)   Things aren't as bad as they seem. You're just in an intense and passionate mood. By tomorrow, you'll feel better.

Monday, December 18 (Moon in Scorpio to Sagittarius 4:10 a.m.)   The moon moves into Sagittarius and your seventh house. This transit highlights your love life and your professional partnerships. You and your spouse or partner have a heart-to-heart and your relationship is better for it.

Tuesday, December 19 (Moon in Sagittarius)   With the holidays now upon you, you rush out today to do last-minute gift shopping. You'll have surprise visitors this year, so pick up a couple of extra gifts too.

Wednesday, December 20 (Moon in Sagittarius to Capricorn 11:39 a.m.)   Here come your surprise visitors. They're older, established. Your parents perhaps? Or perhaps a man and woman who are like parents to you?

Thursday, December 21 (Moon in Capricorn)   Your spouse makes a large expenditure for something you need. It's a major appliance or perhaps a better printer or computer.

Friday, December 22 (Moon in Capricorn to Aquarius 4:49 p.m.)   As the moon moves into your ninth house, news from abroad arrives. Or to confuse matters, it could be visitors from abroad. Accept the situation gracefully and resign yourself to having fun!

Saturday, December 23 (Moon in Aquarius)   Your spiritual beliefs play into your affairs today. Everyone in your house disagrees on politics, but you find allies concerning your metaphysical studies in your midst.

Sunday, December 24 (Moon in Aquarius to Pisces 8:44 p.m.)   Career matters are the last thing on your mind. But due to the generosity of the season, you'll find that any contacts you make now are to your advantage next year.

Monday, December 25 (Moon in Pisces) Imagination, intuition, and your spiritual beliefs all play into the picture today. A boss or colleague calls to wish you a merry Christmas.

Tuesday, December 26 (Moon in Pisces) If your feet are bothering you, soak them in hot Epsom salts. Take a couple of zinc tablets and some vitamin C.

Wednesday, December 27 (Moon in Pisces to Aries 12:05 a.m.) You're looking for last-minute tax breaks. Your accountant comes up with one that may save you a healthy chunk of change.

Thursday, December 28 (Moon in Aries) Your wishes and dreams are highlighted today. Perhaps you received something for Christmas that you can use to achieve these dreams.

Friday, December 29 (Moon in Aries to Taurus 3:09 a.m.) Get your resolutions written down. Make sure they are resolutions that you can live with.

Saturday, December 30 (Moon in Taurus) Go off by yourself today for reflection and solitude. Sometimes, bliss can be nothing more than a walk through a winter wonderland.

Sunday, December 31 (Moon in Taurus to Gemini 6:17 a.m.) It's a perfect way to end a year, with the moon going into your sign. You know the drill on this one, Gemini. Now just make all that potential come to fruition.

HAPPY NEW YEAR!

Monday, January 1 (Moon in Gemini)   Lucky you! You're beginning the year with the moon in your sign. Your self-confidence and sex appeal are at their peak; everyone around you notices. You may launch a new idea or project.

Tuesday, January 2 (Moon in Gemini to Cancer 10:15 a.m.)   Back to the reality of ordinary life after the holidays. The moon has moved into your solar second house of money. What makes you feel most secure emotionally, Gemini? What do you value most? These are the day's questions.

Wednesday, January 3 (Moon in Cancer)   Venus moves into Aquarius and your solar ninth house, a beautiful transit for romance abroad. If you happen to be on your own turf, romance could be with a foreign-born person or someone you meet through a workshop, seminar, or class. If you're a writer trying to get published, this transit helps things move forward.

Thursday, January 4 (Moon in Cancer to Leo 4:15 p.m.)   The Leo moon puts you in the limelight. It may not be where you usually like to be, but you enjoy it. Your neighbors and relatives all seem to want your attention. Is there enough of you to go around?

Friday, January 5 (Moon in Leo)   You communicate concisely and well; just about everything you say is well received by the people around you. They don't have to ask themselves which Gemini twin is talking; they know. Start keeping a journal, Gemini. You need that outlet.

Saturday, January 6 (Moon in Leo)   You get involved in beautifying your neighborhood. People think you're the person to lead the project, and although you're tempted to rise to the occasion, you had better think twice. Tomorrow you'll realize you don't have the time to spare.

Sunday, January 7 (Moon in Leo to Virgo 1:19 a.m.) Home demands your attention. Whether it's housecleaning or tending to someone who isn't feeling well, you are in charge. You may want to paint several rooms.

Monday, January 8 (Moon in Virgo) Your attention to details serves you well. By noticing ways in which you can perform more efficiently at work, you free up more time at home. Your children or perhaps your mom need some emotional bolstering.

Tuesday, January 9 (Moon in Virgo to Libra 1:15 p.m.) A bit of tact and diplomacy will take you a very long way. Since you have romance on your mind, be as cooperative as possible without compromising yourself. Your creative adrenaline is flowing. Make good use of it!

Wednesday, January 10 (Moon in Libra) Your artistic, literary, or musical endeavors are heightened. Even if you think you don't have talent in any of these areas, experiment with one or all of them. You'll surprise yourself!

Thursday, January 11 (Moon in Libra) You're able to access the source of your creative inspiration. To do so, you must put your left brain on hold and allow your intuition to speak.

Friday, January 12 (Moon in Libra to Scorpio 2:08 a.m.) You dig for something—information, illumination, you aren't sure exactly what it is. But you'll recognize it when you find it. Call on your network of friends and acquaintances. Doing so may prove helpful.

Saturday, January 13 (Moon in Scorpio) Your emotions are intense and vivid, like bold dabs of color on an otherwise blank canvas. A situation that gets you riled up may involve a coworker. Take a few deep breaths and step back from the situation. Deal with it tomorrow afternoon.

Sunday, January 14 (Moon in Scorpio to Sagittarius 1:12 p.m.)   The moon joins Jupiter and Pluto in your seventh house, boosting your optimism about a relationship. You feel the big picture, and you are secure enough to act on what you know.

Monday, January 15 (Moon in Sagittarius)   Mercury moves into Aquarius, joining Neptune and Venus in your ninth house. Pack your bags, Gemini, and head overseas. If you can't spare the time or the money, at least sign up for a class or workshop to learn about something that fascinates you.

Tuesday, January 16 (Moon in Sagittarius to Capricorn 8:50 p.m.)   Mars moves into Capricorn and your eighth house. This may be a tricky transit because it energizes taxes, insurance, inheritances, and wills. The eighth house is also about metaphysics. Channel the energy into psychic development!

Wednesday, January 17 (Moon in Capricorn)   With the moon joining Mars in Capricorn in your eighth house, focus on cosmic questions. Why are you here? What happens after death? Have you had past lives? These questions prompt you to buy books on these topics or to take a workshop dealing with metaphysics.

Thursday, January 18 (Moon in Capricorn)   Unless you have a natal Capricorn moon or a natal rising in Capricorn, this lunar transit can feel uncomfortable. It urges you to plan and strategize, to become more grounded and efficient.

Friday, January 19 (Moon in Capricorn to Aquarius 1:16 a.m.)   Finally, a moon that feels almost like home. You seek your personal mythology, the experiences and beliefs that make you unique, but which also tie you to something larger than yourself. A Virgo may prove helpful.

Saturday, January 20 (Moon in Aquarius) In search of the truth, you can't be distracted by petty concerns. But the truth is slippery and may lie in the minute details you would rather avoid. You get help from a woman who shares your interests and dedication.

Sunday, January 21 (Moon in Aquarius to Pisces 3:49 a.m.) Even though it's Sunday, career concerns take center stage. You may have to work several hours to get things on track for tomorrow. It could cause some friction at home but you're able to deal.

Monday, January 22 (Moon in Pisces) Your presentation or project goes well. You get help from a secretive Scorpio who knows the score. You could feel somewhat torn between professional and domestic obligations. Try to go with the flow, Gemini. You're good at that.

Tuesday, January 23 (Moon in Pisces to Aries 5:53 a.m.) There are places in your heart no one knows about. Sometimes, these places mystify even you! By next month, however, you'll have a better handle on what's what in terms of certain friendships. You'll know how to proceed.

Wednesday, January 24 (Moon in Aries) You get together with friends this evening for some mutual support and an exchange of ideas. You're the consummate communicator when it comes to instilling enthusiasm in others, and you'll do it well!

Thursday, January 25 (Moon in Aries to Taurus 8:29 a.m.) Feeling a bit more stubborn than usual? That's

252

good. The Taurus moon helps you ground your feelings and opinions and to stick to what you know is true.

Friday, January 26 (Moon in Taurus) You could feel the need for some solitude. There's a stack of books on your nightstand waiting for you to read them. If you don't have anything to read, watch a movie you've been meaning to see. Or maybe just catch up with all those taped episodes of your favorite show you haven't had time to watch.

Saturday, January 27 (Moon in Taurus to Gemini 12:10 p.m.) Venus moves into Pisces and your solar tenth house. This transit is sure to boost your professional standing in some way. It could also bring about a romance with a peer or boss. Be careful, Gemini! Don't commit to something that doesn't meet your standards. The moon moves into your sign!

Sunday, January 28 (Moon in Gemini) With the moon in your sign, you're eager to get out and socialize. Bookstores and cafés are at the top of your list. Update your e-mail address book, tidy your home office!

Monday, January 29 (Moon in Gemini to Cancer 5:17 p.m.) Balance your checkbook before you make a major purchase. If you're financially solvent this month, buy the item. Otherwise, delay your gratification until February.

Tuesday, January 30 (Moon in Cancer) Your mother or your own nurturing instincts play a role. It's possible that you've strayed a bit far from supporting someone who needs you. Your intuition is surprisingly strong. Listen to it!

Wednesday, January 31 (Moon in Cancer) The month ends on a positive note. Your nostalgia for some element in your past surfaces. You finally grasp the reason why this event or person makes you feel the way you do. This is progress, Gemini!

Thursday, February 1 (Moon in Cancer to Leo 12:15 a.m.) You can relate to this moon, Gemini. It galvanizes your natural communication abilities and triggers activity with neighbors and siblings. Your brother or sister may drop by for a surprise visit.

Friday, February 2 (Moon in Leo) Mercury joins Venus in Pisces in your solar tenth house. Your mind becomes more attuned to what is unspoken, sensed, intuited. This transit could trigger travel related to your profession. If you're a writer, it's a fine transit for entering the flow of language and letting it pour out of you.

Saturday, February 3 (Moon in Leo to Virgo 9:34 a.m.) You're a regular busy bee, tending to family details, running errands, taking care of unfinished business. You've procrastinated the last few weeks; now you'll pay the price!

Sunday, February 4 (Moon in Virgo) You're in the mood to rearrange furniture, paint rooms, and generally spiff up your house. What colors should you use? Which rooms need the most work? Try not to spend so much time getting ready that the actual work is put off until next weekend.

Monday, February 5 (Moon in Virgo to Libra 9:15 p.m.) With Venus still in your solar tenth house, things with work should be smoother. A romance could be budding between you and a peer. And with the moon in the house of romance, one of you might make a move.

Tuesday, February 6 (Moon in Libra) One of your children may need more balance. Pay attention to what the child isn't saying. Your creative adrenaline is pumping hard and furious; you're on a roll. Take advantage of it!

Wednesday, February 7 (Moon in Libra)   These Libra moon days are reminders that you need to have fun. So do what brings you pleasure, Gemini. Treat yourself to something that will make you smile.

Thursday, February 8 (Moon in Libra to Scorpio 10:10 a.m.)   The Scorpio moon is likely to make you feel emotional or more secretive than you usually are. Emotions could center around an event or a person at work or perhaps a situation that you've ignored. Deal with whatever it is on Monday, when the moon will be in a more compatible sign.

Friday, February 9 (Moon in Scorpio)   Detach and wait. That's the best way to navigate a situation. If you try to push your way through, you may get mired. And that can mean only trouble!

Saturday, February 10 (Moon in Scorpio to Sagittarius 10:02 p.m.)   This evening, you feel as if a weight has been lifted. And it has! The moon has moved into Sagittarius, a gregarious and optimistic sign that certainly boosts your morale and your social life.

Sunday, February 11 (Moon in Sagittarius)   You can see the forest instead of just the trees. And the forest is a certain relationship that may need some attention. Is it worth your time? That's the decision you have to make.

Monday, February 12 (Moon in Sagittarius)   Finish up your travel plans, your projects, and whatever else has been brewing. Tomorrow, Mercury turns retrograde in Pisces and your solar tenth house. On other fronts, things at home may be a bit tense. Iron out whatever the core issues are.

Tuesday, February 13 (Moon in Sagittarius to Capricorn 6:43 a.m.)   Mercury turns retrograde in Pisces. Generally, this means to be clear and concise about everything you say, especially as it pertains to your professional life. During this period, which lasts until March 7, you may be revisiting projects you thought were completed.

Wednesday, February 14 (Moon in Capricorn)   Happy Valentine's Day! Be sure to do something that shows your appreciation for the special people in your life. Other people are willing to share their resources with you, so you should do the same.

Thursday, February 15 (Moon in Capricorn to Aquarius 11:36 a.m.)   You're quite the intellectual, able to engage in highbrow discussions about literature, foreign cultures, politics, even mythology. It's as if your smattering of knowledge about many things deepens and expands.

Friday, February 16 (Moon in Aquarius)   Your solar ninth house is pretty crowded with the moon, Mercury, and Neptune all in Aquarius. This energy provides the needed impetus to detach emotionally and live entirely in your head. Enjoy it while it lasts, Gemini!

Saturday, February 17 (Moon in Aquarius to Pisces 1:31 p.m.)   As the moon joins Mercury retrograde in your solar tenth house, you may feel somewhat discombobulated. Your emotions color your conscious actions and thoughts. Your intuition probably sings loudly enough for you to hear it.

Sunday, February 18 (Moon in Pisces)   It could be a dreamy day for you. You long for a peaceful field somewhere far removed from the rat race. Chances are that, even if you find that peaceful field, you'll be happy with it for about five minutes. Then you'll rush back to your life, eager to be on the inside track again.

Monday, February 19 (Moon in Pisces to Aries 2:07 p.m.)   This moon energizes your naturally affable nature. You're ready to party with like-minded friends. Your goals and dreams could be in flux, as you examine where you are and where you would like to be in a year.

Tuesday, February 20 (Moon in Aries)   If you come up against opposition, don't blurt out the first thing that pops into your head because you may regret it. Instead, mull over what the other person said and intuitively test it against what you really feel.

Wednesday, February 21 (Moon in Aries to Taurus 3:04 p.m.)   Venus moves into Aries, a beautiful transit for meeting new friends and for romance with someone who has been a friend. The shuffling of your goals and dreams becomes easier, softer, less urgent.

Thursday, February 22 (Moon in Taurus)   Prepare for when the moon moves into your sign tomorrow. You need to replenish your inner resources and gather your strength so you're rested and alert by Friday afternoon. Choose a good book for the evening. Or chill the way that suits you best.

Friday, February 23 (Moon in Taurus to Gemini 5:42 p.m.)   When the moon moves into your sign this afternoon, you feel a sudden lightness. Since it's the beginning of the weekend, get out with your significant other and have some fun!

Saturday, February 24 (Moon in Gemini)   With Venus in fiery Aries and the moon in your sign, this should be a terrific day. Your passions run high, and you have more interactions than usual with friends. A special someone has caught your eye. The big question is who will make the first move.

Sunday, February 25 (Moon in Gemini to Cancer 10:48 p.m.)   Mars moves into Aquarius, joining Neptune in

257

your solar ninth house. This combination triggers your high ideals and urges you to put them into action. You may join a political or spiritual group that is working for change.

Monday, February 26 (Moon in Cancer)   Tackle questions and issues about emotional security. You may have to deal with a person who brings these issues to light. Allow your intuition to guide you in how to deal with this individual.

Tuesday, February 27 (Moon in Cancer)   Resist feeling stingy. Prosperity begins in your deepest beliefs. Rather than withhold money, dig within to find the root belief that causes you to feel you don't have enough.

Wednesday, February 28 (Moon in Cancer to Leo 6:30 a.m.)   With the transiting moon forming a beautiful angle to Venus, romance is at the top of your list. It's possible that a neighbor or friend suddenly becomes something more.

MARCH 2007

Thursday, March 1 (Moon in Leo)   You can taste spring in the air, and just that taste is enough to lift your spirits. Your high energy and optimism are focused on your community. You could be instrumental in beautifying your neighborhood in some way.

Friday, March 2 (Moon in Leo to Virgo 4:32 p.m.) You may feel picky and critical. If so, keep your criticisms to yourself. Turn this lunar energy toward attention to details in your daily work routine.

Saturday, March 3 (Moon in Virgo)   The lunar eclipse in Virgo could bring up an emotional issue related to your daily work routine or to your health. The best way to use this eclipse energy is to start a regular exercise program if you don't have one already.

Sunday, March 4 (Moon in Virgo)   You're fixing up your home office. It may be something as simple as tidying up files or something as complex as painting walls or putting down a new floor. Prepare the way for the moon in your sign on March 23.

Monday, March 5 (Moon in Virgo to Libra 4:26 a.m.)
Focus on contracts and contractual obligations. Cooperation moves you closer to your goal. Don't be so accommodating that you bend over backward to please the other person. And do not sign on the dotted line until after Mercury turns on March 7.

Tuesday, March 6 (Moon in Libra)   If you feel emotionally vulnerable, deal with it. Understand that, by tomorrow, the feeling will be nothing more than a memory. Do something special for the one you love.

Wednesday, March 7 (Moon in Libra to Scorpio 5:18 p.m.)   Mercury turns direct, and you feel an immediate sense of relief. Finally, you're on track again. You have resolved old issues, and you are ready to move forward.

Thursday, March 8 (Moon in Scorpio)   Feeling a bit intense, Gemini? Then apply a few visualization techniques to turn down the emotional barometer. Or spend a few minutes meditating during the day.

Friday, March 9 (Moon in Scorpio)   If you feel a strangeness in the air, use your intuition to guide you toward greater fulfillment. Your psychic antenna is twitching constantly.

Saturday, March 10 (Moon in Scorpio to Sagittarius 5:38 a.m.)   The moon joins Jupiter and Pluto in Sagittarius in your seventh house. This trio is sure to put some pressure on your romantic and professional partnerships. The pressure is positive, and you and your partner reach a mutually satisfying agreement about some issue that has troubled you.

Sunday, March 11—Daylight Saving Time Begins (Moon in Sagittarius)   You have the big picture concerning a relationship. If you don't like this picture, do something to change it. Back up your ideas with action.

Monday, March 12 (Moon in Sagittarius to Capricorn 3:35 p.m.)   You discover a way to incorporate your interest in metaphysics into your career or professional life. It may not be the easiest thing to do, but that doesn't worry you. Your plan is sound, your strategy excellent.

Tuesday, March 13 (Moon in Capricorn)   You're emotionally grounded, so it's easy to deal with an irritating issue concerning taxes or insurance. Be sure your mortgage and other payments are up-to-date.

Wednesday, March 14 (Moon in Capricorn to Aquarius 10:53 p.m.)   It's not enough to keep your worldview or political views to yourself. Act on them, defend them if necessary. Your verbal skills are strong; your opponent doesn't stand a chance!

Thursday, March 15 (Moon in Aquarius)   Your booster rocket is your spirituality. Sounds odd, but your spiritual foundations get you through a trying situation. Could it be jury duty or dealings with a lawyer or an educator?

Friday, March 16 (Moon in Aquarius)   If you're traveling overseas, expect a pleasant day. You track down some odd myth or story that you can use in your writing or to expand your worldview. Your partner is interested in and supportive of your search.

Saturday, March 17 (Moon in Aquarius to Pisces 1:31 a.m)   Venus moves into Taurus. This transit, which lasts until April 11, could attract a secretive romance. It won't be secretive once Venus moves into your sign. You excel at any work done behind the scenes.

Sunday, March 18 (Moon in Pisces) The moon joins Uranus in Pisces in your solar tenth house. Your emotional reactions to professional issues are unusual, so you see situations and relationships from a new perspective.

Monday, March 19 (Moon in Pisces to Aries 1:42 a.m.) You feel sexy and charismatic; and other people notice. In fact, a special someone may make a move. Are you ready for pure enjoyment, Gemini?

Tuesday, March 20 (Moon in Aries) You and some friends head out for a day of adventure. You may attend a book or film festival in another town or drive into the mountains or to the ocean for relaxation and fun. Strengthen your network of acquaintances and the bonds of friendship.

Wednesday, March 21 (Moon in Aries to Taurus 1:16 a.m.) You obstinately refuse to change your mind about something. Doing so annoys the people around you, but so what? You aren't in a cooperative mood. You feel as if you're being coerced.

Thursday, March 22 (Moon in Taurus) Take up meditation. If you don't think you can sit for a prolonged period trying to blank your mind, start walking each day. Make the walk itself your meditation.

Friday, March 23 (Moon in Taurus to Gemini 2:07 a.m.) With the moon in your sign, Mars in friendly Aquarius, and Jupiter in compatible Sagittarius, the stars are stacked in your favor. How will you use all this favorable energy? Maybe it's time to pull out that manuscript you were working on and get back to writing.

Saturday, March 24 (Moon in Gemini)   You're filled with positive energy; there's just no stopping you. Regardless of what you pursue, do it with typical Gemini vigor and enthusiasm.

Sunday, March 25 (Moon in Gemini to Cancer 5:49 a.m.) Protect what you have. It's not as if you're surrounded by enemies or in danger. Take a deeper look at why you feel this way.

Monday, March 26 (Moon in Cancer)   Yesterday's introspection leads to enlightenment. Your feelings about protecting what you have may date back to events in your early childhood. Release that childhood belief. Your point of power lies in the present.

Tuesday, March 27 (Moon in Cancer to Leo 1:05 p.m.)   The moon joins Saturn in Leo in your third house. You may feel restrained or restricted. The truth is that you have placed these restrictions on yourself. Find out why.

Wednesday, March 28 (Moon in Leo)   You're moving ahead on your screenplay or book. You seem to have found the perfect structure for it. All you have to do is race to the finish. Rewrite during the next Mercury retrograde.

Thursday, March 29 (Moon in Leo to Virgo 11:28 p.m.)   Late tonight, the moon moves into Virgo. This may not be your favorite moon. Learn to use its energies wisely. Set an agenda for tomorrow, and tend to details you've put off.

Friday, March 30 (Moon in Virgo)   Your agenda works! You can leave work this afternoon with a clean slate for Monday. Enjoy the weekend!

Saturday, March 31 (Moon in Virgo)   You could feel the residue of the lunar eclipse in Virgo earlier this month. Some emotional issue surfaces that concerns a coworker or an employee. Roll with the punches, Gemini. Tomorrow will be a better day!

APRIL 2007

Sunday, April 1 (Moon in Virgo to Libra 11:45 a.m.) Lounge around with your partner or a group of friends. You may have to mediate a dispute or disagreement; you're up to the challenge.

Monday, April 2 (Moon in Libra)   To move forward step by step isn't your thing. You would rather fly between two points than get there by taking baby steps. Use a combination of both to succeed.

Tuesday, April 3 (Moon in Libra)   As the moon makes its transition from Libra to Scorpio, your best bet is to sleep! This way you can draw on the energies of this intensely emotional and intuitive sign in the dream state.

Wednesday, April 4 (Moon in Libra to Scorpio 12:37 a.m.)   You're downright psychic. You seem to be so deep in the flow of events that you're able to predict something for yourself or someone else. Synchronicities abound. Pay attention!

Thursday, April 5 (Moon in Scorpio)   Jupiter turns retrograde in Sagittarius and your seventh house. Its expansive energy won't work smoothly, so you could experience a few bumps in your personal and professional partnerships until August 6, when Jupiter turns direct. Don't obsess about it. You have good things going on.

Friday, April 6 (Moon in Scorpio to Sagittarius 12:57 a.m.)   Mars joins Uranus in Pisces and your tenth house.

This may feel like an itch you can't scratch. But it's sure to attract unusual people and opportunities. A lot of your energy until May 15 is poured into your career.

Saturday, April 7 (Moon in Sagittarius)   This transit is excellent for publishing ventures and anything to do with higher education. You may decide to enroll in a class to upgrade your skills or simply because the topic interests you.

Sunday, April 8 (Moon in Sagittarius to Capricorn 11:36 p.m.)   Feel a bit frustrated, Gemini? Don't fret. It's all that earthy energy of the Capricorn moon trying to dampen your spirits. Use this energy to ground and orient yourself rather than resist what it's telling you.

Monday, April 9 (Moon in Capricorn)   With tax day creeping up so quickly, be sure your tax papers are in order. While you're at it, get a reality check on your insurance policies and your will as well. An older person has words of wisdom for you.

Tuesday, April 10 (Moon in Capricorn)   Mercury moves into Aries. For the next seventeen days, you'll be a regular social butterfly. A party? You'll be there. A café gathering for your writing group? You're there. After-school drama auditions? You're first in line.

Wednesday, April 11 (Moon in Capricorn to Aquarius 7:23 a.m.) Venus moves into your sign, and you pull out all the stops. Expect romance, good fortune in the arts, and ease with friends. It rarely gets much better than this. Other people take notice.

Thursday, April 12 (Moon in Aquarius)   Dig around in your belief system. You could start doing this by writing down what you think your beliefs are and playing around with them. Which beliefs are really yours and which ones have you accepted from parents, school, and friends?

Friday, April 13 (Moon in Aquarius to Pisces 11:39 a.m.) As you get into your professional mode this morning, your intuition speaks loud and clear. Listen. Doing so will save you heartache.

Saturday, April 14 (Moon in Pisces) Haven't you finished your taxes yet? Get your forms ready to mail on Monday. Be sure you have taken every deduction allowed under the law. If you owe a substantial amount, cut back for the next few months.

Sunday, April 15 (Moon in Pisces to Aries 12:47 p.m.) You're in an active frame of mind; you may head out for an early-morning jog or even a swim. A gathering with friends is in order. They may meet at your place, Gemini, so be ready.

Monday, April 16 (Moon in Aries) Your passions increase tenfold. You want results yesterday, which can make you careless. Slow down. Pace yourself. You'll be happy you did.

Tuesday, April 17 (Moon in Aries to Taurus 12:12 p.m.) You're consumed by a particular project or issue. A little obsession is probably a good thing as long as you don't go to extremes.

Wednesday, April 18 (Moon in Taurus) You're a flexible person who adapts well to change, but you may be stubborn about an important issue. It's not blind stubbornness; you simply know you're right.

Thursday, April 19 (Moon in Taurus to Gemini 11:52 a.m.) Saturn turns direct in Leo and your solar third house. This is positive news for your communications skills and for your relationships with neighbors and siblings. Saturn brings a structure to your writing.

Friday, April 20 (Moon in Gemini) The moon is finally in your sign. You soar, your sex appeal is high, and the possibilities of romance are excellent. Do whatever brings you pleasure. Work on your book, screenplay, or creative project.

Saturday, April 21 (Moon in Gemini to Cancer 1:51 p.m.) You usually feel a bit blue when the moon leaves your sign and moves into Cancer. You shouldn't. Each lunar transit has its purpose in our lives; the Cancer moon asks that you place your home and family above all else.

Sunday, April 22 (Moon in Cancer) If you want to trace your genealogical roots, start on the Internet. You might also talk to your parents or grandparents. You may be surprised by what they have to say.

Monday, April 23 (Moon in Cancer to Leo 7:39 p.m.) The moon joins Saturn in Leo. You find the perfect structure for a project. Saturn helps bring your ideas into line; the moon provides you with the intuitive certainty you need.

Tuesday, April 24 (Moon in Leo) How far can you take your optimism? Surprise yourself. Find out what happens to your personal world when you pass on the goodwill others show you. Change begins with just one person.

Wednesday, April 25 (Moon in Leo) A neighbor who has had an ax to grind may lay aside hostilities. Or perhaps you've had a rough and bumpy road with a brother or sister, and you mend fences. Think clichés, Gemini. Play it safe!

Thursday, April 26 (Moon in Leo to Virgo 5:25 a.m.)　Even though the moon moves into a sign that forms a challenging angle with your sun, you still have Venus in Gemini on your side. Venus is where you should put your energies. Think romance. Think prosperity. Manifest what you desire.

Friday, April 27 (Moon in Virgo)　Mercury moves into Taurus and your solar twelfth house. Think privacy. Work behind the scenes. If you're a writer, finish up a book, screenplay, memos, or projects. You're mentally stubborn, and that's exactly what you need.

Saturday, April 28 (Moon in Virgo to Libra 5:46 p.m.)　Breathe easy, Gemini. You and the Libra moon get along just fine. You're sociable and willing to listen to others; you can delve into your creative projects with complete ease.

Sunday, April 29 (Moon in Libra)　Your creativity takes center stage. Your muse cheers you on, and everyone around you cooperates to make the process easy. You'll be pleased with the outcome.

Monday, April 30 (Moon in Libra)　If you try to please everyone, you lose. Reserve a little something for yourself; try to please only one or two people. Use the energies of this lunar transit to focus on world peace.

MAY 2007

Tuesday, May 1 (Moon in Libra to Scorpio 6:42 a.m.)　Here's that intense Scorpio moon. The best way to deal with these passionate energies is to focus on psychic and intuitive elements. Design an intuitive test for yourself. Teach yourself how to see auras. You know the drill, Gemini.

Wednesday, May 2 (Moon in Scorpio)   Worn out by the passionate Scorpio moon? Chill out with a good book. If reading sounds too taxing, catch up on the latest movies or TV. Or get out and enjoy the spring weather.

Thursday, May 3 (Moon in Scorpio to Sagittarius 6:48 p.m.)   You suddenly have the itch to travel or to study something new. If you travel, an exotic destination should cure your restlessness. Travel before June 15, when Mercury turns retrograde, or after July 9, when it turns direct.

Friday, May 4 (Moon in Sagittarius)   The moon opposed to your sun can be challenging, but you know how to maximize this energy. Further your studies and knowledge. Remain upbeat and optimistic, and let this fire moon act as your booster rocket.

Saturday, May 5 (Moon in Sagittarius)   Whenever the moon joins Pluto in your seventh house, sparks fly. You can be in the dumps one moment and in the clouds the next. Power issues may surface with a partner.

Sunday, May 6 (Moon in Sagittarius to Capricorn 5:21 a.m.)   Mars, Pisces, and the moon in Capricorn seem to be shaking hands across the heavens. This is excellent news, Gemini. Your intuition is grounded and efficient. You're able to plan, strategize, and make things happen.

Monday, May 7 (Moon in Capricorn)   If you feel like running away, get off by yourself to think things over. Uncover the reasons you feel the way you do. Be honest. What you discover may surprise you.

Tuesday, May 8 (Moon in Capricorn to Aquarius 1:48 p.m.)   Venus moves into Cancer, and until June 5, you should be in good financial shape. Checks finally arrive. Your love life may pick up, in strange ways.

Wednesday, May 9 (Moon in Aquarius)   Your concern extends to those less fortunate than you and to stray animals. What can you do to help? Maybe you can satisfy your social conscience by contributing money to charity and by volunteering at an animal shelter.

Thursday, May 10 (Moon in Aquarius to Pisces 7:32 p.m.)   Divination is in order. It can be anything—astrology, runes, or tarot cards. If you're in the right frame of mind, you probably can glean information from grains of sand. The point is that you're searching for guidance.

Friday, May 11 (Moon in Pisces)   Batten down the hatches. Your ruler moves into your sign. Everything that is Gemini surges to the surface of your life. Until May 28, you're on the go constantly. There are so many people to see, so many books to read, so many plays and movies to watch.

Saturday, May 12 (Moon in Pisces to Aries 10:20 p.m.)   With the moon in Aries and Venus in your own sign, you are one hot ticket. No telling how this day will pan out, but it will be memorable—that's for sure!

Sunday, May 13 (Moon in Aries)   In case you find yourself with free time, check in with your family to make sure everyone is well and that life is good. While you're at it, make a reality check. Are your friendships where you want them to be?

Monday, May 14 (Moon in Aries to Taurus 10:50 p.m.) Are we becoming—or have we already become—a nation of sleepwalkers? Are we so caught up in the frantic pace of our lives that we overlook the obvious? Even you may have trouble processing what you experience. Slow down. Reflect.

Tuesday, May 15 (Moon in Taurus)   Mars moves into Aries, creating quite an action-packed lineup for you. Romance, friends, networks, partnerships, profound change—they're all on the table. Where do you begin?

Wednesday, May 16 (Moon in Taurus to Gemini 10:35 p.m.)   Tonight, the moon moves into your sign, adding to the terrific lineup of planets that favor you and your endeavors. Pace yourself. You may be tempted to overcommit, thus scattering your energy.

Thursday, May 17 (Moon in Gemini)   Checks aren't just in the mail. They're in your mailbox. Your love life is picking up, several people vie for your attention. It's a nice place to be, isn't it, Gemini?

Friday, May 18 (Moon in Gemini to Cancer 11:39 p.m.)   Late tonight, the moon joins Venus in Cancer. This energy certainly energizes your finances. Postpone the purchase of large-ticket items until Venus has left your second house because Venus can make you extravagant!

Saturday, May 19 (Moon in Cancer)   Shopping, anyone? Hit the bargain stores, Gemini. At the end of the day, you'll be glad you did. On other fronts, your mother or another nurturing female in your life has some words of wisdom you should heed.

Sunday, May 20 (Moon in Cancer)   The moon and Venus team up to bring you an attractive financial or investment opportunity. Make your decision about this before Mercury turns retrograde on June 15. Overall, it's a pleasant day to putter around your house, perhaps doing some touch-up painting or beautifying your yard.

Monday, May 21 (Moon in Cancer to Leo 3:57 a.m.)   The moon joins Saturn in Leo in your third house. Some of your relationships with neighbors could feel strained. Try not to alienate anyone. The strains will pass of their own accord.

Tuesday, May 22 (Moon in Leo)   Sometimes it is difficult to shine in your own backyard, Gemini, but you do it. You become involved in a community project that places you in front of the public.

Wednesday, May 23 (Moon in Leo to Virgo 12:27 p.m.)   Home is your focus. Some issue or concern connected with your family needs your attention. If you're setting up a home-based business, tend to small details, and make sure everything is in order.

Thursday, May 24 (Moon in Virgo)   Neptune turns retrograde in Aquarius and your ninth house. The effects of this movement, which lasts until Halloween, will be subtle. You may be somewhat confused about your worldview or spiritual beliefs. In puzzling through your confusion, you come out the other side with great clarity.

Friday, May 25 (Moon in Virgo)   Late this evening, the moon shifts into a sign compatible with yours. This transit, which lasts for the next two days, enhances your creative abilities, your love life, and whatever you do for pleasure.

Saturday, May 26 (Moon in Virgo to Libra 12:17 a.m.)   You're on fire, eager to get started on a home-improvement project. The improvement part of the equation is questionable; what you're really after is an enhanced aesthetic quality to your home. Time to practice some feng shui?

Sunday, May 27 (Moon in Libra)   Yesterday's home beautification project has been replaced by a drive for creative excellence. One of your children needs your attention and support—perhaps with creative endeavors.

Monday, May 28 (Moon in Libra to Scorpio 12:12 p.m.) Mercury joins Venus in Cancer in your second house. Your thoughts turn to what you value most. In some way, this issue becomes clear for you over the next few weeks.

Tuesday, May 29 (Moon in Scorpio) The moon and Venus form a harmonious angle to each other. This combination facilitates your psychic development. You're digging for a bottom line in terms of work, and by the day's end, you find it!

Wednesday, May 30 (Moon in Scorpio) The detective in you is eager and persistent to uncover some bit of information you need. It could involve a colleague or employee. Your passion is running high, so make time for your partner this evening.

Thursday, May 31 (Moon in Scorpio to Sagittarius 1:07 a.m.) It's a relief to leave the Scorpio moon behind. All that intense emotion has left you exhausted. By tomorrow, you'll be in a much better state of mind.

JUNE 2007

Friday, June 1 (Moon in Sagittarius) Even though the Sagittarius moon is opposed to your sun sign, its fire and your air elements mix well. Besides, it's hard to resist the gregarious nature of this lunar transit. Get out there and have some fun, Gemini!

Saturday, June 2 (Moon in Sagittarius to Capricorn 11:10 a.m.) You may come up against resistance related to taxes or insurance. An adjustment is required in your attitude or actions. Just do what's required, don't fight the flow of events.

Sunday, June 3 (Moon in Capricorn)　　The moon and Venus form a harmonious angle to each other. Any romance that begins under this combination would be intuitive, yet grounded. Explore all the possibilities that come your way, but don't make a decision yet.

Monday, June 4 (Moon in Capricorn to Aquarius 7:16 p.m.)　　Break your routine and head out for parts unknown. The journey doesn't have to be distant. You are simply too restless to stick to what is tried and true.

Tuesday, June 5 (Moon in Aquarius)　　Venus moves into Leo and your solar third house. This transit, favorable for you, could spur a romance with a neighbor or a friend. It puts you in the spotlight and enhances your sex appeal.

Wednesday, June 6 (Moon in Aquarius)　　You get together with your support group this evening and plan a trip to some exotic locale. Be sure that your travel plans fall before June 15 and after July 9, the Mercury retrograde period.

Thursday, June 7 (Moon in Aquarius to Pisces 1:25 a.m.)　　The moon meets up with Uranus in Pisces again, bringing a surprise twist to the plot of your professional life. This little surprise involves a peer who has been watching you for some time, perhaps with a touch of envy!

Friday, June 8 (Moon in Pisces)　　Synchronicities have you puzzling over the hidden order of things. Think of these synchronicities as signs that direct you on your path toward a particular professional or personal goal.

Saturday, June 9 (Moon in Pisces to Aries 5:27 a.m.)　　You always feel more gregarious and bold when the moon is in Aries. It brings out the daring and courageous part of you that loves risk. That character trait attracts someone special.

Sunday, June 10 (Moon in Aries)   Drama, drama, drama! Some friendship issue is right in the center of activities. It generates a lot of attention from the people around you. You inadvertently feed into it when you offer your opinion.

Monday, June 11 (Moon in Aries to Taurus 7:30 a.m.)   A bit of stability and solitude is called for. Settle in with your partner and enjoy a sensuous and relaxing evening. Tonight, your dream recall should be good, so pose a question before you fall asleep and ask for an answer by dawn.

Tuesday, June 12 (Moon in Taurus)   If you feel stubborn, blame the Taurus moon. You refuse to budge on an important issue. You may not be right, but that's beside the point.

Wednesday, June 13 (Moon in Taurus to Gemini 8:24 a.m.)   Your relief is palpable. The moon is in your sign, and you're all over the place, doing your Gemini thing. Your body is revved up, raring to go. Be sure to include a period of exercise. You'll need it to center yourself.

Thursday, June 14 (Moon in Gemini)   Tomorrow, your ruler, Mercury, turns retrograde. Finish up projects, get manuscripts sent off. If you have to travel, try to be home before tomorrow or be prepared for unexpected changes in your schedule.

Friday, June 15 (Moon in Gemini to Cancer 9:46 a.m.) Mercury turns retrograde in your second house. Until July 9, checks may be delayed. Scrutinize bank and other financial accounts and bills for errors. Back up all your computer data.

Saturday, June 16 (Moon in Cancer)   The Cancer moon is tossed into the Mercury-retrograde muddle. Your emotions are triggered over an error you find on an insurance or tax statement. Take a couple deep breaths, back off, and wait until tomorrow to deal with it.

Sunday, June 17 (Moon in Cancer to Leo 1:25 p.m.)   It could be your lucky day. But it's not as if the luck just lands in your lap. You have to follow hunches and synchronicities, navigating your way through a strange landscape of inexplicable events or situations.

Monday, June 18 (Moon in Leo)   Since this moon is in your solar third house of communications, which includes books, sit down and finish whatever you're reading. If you're not reading anything, maybe you should pick up that novel you've always wanted to read.

Tuesday, June 19 (Moon in Leo to Virgo 8:46 p.m.)   You're protective of your family and home. If you think these concerns are tied to events in your childhood, talk to your mother or father. Then again, there may not be any deep, dark reason for the feelings.

Wednesday, June 20 (Moon in Virgo)   Time to tidy up the house; get everyone else to pitch in. Start that home-improvement or -beautification project before you go on vacation.

Thursday, June 21 (Moon in Virgo)   If necessary, hire a cleaning service to sweep through your house. You can afford it, Gemini, and the time you save can be put to better use. Besides, house cleaning isn't something you enjoy.

Friday, June 22 (Moon in Virgo to Libra 7:44 a.m.)   Indulge yourself in your creativity. Your muse is in attendance, whispering in your ear. You may have to convince family and friends to respect your creative time.

275

Saturday, June 23 (Moon in Libra)   Uranus turns retrograde in Pisces until November 24. The effects of this movement are subtle, but you may be rethinking your career goals. If you're romantically involved with a colleague or a boss, things may not go very smoothly for a while.

Sunday, June 24 (Moon in Libra to Scorpio 8:27 p.m.)   Mars moves into Taurus and your solar twelfth house. Until August 7, you may feel irritable. Work alone as much as possible. If you get involved romantically with someone, keep to yourselves.

Monday, June 25 (Moon in Scorpio)   With transiting Mars and the transiting moon opposing each other, today and tomorrow could be challenging for you. Events trigger emotional reactions that are completely out of whack for what happens.

Tuesday, June 26 (Moon in Scorpio)   You and a colleague may disagree on something. You simply can't let go of it. But you should. It isn't worth damaging the relationship over a minor difference in opinion.

Wednesday, June 27 (Moon in Scorpio to Sagittarius 8:25 a.m.)   Finally, a moon that agrees with you. As usual, the Sagittarius moon brings a buoyancy to daily life and allows you to see the larger picture of a relationship.

Thursday, June 28 (Moon in Sagittarius)   The moon and Saturn form a harmonious angle to each other, which benefits you, Gemini. You're able to incorporate your intuitive knowledge with your left-brain logic. A Leo or an Aries may be helpful.

Friday, June 29 (Moon in Sagittarius to Capricorn 6:06 p.m.)   Late this afternoon, you're called in to help an elderly relative or friend. This person may need aid with insurance or tax forms. If this area isn't your expertise, steer the individual toward people who can do what needs to be done.

Saturday, June 30 (Moon in Capricorn)   You could find yourself asking cosmic questions. Are we more than our physical bodies? What happens when we die? Do some research if you're really interested.

JULY 2007

Sunday, July 1 (Moon in Capricorn)   The summer is heating up. But with the moon in Capricorn, you're forced to be grounded and practical today. If you've been thinking of buying a home, don't apply for a mortgage until after Mercury turns direct on July 9.

Monday, July 2 (Moon in Capricorn to Aquarius 1:25 a.m.)   Escape from your routine. Create an adventure. Get out of town. Pretend you're being pursued by government agents who want information that only you possess. Use your imagination, Gemini!

Tuesday, July 3 (Moon in Aquarius)   Continuing with yesterday's journey, you're in a town you've never visited. You aren't sure which way to turn. But you find friends in unlikely places, and you are able to rest for the night.

Wednesday, July 4 (Moon in Aquarius to Pisces 6:53 a.m.) Happy Independence Day! Stop thinking about your career. It's not time for that, Gemini. Today is for family, friends, neighborhoods, celebrations. It's about understanding the Bill of Rights and what constitutes a democracy.

Thursday, July 5 (Moon in Pisces)   If you have the day off, indulge yourself by doing something that appeals to your artistic or intuitive senses. It could be something as simple as visiting an art museum or as complex as taking a workshop on intuitive development.

Friday, July 6 (Moon in Pisces to Aries 10:57 a.m.)
Good thing it's Friday! From midmorning forward, you'll
be restless. Whether you hang with friends this evening or
head to a class or a bookstore or seek out the company of
a special romantic partner, the day will be enjoyable.

Saturday, July 7 (Moon in Aries)   In two days, your
ruler, Mercury, will turn direct. You may be feeling a slight
difference in the air already, but don't pack your bags just
yet. If the weather is good, go hiking or canoeing or rafting.

*Sunday, July 8 (Moon in Aries to Taurus 1:54
p.m.)*   This afternoon, the moon joins Mars in Taurus in
your solar twelfth house. This combination of planets may
grate on you. Best to take the energy and head to the gym
or pour it into some other form of physical activity.

Monday, July 9 (Moon in Taurus)   Mercury turns direct. Checks you've expected start to arrive, and any financial hassles you've had straighten out. Put on your traveling
shoes and get out of town!

*Tuesday, July 10 (Moon in Taurus to Gemini 4:10
p.m.)*   By this afternoon, you're swinging from the trees!
The moon is in your sign, and you certainly need the energy
it brings. Gone is the angst of the past few weeks. You're
rushing ahead on a half dozen projects; your main dilemma
is deciding which is most important.

Wednesday, July 11 (Moon in Gemini)   You and your
partner steal away for an evening together. But your idea
of an evening together may not be a candlelight dinner; it's
probably the newest art film or a bookstore with a great
café. Be sure your partner has the same agenda.

*Thursday, July 12 (Moon in Gemini to Cancer 6:40
p.m.)*   As the moon joins Mercury in your solar second
house, your intuitive certainty about an investment or fi-

nancial opportunity may be at odds with what your left brain is telling you. Wait until the moon or Mercury moves out of Cancer before you decide.

Friday, July 13 (Moon in Cancer)   Putter around your house, fix what needs to be fixed, and generally tidy things up. You should enhance the prosperity area of your house through some feng shui techniques. If you work at home, determine which area of your office is your prosperity corner.

Saturday, July 14 (Moon in Cancer to Leo 10:44 p.m.)   Venus moves into Virgo and your solar fourth house. If you and your partner live together, this transit should spell smooth sailing. Your relationship with your family improves. You may feel compelled to beautify your home before this transit ends in November.

Sunday, July 15 (Moon in Leo)   Talk over that investment opportunity with a trusted friend or sibling, and make your decision. Still thinking about how much fun you had on the Fourth of July? Start planning for just as much pleasure over Labor Day weekend.

Monday, July 16 (Moon in Leo)   If you have an anniversary, be sure to do something special for and with your partner. Whether you've been together three months or thirty years, renew your commitment.

Tuesday, July 17 (Moon in Leo to Virgo 5:40 a.m.)   As the moon joins Venus in Virgo, you're in the mood for romance and nurturing. If you're not involved with anyone, this energy may manifest itself as good fortune in the arts or money. If you're going to buy a new appliance or some other expensive item, do it before Venus turns retrograde on July 27.

Wednesday, July 18 (Moon in Virgo)   If you can, work out of your house. After all, if you performed feng shui magic on your home office, the energy is excellent. You may have to shut the door to your office so you can maintain your privacy.

Thursday, July 19 (Moon in Virgo to Libra 3:54 p.m.)   It's a fine day for your creative projects. In fact, you won't be able to avoid being artistic. Your aesthetic senses are enhanced; you have the drive and will to follow your heart.

Friday, July 20 (Moon in Libra)   You may find yourself in the midst of a dispute. If so, appoint yourself the mediator. You'll be able to argue both sides. Your intervention won't be immediately appreciated, but by tomorrow, hard feelings on both sides will be gone.

Saturday, July 21 (Moon in Libra)   Balance is the toughest quality to find. You may need to ask for help, perhaps by assigning duties or tasks to the people around you, thus freeing your time for something else.

Sunday, July 22 (Moon in Libra to Scorpio 4:19 a.m.)   Information is power. So you're empowered because you simply won't relinquish your search for something you or someone else needs. You dig, research, and investigate.

Monday, July 23 (Moon in Scorpio)   Just think, Gemini. The intensity of your will and emotions can shatter obstacles. If there are things you don't like about your daily work environment, apply your powerful will to change them. Your point of power lies in the present.

Tuesday, July 24 (Moon in Scorpio to Sagittarius 4:31 p.m.)   Sign contracts. You have the larger picture of the issues involved; the Sagittarius moon fills you with optimism. Even though this moon is opposed to your sun, it lights up your seventh house of partnerships.

Wednesday, July 25 (Moon in Sagittarius)   The deeper truth you're looking for is spiritual. As a Gemini, you're seeking ways to incorporate that spirituality into your ordinary life and to teach it without being dogmatic. Obviously, this can't be done in a day. Commit to a long-term quest.

Thursday, July 26 (Moon in Sagittarius)   Set your course. Be clear about where you want to go. Then connect the dots between the two points and make it happen. This requires commitment and pure intention on your part. Are you up to the challenge?

Friday, July 27 (Moon in Sagittarius to Capricorn 2:23 a.m.)   Venus turns retrograde in Virgo, your solar fourth house. This doesn't mean that your love life, home life, or family life is going to hit the skids. It doesn't mean your marriage will unravel. You may be revisiting your concepts and feelings about relationships, the arts, and even your attitude toward money. The retrograde period lasts until September 8.

Saturday, July 28 (Moon in Capricorn)   You could be spending time with an elderly person who needs help and emotional support. Don't resist the flow of events. Try to remain emotionally detached.

Sunday, July 29 (Moon in Capricorn to Aquarius 9:14 a.m.)   The Aquarius moon suits you much better than earth-sign moons. It's all about mind, groups, and the individual's place within the universe. How you apply Aquarius principles will determine how you live.

Monday, July 30 (Moon in Aquarius)   What can you do for people who are less fortunate or stray animals? Do something that helps someone else. Volunteer your time or make a charitable contribution.

Tuesday, July 31 (Moon in Aquarius to Pisces 1:41 p.m.) As the moon changes signs, your career comes into play. Or you may have to deal with some aspect of authority. Deal with the person directly. In the end, that will get you past the situation much faster.

AUGUST 2007

Wednesday, August 1 (Moon in Pisces) Whenever the moon joins Uranus in your solar tenth house, your emotional reactions are unusual. A colleague or boss annoys you with unfair criticism. Keep your opinion to yourself. It's not worth arguing about.

Thursday, August 2 (Moon in Pisces to Aries 4:43 p.m.) As the moon moves into your solar eleventh house, you have several invitations from friends. Any publicity or public speaking you do is well-received. Promote yourself or your product.

Friday, August 3 (Moon in Aries) With Venus still moving retrograde in your solar fourth house and the moon in your eleventh, you're restless for change. Don't make any renovations to your home. Wait until after Venus turns direct on September 8.

Saturday, August 4 (Moon in Aries to Taurus 7:16 p.m.) Mercury moves into Leo, stimulating all of your communications abilities. If you're a writer, this transit should light a fire under you. Things really pick up in about four days, when Mars moves into your sign.

Sunday, August 5 (Moon in Taurus) With the moon in your solar twelfth house, you need time for solitude and reflection. Security issues may surface. You could worry about money or insurance coverage. Try not to fret and obsess. It's just the Taurus moon reminding you to pay attention to what makes you feel emotionally secure.

Monday, August 6 (Moon in Taurus to Gemini 10:02 p.m.)   Jupiter turns direct in Sagittarius and your solar ninth house. This movement should feel very good for you. Opportunities in publishing, education, and overseas travel surface until the end of the year.

Tuesday, August 7 (Moon in Gemini)   Mars moves into your sign, a booster rocket that impacts every area of your life. Your energy and sexuality are at a high. You feel as if you can do anything; you won't shy away from anything that comes your way. Be careful not to overcommit. Otherwise you'll find yourself in a time crunch.

Wednesday, August 8 (Moon in Gemini)   With the moon and Mars in your sign, you have a powerful combination at your fingertips. Mars may make you impatient. If you're in a hurry, you could be more accident-prone. Slow down!

Thursday, August 9 (Moon in Gemini to Cancer 1:37 a.m.)   The moon moves into your solar second house. This lunar transit compels you to bring your ideas down to earth, to be more practical and efficient. Anything you take on will be done with those attributes in mind.

Friday, August 10 (Moon in Cancer)   If there are minor issues surfacing at home, deal with them directly and immediately. You may have to slow down on your spending until checks arrive.

Saturday, August 11 (Moon in Cancer to Leo 6:42 a.m.)   The Leo moon may accelerate things, just as Mars in your sign does. Slow down; pace yourself. There's plenty of time to get things done.

Sunday, August 12 (Moon in Leo)   You have plenty of star power. Finish your novel or screenplay, complete any communications projects. Your partnerships are humming right along now that Jupiter is moving direct in your solar seventh house.

Monday, August 13 (Moon in Leo to Virgo 2:04 p.m.)   Finish up projects and get emotional issues straightened out before September 2, when Saturn moves into Virgo and your fourth house. For the next two and a half years, Saturn will impose structures through which you and your family must live.

Tuesday, August 14 (Moon in Virgo)   Since Mars will be in your sign until September 28, make a list of everything you would like to accomplish by that date. This can include anything from practicalities to the esoteric, from home improvement to self-improvement.

Wednesday, August 15 (Moon in Virgo)   When the moon moves into Libra early tomorrow, you'll feel the shift. Stay up a little later, and figure out how you can clear your schedule so that you can devote tomorrow and the next day to *your* creativity.

Thursday, August 16 (Moon in Virgo to Libra 12:05 a.m.)   If you did clear your schedule, where will you start with your creativity? The question won't puzzle you for very long. Like many Geminis, you probably have a number of writing projects you've started and stuck away somewhere. Dust them off and set to work.

Friday, August 17 (Moon in Libra)   Your kids take up part of your day, but you love every second of it. After all, time is marching inexorably forward, and they won't be at home forever. Enjoy them while you can.

Saturday, August 18 (Moon in Libra to Scorpio 12:14 p.m.)   Detach from emotional issues as much as possible. It's all too easy to be led into an argument about some hot topic, and then find yourself boxed in, with no way out. This is particularly true if the topic involves religion or politics.

Sunday, August 19 (Moon in Scorpio)   Mercury moves into Virgo and your fourth house. This transit should stimulate activity on the home front. Out-of-town visitors are possible before September 5; there are more e-mails than usual in your in-box.

Monday, August 20 (Moon in Scorpio)   Your spiritual beliefs or worldview comes into play. You may try to incorporate one or both of these areas into your ordinary life. An Aries or a Leo has advice you should listen to.

Tuesday, August 21 (Moon in Scorpio to Sagittarius 12:45 a.m.)   You really do enjoy this moon. It's especially fine because it shares space with direct-moving Jupiter. Your opportunities in education, publishing, and overseas travel are expanding. You may also be called for jury duty!

Wednesday, August 22 (Moon in Sagittarius)   How far can you run with an idea? Discover just how passionate you feel about an idea or project and how determined you are to make this idea or project a reality.

Thursday, August 23 (Moon in Sagittarius to Capricorn 11:20 a.m.)   As the moon moves into Capricorn, you suddenly feel fatigued. The Capricorn moon is dampening your spirits and great mood. But this moon also compels you to become more grounded and aware of your surroundings.

Friday, August 24 (Moon in Capricorn)   If you pay quarterly taxes, get your tax forms in order. You may sign up for a course in something as mundane as estate law or as mysterious as past lives.

Saturday, August 25 (Moon in Capricorn to Aquarius 6:35 p.m.) When the moon joins Neptune in your ninth house, you can expect some vagueness and confusion about what you feel and experience. Higher inspiration and spirituality ride along with this combination.

Sunday, August 26 (Moon in Aquarius) You feel exhilarated by the promise of newness in the air. Friends figure into the activities, specifically those whose goals are like yours. Your political involvement may increase this fall.

Monday, August 27 (Moon in Aquarius to Pisces 10:35 p.m.) Try to chill out; don't run yourself ragged. A colleague may turn to you for advice or emotional support. Be as gentle with this person as possible. Listen.

Tuesday, August 28 (Moon in Pisces) The insight you have from dreams and meditation concerns a professional issue or someone involved in your professional life. Take the insight into account, weigh the issues, and make your decision when the moon moves into Aries.

Wednesday, August 29 (Moon in Pisces) Be prepared for the moon's transit into Aries. Make lists, contact people by e-mail, and check your schedule for the next few days. Any public speaking you do in the next two days is well-received.

Thursday, August 30 (Moon in Pisces to Aries 12:25 a.m.) A visit to a psychic may be in order. This person will be able to provide you with information or insight you need concerning a friendship or perhaps one of your goals. List your questions before you go. If the psychic is really good, you won't even have to ask the questions.

286

Friday, August 31 (Moon in Aries) It's the end of another month, and your energy might be low. Kick back and relax this weekend if you don't have plans. Fall is coming, so enjoy the good weather while you can.

SEPTEMBER 2007

Saturday, September 1 (Moon in Aries to Taurus 1:36 a.m.) Tomorrow, Saturn moves into Virgo and remains there for about two and a half years. You can prepare for this by listing the goals you have for your home and family.

Sunday, September 2 (Moon in Taurus) Saturn moves into Virgo and your solar fourth house. This transit may delay any moves you had hoped to make, but brings the proper structure into your life. With Venus still moving retrograde in your fourth house, you may encounter physical discomforts that relate to the environment.

Monday, September 3 (Moon in Taurus to Gemini 3:31 a.m.) Early this morning, the moon moves into your sign, signaling a high time of the month. Look to friends to help you achieve your goals. Don't hesitate to delegate.

Tuesday, September 4 (Moon in Gemini) You do your share of catching up with friends you haven't seen for a while. A Libra or an Aquarius brings you information you've been searching for. If you can squeeze in time to read, get to that book you haven't yet started.

Wednesday, September 5 (Moon in Gemini to Cancer 7:09 a.m.) Mercury moves into Libra; this transit feels very good! It stimulates activity in your love life and with your creativity. In fact, get busy with your book.

Thursday, September 6 (Moon in Cancer) Feeling somewhat security conscious, Gemini? Blame the Cancer moon. This moon also enhances your intuition and your nurturing instincts.

Friday, September 7 (Moon in Cancer to Leo 1:00 p.m.)   Pluto turns direct in your seventh house. This movement benefits both personal and professional partnerships. Whether partnerships begin or end, the transformation is profound and, in the long run, works to your benefit.

Saturday, September 8 (Moon in Leo)   Venus turns direct, so whatever bumps you've been experiencing at home will iron out. Friends gather at your place this evening, perhaps for a cookout. You end up on center stage as a storyteller.

Sunday, September 9 (Moon in Leo to Virgo 9:11 p.m.)   In two days, there's a solar eclipse in Virgo and your solar fourth house. Take steps to maximize this eclipse's energy. You'll be glad you did.

Monday, September 10 (Moon in Virgo)   Make your lists, prioritize, and tackle one item at a time. Be a perfectionist. As long as you don't criticize others for not living up to your ideal of perfection, you can achieve a great deal.

Tuesday, September 11 (Moon in Virgo)   You might feel like getting off by yourself for some meditation. You'll be glad you did. Spend the rest of the day with loved ones.

Wednesday, September 12 (Moon in Virgo to Libra 7:32 a.m.)   You're looking for balance in your creative work and your personal life. How you achieve the balance depends on how you allot your time. Get to work!

Thursday, September 13 (Moon in Libra)   You're on a creative roll! With both the moon and Mercury in your solar fifth house, you express yourself well regardless of what creative venue you're pursuing.

Friday, September 14 (Moon in Libra to Scorpio 7:37 p.m.) An emotional issue related to employees surfaces. Postpone any decision until Monday, when the moon is in Sagittarius. Then you'll be able to see the larger picture.

Saturday, September 15 (Moon in Scorpio) Head to the gym or to an aerobics class. Do something to strengthen and tone your body and start to do it regularly. The issues that the solar eclipse raised are evident in your home life. Deal with them.

Sunday, September 16 (Moon in Scorpio) Chill, Gemini. In the long run, keeping to yourself and completing work from home will benefit you. Take at least an hour to follow your regular exercise routine.

Monday, September 17 (Moon in Scorpio to Sagittarius 8:21 a.m.) Make your decision about last week's trouble at work. You and your partner reach an agreement. You may sign up for a workshop or seminar on some aspect of the legal system.

Tuesday, September 18 (Moon in Sagittarius) If you're in contract negotiations, you may sign on the dotted lines. Discuss things first with your partner or significant other.

Wednesday, September 19 (Moon in Sagittarius to Capricorn 7:52 p.m.) The convergence of energies focuses on your finances—not just what you earn and spend, but on the financial resources you share with others. A spouse or business partner has financial advice you should listen to.

Thursday, September 20 (Moon in Capricorn) Gather your information, and then lay down your strategy or plan. Be detailed, but not so detailed that there's no room for change. You're a mutable sign, which means that flexibility and adaptability are your greatest survival tools.

Friday, September 21 (Moon in Capricorn)   You may feel somewhat down in the dumps. Try to roll with the mood, Gemini, and know that by tomorrow, when the moon moves into a more compatible sign, your disposition will be much improved.

Saturday, September 22 (Moon in Capricorn to Aquarius 4:18 a.m.)   The moon joins Neptune in Aquarius in your solar ninth house. This combination of planets softens your mood and adds a spiritual flavor to whatever you do. You're aware of synchronicities and the hidden order of things.

Sunday, September 23 (Moon in Aquarius)   Friends figure prominently in events. This could spell involvement in a political group, a film group, or even an educational group. Whatever your involvement, you bring your knowledge and expertise to the group.

Monday, September 24 (Moon in Aquarius to Pisces 8:56 a.m.)   It's a career day that presents some intriguing challenges. Your best bet is to deal with each challenge as it surfaces and then to move on. Use your imagination to find creative solutions to problems.

Tuesday, September 25 (Moon in Pisces)   Your imagination and intuition work in tandem, leading you toward a new way to do your job. If you've been bored with your career, spice it up.

Wednesday, September 26 (Moon in Pisces to Aries 10:23 a.m.)   Mars won't be in your sign for much longer. Make the most of the planet's energy to complete long-standing projects or to tackle things on which you have procrastinated.

Thursday, September 27 (Moon in Aries)   Mercury moves into Scorpio and your solar sixth house. This transit deepens your intuition and your investigative and research abilities. You come across with a certain intensity that makes whatever you say or write convincing.

Friday, September 28 (Moon in Aries to Taurus 10:18 a.m.)   Mars moves into Cancer and your second house. Fasten your seat belt. Until the end of the year, a lot of your energy goes into earning money; you may even take a second job. And new financial opportunities may come your way.

Saturday, September 29 (Moon in Taurus)   Your second job or your new job could be something you do from your home. You benefit from solitude and reflection.

Sunday, September 30 (Moon in Taurus to Gemini 10:35 a.m.)   Lucky you! The month ends with the moon in your sign, and you're in a social mood. You reconnect with friends through e-mail; you may accept an invitation for dinner or drinks.

OCTOBER 2007

Monday, October 1 (Moon in Gemini)   Your sex appeal, self-confidence, and general mood are great. Launch any work projects now. By the time Mercury turns retrograde on October 11, you'll be in the right frame of mind to revise and rewrite.

Tuesday, October 2 (Moon in Gemini to Cancer 12:58 p.m.)   As the moon moves into your solar second house, it's money issues again! This time, the news should be in your favor. You also take a deep inner look at whether you actually walk your talk.

291

Wednesday, October 3 (Moon in Cancer) A family discussion highlights your deepest values. Have you been as compassionate as possible? Have you done at least one nice thing for someone else?

Thursday, October 4 (Moon in Cancer to Leo 6:28 p.m.) Divination tools are on your mind. You have some burning question that needs an answer or, at the very least, additional insight. Try the tarot or even astrology! There are also oracles on the Web.

Friday, October 5 (Moon in Leo) You usually love the Leo moon. It gives you an opportunity to shine. If you feel a bit down, look within for the answer. It may date back to when the moon was in Scorpio or Pisces.

Saturday, October 6 (Moon in Leo) Get moving on your manuscript, Gemini. The lunar energies favor writing and communications. Keep a notebook handy to jot down ideas. You could get additional input from relatives.

Sunday, October 7 (Moon in Leo to Virgo 3:04 a.m.) With Saturn in Virgo, the Virgo moon adds pressure on you to tend to details. You become finicky about your home and family. Resist the temptation to become obsessive!

Monday, October 8 (Moon in Virgo) Along comes Venus in Virgo to place pressure on you to be a perfectionist. This transit certainly favors romance and smooth sailing at home. You may be fastidious about how your home looks or how you organize your home office.

Tuesday, October 9 (Moon in Virgo to Libra 1:58 p.m.) If you awaken frustrated and small things immediately start going wrong, you probably feel the effects of the Mercury retrograde a bit early. It happens sometimes.

But when it happens to you, it could mean that the retrograde period will be filled with challenges.

Wednesday, October 10 (Moon in Libra) Your artistic sensibilities may accelerate to the point where you keep working until you're finished. Starting tomorrow, when Mercury turns retrograde, revise what you've worked on.

Thursday, October 11 (Moon in Libra) Mercury turns retrograde in Scorpio and your solar sixth house. This movement impacts your daily work routine and health. One of the most constructive ways to use the energy is to continue your regular exercise routine.

Friday, October 12 (Moon in Libra to Scorpio 2:14 a.m.) With Mars and the moon forming harmonious angles to each other, your intuition and imagination zip along. You're able to bypass your left brain and dive straight into the heart of whatever you need.

Saturday, October 13 (Moon in Scorpio) Stay on track. Don't allow coworkers or anyone else at work to distract you from what's important. You know the score.

Sunday, October 14 (Moon in Scorpio to Sagittarius 2:58 p.m.) With the moon in optimistic Sagittarius, conjunct expansive Jupiter, you're in fine shape. Even though this moon is opposed to your sun, the fire element is compatible with your sun's element. Enjoy yourself!

Monday, October 15 (Moon in Sagittarius) You and your partner grasp the big picture of your relationship. The understanding may not come all at once, but you each have a clearer understanding of your individual needs.

Tuesday, October 16 (Moon in Sagittarius) Don't sign the contract just yet. Don't negotiate either if you can help it. Wait until Mercury turns direct on November 1. If you must sign, do so with the understanding that you will have to revisit the contract at some point.

Wednesday, October 17 (Moon in Sagittarius to Capricorn 3:04 a.m.)   Venus and Saturn in Virgo and Mars in Cancer form harmonious angles to this transiting moon, but not to your sun sign. The combination favors a more grounded and realistic approach to the financial obligations that you and your partner share. Maybe it's time to set aside money for a child's college education.

Thursday, October 18 (Moon in Capricorn)   You help out an elderly relative or someone else who needs financial or emotional support. You have a need to balance the various parts of your life; the Capricorn moon may help you to do exactly that.

Friday, October 19 (Moon in Capricorn to Aquarius 12:52 p.m.)   You chafe at the restrictions that Saturn in your solar fourth house is imposing on you. The Aquarius moon provides the opportunity to break free of the status quo for a few days. Let the cosmos shake up your world. Embrace chaos.

Saturday, October 20 (Moon in Aquarius)   If a special Libra in your life celebrates a birthday, go all out to make the occasion memorable for that person. Life, after all, isn't just about you.

Sunday, October 21 (Moon in Aquarius to Pisces 7:03 p.m.)   Once again, the moon joins Uranus in Pisces in your solar tenth house. These transits may not be especially comfortable for you, but they definitely get your imagination moving in the right direction. Use your imagination to approach your career in a new way.

Monday, October 22 (Moon in Pisces)   You're deep in Mercury-retrograde country. If you have to travel, be sure to check your schedule because things may change without warning. Also, check on e-mails and letters you have sent to be sure the other person has received them.

Tuesday, October 23 (Moon in Pisces to Aries 9:25 p.m.)   Finally, a lunar transit that energizes you. This is a wonderful time for publicity and promotion. You have your finger on the public pulse, and it comes through in your public speaking. Get together with friends and celebrate autumn!

Wednesday, October 24 (Moon in Aries)   Celebration, daring, risk, courage—all these attributes come into play, but in an inner, emotional sense. You fully grasp the concept that you write the script of your life from the inside out. Be careful what you wish for. You might just get it!

Thursday, October 25 (Moon in Aries to Taurus 9:08 p.m.)   This lunar transit provides the perfect excuse to take a long weekend, kick back, and relax. You've earned the time off. Never forget to nurture yourself.

Friday, October 26 (Moon in Taurus)   You participate in an outdoor activity that takes you deep into the heart of nature. Finally, you can hear yourself think and let your feelings flow through you.

Saturday, October 27 (Moon in Taurus to Gemini 8:12 p.m.)   You're free to do pretty much whatever you want. You won't have a list; you'll be spontaneous and go wherever your spirit leads you. Synchronicities may signal the path to follow!

Sunday, October 28 (Moon in Gemini)   Your head and heart are in complete agreement over a personal issue. You're firm about the course you would like to follow, yet you're not so firm that you lose your flexibility.

Monday, October 29 (Moon in Gemini to Cancer 8:50 p.m.)   As the moon moves into nurturing Cancer and your solar second house, you feel the need to protect your assets in some way. It could be as simple as taking out more insurance coverage on your home.

Tuesday, October 30 (Moon in Cancer)   Your mom or another nurturing female relates a dream or intuitive hunch; you are compelled to listen because the message is for you. Whether you heed it or not is entirely up to you. Free will is always the bottom line.

Wednesday, October 31 (Moon in Cancer)   Happy Halloween! Even though the moon doesn't move into flamboyant Leo until after midnight, dress and go trick or treating with your kids. If you don't have children, don a costume in which you can greet trick or treaters.

NOVEMBER 2007

Thursday, November 1 (Moon in Cancer to Leo 12:48 a.m.) Mercury turns direct. Travel, sign contracts, and communicate to your heart's content. The Leo moon galvanizes you to connect with neighbors and relatives.

Friday, November 2 (Moon in Leo)   Time to dust off that manuscript or screenplay. The lunar energy favors writers and writing. Your creativity puts you on center stage.

Saturday, November 3 (Moon in Leo to Virgo 8:45 a.m.) With the moon joining both Saturn and Venus in your solar fourth house, the heat is on to get your home in order. This could entail any number of things from a simple cleaning of your house to improvements and new furniture. But first and foremost, it concerns your family.

Sunday, November 4—Daylight Saving Time Ends (Moon in Virgo) You and your loved ones stick close to home. You may invite neighbors and relatives over, your kids may have friends over, and generally, the atmosphere is festive. Think of this as a precursor to the Thanksgiving holidays.

Monday, November 5 (Moon in Virgo to Libra 6:47 p.m.) This evening, you steal away for a while to dive into your creative projects. Your challenge will be to focus on one thing and pour your energies into that. Friends may help you define the project.

Tuesday, November 6 (Moon in Libra) In two days, Venus moves into Libra. Get ready for this one by putting your creative priorities in order. The Venus transit, which will last until early December, will bring in new creative opportunities.

Wednesday, November 7 (Moon in Libra) Uranus turns direct in your solar tenth house on November 24. Prepare by applying your creative drive to your career so that when Uranus changes directions, you begin to see results.

Thursday, November 8 (Moon in Libra to Scorpio 7:19 a.m.) Venus moves into Libra and remains there until December 5. This period should be incredibly romantic for you, as long as you aren't looking for commitment in a new relationship. It's also a deeply creative time for you.

Friday, November 9 (Moon in Scorpio) The moon forms a harmonious angle with Mars in Cancer in your second house. This combination could help you grasp the bottom line on an investment opportunity or on some issue at work. Your energy is fluid and intuitive. Use it to your advantage.

Saturday, November 10 (Moon in Scorpio to Sagittarius 7:59 p.m.) The moon joins Jupiter in your solar seventh house. This combination should create an intriguing day with your personal or professional partner. You're able to see the larger scope of your relationship and to make decisions accordingly.

Sunday, November 11 (Moon in Sagittarius) You and a partner attend a seminar or workshop. In some way, you'll gain insights about yourselves and your relationship that may not even be related to the topic. Use these insights to improve your communications with each other.

Monday, November 12 (Moon in Sagittarius) With Mercury moving direct, you should proceed with contract negotiations. With Venus in Libra, the sign of justice and balance, don't hesitate to request everything that you want in the contract. Be fair to yourself!

Tuesday, November 13 (Moon in Sagittarius to Capricorn 8:01 a.m.) Mars and the moon form a harmonious angle to each other, but not to your sun sign. Still, you can use this energy to focus on areas of your life that need attention. Some of these areas might be finances, shared resources, insurance and taxes, and your fundamental values.

Wednesday, November 14 (Moon in Capricorn) Your thoughts turn toward cosmic questions. What happens when we die? Is the soul reborn? What is karma? Try to recall your dreams tonight. Answers may come to you through them.

Thursday, November 15 (Moon in Capricorn to Aquarius 6:31 p.m.) Mars turns retrograde in Cancer and remains that way through the end of the year. This transit could delay any checks that you're expecting to arrive through the mail. Your physical energy may not be quite as robust as it usually is. Keep up your regular exercise routine.

Friday, November 16 (Moon in Aquarius)   You and a group of friends could be planning an overseas trip. You may not be traveling for sheer pleasure. There's a deep meaning to the journey. It may be to study some aspect of a foreign culture or country.

Saturday, November 17 (Moon in Aquarius)   On November 24, Uranus turns direct in Pisces and your solar tenth house. This is good news for your career. You can expect events to move forward smoothly. You can prepare for this movement by listing your priorities for November 24 or November 26.

Sunday, November 18 (Moon in Aquarius to Pisces 2:15 a.m.)   The moon moves into your solar tenth house, stimulating professional matters. You may feel somewhat vulnerable today with a colleague or a boss. Go with the flow of events; try not to get upset about things over which you have no control. Use your imagination and intuition to navigate events successfully.

Monday, November 19 (Moon in Pisces)   Be careful about an emotional display in public. It will come about suddenly, if it happens at all, and will catch you off guard. You may provide support and compassion for a colleague who is going through a rough time.

Tuesday, November 20 (Moon in Pisces to Aries 6:25 a.m.)   Here's that wonderful Aries moon you enjoy so much. Your friends are important to you. You may spend time connecting with them through e-mail, by phone, or in person.

Wednesday, November 21 (Moon in Aries)   Party time! The festivities are spontaneous, but enjoyable. You and someone you considered a friend may discover that you have more in common than you thought. Is this the beginning of a romance?

Thursday, November 22 (Moon in Aries to Taurus 7:19 a.m.) Happy Thanksgiving! The company you keep will be more important than the location or even what you eat! Take a look at the faces around you. What kind of people are they? What do they reflect about you?

Friday, November 23 (Moon in Taurus) Can you keep a secret? Well, you will. And it may not even be your secret, but one that someone else has entrusted to you. Follow your instincts; listen to your intuition.

Saturday, November 24 (Moon in Taurus to Gemini 6:29 a.m.) Uranus turns direct in your solar tenth house and the moon moves into your sign! Events could be exciting in a strange way. You attract unusual, idiosyncratic people.

Sunday, November 25 (Moon in Gemini) A positive and uplifting day overall. You're in the groove, and you're able to do just about everything quickly. Be careful that you don't move so fast that the day passes in a blur. Pause to enjoy the smaller things in life.

Monday, November 26 (Moon in Gemini to Cancer 6:07 a.m.) Compared to yesterday, nothing seems to move quickly. It's as if you woke in a slow-motion dream. Don't resist. Move with it and see where this strange state takes you.

Tuesday, November 27 (Moon in Cancer) You should have a pretty good idea how you experience this lunar transit. You're more sensitive than usual and maybe more concerned about emotional security issues. You could be nostalgic for some part of your past. One good way to use this energy is to create a collage from old photos.

Wednesday, November 28 (Moon in Cancer to Leo 8:23 a.m.)   Finally, another fire-sign moon! The Leo moon makes you flamboyant in some way. Perhaps you wear flashier clothes. Maybe you talk to strangers. Or it could be that you act like a political candidate on the campaign trail.

Thursday, November 29 (Moon in Leo)   You help out around your neighborhood or in your community. Stray animals could be included in what you're doing. Does this volunteer effort come from the heart?

Friday, November 30 (Moon in Leo to Virgo 2:45 p.m.)   The moon joins Saturn in Virgo and your solar fourth house. You may feel somewhat oppressed, particularly about a family issue. Deal with it, pretty soon, this feeling will pass.

DECEMBER 2007

Saturday, December 1 (Moon in Virgo)   Mercury moves into Sagittarius. This transit lasts until December 20 and should be a good one for communications with both personal and professional partners. However, the energy under this transit can be volatile at times, with each person eager to say what has to be said.

Sunday, December 2 (Moon in Virgo)   Things may feel surreal, with your mood lifting, then plunging. But you and a family member talk honestly about a particular issue. That's something to cheer about!

Monday, December 3 (Moon in Virgo to Libra 1:02 a.m.)   It's hard to miss the festive feel to the air. It's either the proximity of the holidays or a special look from someone you would like to get to know. You're in the sort of mood where you may even decide to write poetry this evening. Keep a journal of your musings for the next few days.

Tuesday, December 4 (Moon in Libra)　　You find this journal business compelling and decide to keep making entries for the next six months. It's a good way to get in touch with your feelings, your deepest beliefs, your creative aspirations, and what you're looking for in a mate.

Wednesday, December 5 (Moon in Libra to Scorpio 1:32 p.m.)　　Both the moon and Venus move into Scorpio. This double whammy is excellent for romance at work. But this romance, if it happens, will be intense. Until December 30, when Venus changes signs again, things at work should go smoothly for you. You receive help from women.

Thursday, December 6 (Moon in Scorpio)　　Your emotions rush like a swollen river. You may be secretive about what you do (or whom you see); if you want to strike back at someone, don't. Wait until the moon has moved into Sagittarius.

Friday, December 7 (Moon in Scorpio)　　You're on the prowl for information. You may research something—or someone—and pull out all the stops. Take notes on what you uncover. You're the consummate detective.

Saturday, December 8 (Moon in Scorpio to Sagittarius 2:12 a.m.)　　Do you still feel like striking back or getting even with anyone involved in Thursday's events? If so, evaluate what your reaction might mean for your relationship with this person. Is it still worth having your say?

Sunday, December 9 (Moon in Sagittarius)　　Your spiritual values come into play. You may try to integrate these values into your most intimate relationships. But you can't force this sort of integration. It has to happen on its own.

Monday, December 10 (Moon in Sagittarius to Capricorn 1:51 p.m.)　　With Mars moving retrograde in Cancer and the moon in Capricorn, your day could be a bit weird. But you don't mind weird as long as it keeps life interesting. A few things to watch out for: financial advice from people whose personal finances are a mess and errors on your bank statement.

Tuesday, December 11 (Moon in Capricorn)   If you have your natal moon or ascendant in Capricorn, this may be a good day. You'll be emotionally strong and resilient; others won't mess with you. But if you don't have any natal planets in Capricorn, act like you know what you're doing so that no one questions your authority.

Wednesday, December 12 (Moon in Capricorn)   You know you don't have all the answers. You know you don't even have half the answers. But you have something else: adaptability and the ability to win over just about anyone who opposes you.

Thursday, December 13 (Moon in Capricorn to Aquarius 12:02 a.m.)   A friendly moon for you, Gemini. This moon usually gives you the opportunity to explore worlds beyond your own. Whether you travel to these worlds mentally or physically, the journey always expands your belief system.

Friday, December 14 (Moon in Aquarius)   Take heed. On December 18, Jupiter moves into Capricorn for a transit that takes about a year. If you have natal planets in Capricorn or the other earth signs, this should be a very good time for you! Certain areas of your life will expand; new opportunities will pour in.

Saturday, December 15 (Moon in Aquarius to Pisces 8:15 a.m.)   You and a colleague or friends are holiday shopping. Make a day of it and finish up if at all possible. One of your parents needs help getting out to shop. If you brought work home with you, put it off until tomorrow.

303

Sunday, December 16 (Moon in Pisces)   You, like just about everyone else in your office, are in a festive mood. If you're quick and alert, you can take advantage of this goodwill by promoting a project that is near and dear to your heart. You may encounter some opposition, but you're able to overcome it.

Monday, December 17 (Moon in Pisces to Aries 1:53 p.m.)   With the moon moving into fiery Aries, you could be somewhat edgy and temperamental. But overall, this lunar energy fits your lightning-quick mind. You're galvanized to rethink some of your goals and dreams.

Tuesday, December 18 (Moon in Aries)   Jupiter moves into Capricorn. It spends about a year transiting this sign and expanding your interest in metaphysics. You also will have other people's resources at your disposal. A partner or spouse may get a substantial raise.

Wednesday, December 19 (Moon in Aries to Taurus 4:38 p.m.)   Saturn turns retrograde in Virgo and your fourth house. This is hardly welcome news for the holidays. Try to use this energy to review and reevaluate your goals and dreams for yourself and your family.

Thursday, December 20 (Moon in Taurus)   Mercury joins Jupiter in Capricorn, pressuring you to become much more practical in terms of mortgages, loans, insurance, and taxes. Your conscious mind has a harder, more pragmatic edge.

Friday, December 21 (Moon in Taurus to Gemini 5:14 p.m.)   This lunar transit comes just in time for the holidays, buoying your spirits and mitigating some of the Capricorn influence you're experiencing. You head out to the mall or some great specialty shop to do some last-minute shopping.

Saturday, December 22 (Moon in Gemini) If you have a moon rising or other planets in Capricorn, you may be reaping unexpected benefits from the Jupiter transit. If you don't have your natal chart, get yours online through one of the Web sites that offers free natal charts.

Sunday, December 23 (Moon in Gemini to Cancer 5:19 p.m.) It's somehow appropriate that the moon moves into Cancer just as Christmas approaches. Home, hearth, and family are all accentuated. Nostalgia may be thick in the air as family and friends recall bygone days.

Monday, December 24 (Moon in Cancer) Release old grudges, heartaches, and bitterness. Mend damaged relationships with relatives and friends. Then you'll be in great shape for the approaching new year.

Tuesday, December 25 (Moon in Cancer to Leo 6:53 p.m.) Merry Christmas! Regardless of how you celebrate, you shine among your loved ones. Your generous spirit may put a dent in your pocketbook when the credit card bills come due, but it's only money.

Wednesday, December 26 (Moon in Leo) The day after a major holiday is often a blue-funk day. But with a Leo moon in your court, your mood is optimistic and upbeat and infects everyone with whom you come into contact. It's hard to keep a Gemini down for too long!

Thursday, December 27 (Moon in Leo to Virgo 11:45 p.m.) By the time the moon moves into Virgo, try to be asleep. You'll save yourself worry and angst! If you're awake, make lists about new year's goals.

Friday, December 28 (Moon in Virgo) Fret to your heart's content. When you get tired of fretting, put this lunar energy to good use by exercising, perfecting, cleaning, and practicing feng shui on your home. In other words, get things in order.

Saturday, December 29 (Moon in Virgo)   Get with the agenda. It's an organization day. Regardless of whether you have guests over to your place or you're going elsewhere to celebrate, have your priorities set. Line up a babysitter, a caterer, parking—whatever you need.

Sunday, December 30 (Moon in Virgo to Libra 8:38 a.m.) Venus moves into Sagittarius and your solar seventh house. Even though Venus is opposed to your sun, the most serious consequence is a tendency toward overindulgence. If you're in love, you and your partner go overboard. If you're looking for romance, you perhaps look too hard. Generally this transit favors a pleasant time with your partner.

Monday, December 31 (Moon in Libra)   With Venus in Sagittarius and the moon in Libra, the entire day is made to order for your need for variety and versatility. There's an emphasis on romance, hope, and your creativity.

HAPPY NEW YEAR!

SYDNEY OMARR

Born on August 5, 1926, in Philadelphia, Pennsylvania, Sydney Omarr was the only person ever given full-time duty in the U.S. Army as an astrologer. He is regarded as the most erudite astrologer of our time and the best known, through his syndicated column and his radio and television programs (he was Merv Griffin's "resident astrologer"). Omarr has been called the most "knowledgeable astrologer since Evangeline Adams." His forecasts of Nixon's downfall, the end of World War II in mid-August of 1945, the assassination of John F. Kennedy, Roosevelt's election to a fourth term and his death in office . . . these and many others are on the record and quoted enough to be considered "legendary."

ABOUT THE SERIES

This is one of a series of twelve Sydney Omarr®
Day-by-Day Astrological Guides for the signs of
2007. For questions and comments about the
book, e-mail tjmacgregor@booktalk.com.

SYDNEY OMARR'S®
SUN, MOON, AND YOU:
An Astrological Guide to
Your Personality

Discover the effects of the moon and sun on
LOVE, ROMANCE & SUCCESS

Nationally syndicated columnist Sydney
Omarr® shows readers how to turn the tides
in their lives! Included are all the keys to
finding the perfect balance between
day and night, featuring:

- An introduction to the sun and moon signs
- Easy-to-read tables
- How sun/moon signs contribute to personality, likes
and dislikes, finding ideal mates and the perfect jobs

Filled with colorful examples of historical
figures under each sign, and requiring no
familiarity with astrology, this is the
must-have guide for all fans of astrology!

0-451-21454-4

Unlock the Secrets of the Mystical World

Penguin Group (USA) Online

What will you be reading tomorrow?

Tom Clancy, Patricia Cornwell, W.E.B. Griffin,
Nora Roberts, William Gibson, Robin Cook,
Brian Jacques, Catherine Coulter, Stephen King,
Dean Koontz, Ken Follett, Clive Cussler,
Eric Jerome Dickey, John Sandford,
Terry McMillan, Sue Monk Kidd, Amy Tan,
John Berendt…

You'll find them all at
penguin.com

Read excerpts and newsletters,
find tour schedules and reading group guides,
and enter contests.

Subscribe to Penguin Group (USA) newsletters
and get an exclusive inside look
at exciting new titles and the authors you love
long before everyone else does.

PENGUIN GROUP (USA)
us.penguingroup.com